From Typology to Doxology

From Typology to Doxology
Paul's Use of Isaiah and Job in Romans 11:34–35

ANDREW DAVID NASELLI

◦PICKWICK *Publications* • Eugene, Oregon

FROM TYPOLOGY TO DOXOLOGY
Paul's Use of Isaiah and Job in Romans 11:34–35

Copyright © 2012 Andrew David Naselli. All rights reserved. Except for brief quotations in critical publications or reviews, no part of this book may be reproduced in any manner without prior written permission from the publisher. Write: Permissions, Wipf and Stock Publishers, 199 W. 8th Ave., Suite 3, Eugene, OR 97401.

Pickwick Publications
An Imprint of Wipf and Stock Publishers
199 W. 8th Av.e, Suite 3
Eugene, OR 97401

www.wipfandstock.com

ISBN 13: 978-1-61097-769-2

Cataloging-in-Publication data:

Naselli, Andrew David.

    From typology to doxology: Paul's use of Isaiah and Job in Romans 11:34–35 / Andrew David Naselli.

    xii + 202 p. ; 23 cm. Includes bibliographical references.

    ISBN 13: 978-1-61097-769-2

    1. Bible. N.T. Romans XI, 34–35—Criticism, interpreteation, etc. 2. Bible. N.T. Epistles of Paul—Relation to Isaiah. 3. Bible. N.T. Epistles of Paul—Relation to Job. I. Title.

BS2387 N25 2012

Manufactured in the U.S.A.

Unless otherwise indicated, all Scripture quotations are from Scripture quotations are from The Holy Bible, English Standard Version®, copyright © 2011 by Crossway Bibles, a publishing ministry of Good News Publishers. Used by permission. All rights reserved.

*To Jenni,
who fulfills me*

Contents

List of Tables / viii
Foreword by James M. Hamilton Jr./ ix
Preface / xi

1. Introduction / 1
2. Romans 11:34–35 in Context / 7
3. Isaiah 40:13 in Context / 39
4. Job 41:3a in Context / 63
5. Textual Issues / 91
6. Relevant Uses of Isaiah 40:13 and Job 41:3a in Jewish Literature / 99
7. Paul's Hermeneutical Warrant for Using Isaiah 40:13 and Job 41:3a in Romans 11:34–35 / 117
8. Paul's Theological Use of Isaiah 40:13 and Job 41:3a in Romans 11:34–35 / 146
9. Conclusion / 159

Bibliography / 163

Tables

1. Comparison of Isa 40:13 with Rom 11:34 and Job 41:3 with Rom 11:35 / 2
2. Salvation-Historical Twists in Rom 11:11–32: Israel → Gentiles → Israel / 18
3. The Components of Paul's Extended Metaphor of the Olive Tree in Rom 11:16b–24 / 21
4. A Propositional Display of Rom 11:33–36 / 29
5. Textual Issues in Isa 40:13, Job 41:3, and Rom 11:34–35 / 92
6. Significant Differences between Isa 40:13, Job 41:3, and Rom 11:34–35 / 95
7. Isa 40:12–14 in the MT and 1QIsaa / 109
8. Comparing Job 38:4–7 and Isa 40:12–14 / 140
9. OT Quotations in Romans 9–11 / 142

Foreword

The book you hold in your hands deserves close attention for several reasons: it treats a climactic passage in what may be the most important letter ever written by one of the world's most influential authors. Moreover, in Romans 11:33–36 Paul himself quotes two other great texts, the books of Job and Isaiah. In addition to the significance of the material treated, Andy Naselli's treatment is notable: this book explains how Paul uses Isaiah 40:13 and Job 41:3 in Romans 11:34–35, and the explanation is as insightful and responsible as it is daring and exciting.

It's not hard to imagine a published dissertation being responsible and insightful, but daring and exciting? Indeed.

Exciting precisely because Naselli dares to understand. The daring claims made here are that Paul gets the Old Testament right, that as Paul quotes the Old Testament, his citations invoke broader passages, and that the flow of thought in those broader passages corresponds to the argument Paul makes. Insight and courage ignite Naselli's bold contention that the way Paul uses these texts cues us to a wider typological connection that Paul sees between what Isaiah said to the nation of Israel, the experience of Job, and what Paul says the Jewish people will experience in the future. The wood of Naselli's scholarship, arranged with rigorous care, has been set aflame by his sympathetic analysis of Paul's perspective, resulting in a sacrifice of praise with a pleasing aroma. Accounting for all the evidence, whether from primary sources or secondary literature, the blazing book yields light and heat.

How could Paul's citation of Isaiah 40:13 be typological? Because as the quotation of Isaiah 6:9–10 in all four Gospels and Acts indicates, the hardening that led to the exile from the land has not yet been lifted (cf. Rom 11:25). The prophesied new exodus and return from exile have been anticipated and inaugurated but not yet consummated: anticipated in the returns to the land narrated in Ezra and Nehemiah; inaugurated in the death and resurrection of Jesus. There is a sense in which, having rejected the Messiah, Israel remains in exile. Paul is explaining in Romans 11 how God will keep his promise to restore his people, having made them jealous by those who are no people (cf. Deut 32:21 and Rom 11:13–14). The typological pattern of new exodus and return from exile evoked in Isaiah 40, then, is the pattern that will find its antitype, its ultimate fulfillment, when the Redeemer comes from Zion, banishes ungodliness from Jacob, takes away their sin, brings them into the new covenant, "and in this way all Israel will be saved" (Rom 11:26–27). Naselli also draws insightful parallels between the experience of Job and Israel in making the case that Paul's also uses Job 41:3 typologically.

Naselli shows that Paul's use of Isaiah 40:13 and Job 41:3 demonstrates that God established a foundation of judgment on which he built a soaring tower of mercy for the praise of his glory in the life of Job and the history of Israel, and this pattern of events will be fulfilled in the future redemption of Israel to which Paul points. To put it another way, Naselli has demonstrated that Paul's argument here is that God shows his glory in salvation through judgment.

This book deserves the attention of all who care to understand the passages examined here, and more broadly, how the New Testament authors understand the Old. This is an exploration of unsearchable judgments and inscrutable ways (Rom 11:33), pointing to the one whose mind none has mapped, to whom none give counsel or bribes, "For from him and through him and to him are all things. To him be glory forever. Amen" (Rom 11:34–36). Let me keep you from it no longer: God's best to you in this insightful and responsible, daring and exciting read.

James M. Hamilton Jr.
Associate Professor of Biblical Theology
The Southern Baptist Theological Seminary

Preface

THIS BOOK BEGAN AS a paper prepared for D. A. Carson's PhD seminar "The Old Testament in the New" in fall 2006 at Trinity Evangelical Divinity School in Deerfield, Illinois. Carson required each student to write a paper on the use of the OT in a specific NT passage, and I chose Rom 11:34–35, primarily because it is attached to my favorite verse in the Bible: Rom 11:36. I slightly revised the paper and presented it at the national meeting of the Evangelical Theological Society on November 19, 2008. The study was so rewarding that I expanded it into a dissertation, which I have revised as this book.

I am grateful for Carson's wise guidance along the way. It's hard to imagine a better mentor for a doctoral program. He routinely assured me that a PhD program that doesn't make you sweat and feel like a twit at times isn't worth the expense. By this measure I got far more than I paid for. And serving as his research assistant since 2006 has been worth more than the PhD. His gifts and productivity are astonishing, and it's been an honor to leverage his work a bit by helping with copyediting and other projects. One of the first large projects he gave me was to proof *Commentary on the New Testament Use of the Old Testament* (ed. G. K. Beale and D. A. Carson; Grand Rapids: Baker, 2007), and that introduced me, in a fairly comprehensive way, to the complex and variegated ways the NT uses the OT.

I'm grateful also for my dissertation's other two readers: Bob Yarbrough and Willem VanGemeren. Yarbrough is a model NT scholar and churchman. God has gifted this lumberjack with sharp wit, analytical skills, and theological acumen. VanGemeren's warm demeanor made the PhD program at TEDS more bearable. He has rightly pinpointed me as a left-brain guy, so he has at least alerted me that the right brain exists and that this has a bearing on my theological method. I should offer a disclaimer that anything I say about Isaiah (or the whole OT for that matter) is not his fault. He's a Jedi Master when it comes to reading the Hebrew OT, and he makes linguistic, literary, and theological connections with nuance far beyond my ability.

I'm grateful to family and friends who supported me in many ways, but one deserves special thanks with reference to this book: my Dad, Charles Naselli. He proofs almost everything I write for publication, and he eagerly and skillfully provided valuable feedback at every stage of this project.

My godly wife, Jenni, endured two PhDs in our first seven years together (one year of dating and engagement followed by six years of marriage). That's two rounds of coursework, two rounds of comprehensive exams, and two dissertations (and now two children, too). She should get a degree for that. Now, regarding this book's dedication, I should qualify (since that's what PhDs are supposed to do to everything) that referring to Jenni as the one "who fulfills me" is not an allusion to πληρόω as if the hermeneutical warrant for this book is Jenni's typological connection to me. Nor does it mean merely that she satisfies me. It means that she makes me complete by supplying what is lacking. And there's a lot lacking. She unselfishly and patiently encourages, supports, and loves me. She is a delight to love and lead, and I could not have made it this far without her.

My view of God has deepened as a result of studying Rom 11:33–36 (see especially ch. 8). God has enlarged my view of how great and glorious he is and how small and unimpressive we are.

"For from him and through him and to him are all things.
To him be glory forever. Amen." (Rom 11:36)

Andy Naselli
Moore, South Carolina
September 2011

1

Introduction

ROMANS 11:36 IS PERHAPS the grandest, most all-encompassing doxology in the New Testament: "For from him and through him and to him are all things. To him be glory forever. Amen." "Doxologies," Peter T. O'Brien explains, "are short, spontaneous ascriptions of praise to God which frequently appear as concluding formulae to [1] prayers, [2] hymnic expressions and [3] sections of Paul's letters."[1] Paul's doxology in Rom 11:36 concludes what is likely a hymn (Rom 11:33–35) as well as a section of his letter to the Romans (chs. 9–11 and perhaps more broadly, chs. 1–11).

One striking aspect about Paul's doxology in Rom 11:36 is that he prefaces it by quoting two verses from the Old Testament: Isa 40:13 and Job 41:3a.[2] (See table 1.) This raises a host of questions such as the following: What is the context of the OT passages cited? How are those OT passages used in other Jewish literature? Are there any significant textual issues? What is Paul's hermeneutical warrant for using those OT passages in Rom 11? What is Paul's theological use of those OT passages in Rom 11? How—if at all—does Paul's use of the OT in Rom 11:34–35 contribute to the broader discussion on the use of the OT in the NT?

---

1. O'Brien, "Benediction," 69.

2. The English text of Job 41 is numbered differently than the MT. Job 40:25–32 in the MT is 41:1–8 in English, and 41:1–26 in the MT is 41:9–34 in English. This book uses the numbering in the MT (and sometimes also includes in parentheses the numbering in the English text).

TABLE 1: Comparison of Isa 40:13 with Rom 11:34 and Job 41:3 with Rom 11:35

vv.	BHS	LXX (NETS)	NA²⁷
Isa 40:13 & Rom 11:34	מִי־תִכֵּן אֶת־רוּחַ יְהוָה וְאִישׁ עֲצָתוֹ יוֹדִיעֶנּוּ	τίς ἔγνω νοῦν κυρίου καὶ τίς αὐτοῦ σύμβουλος ἐγένετο ὃς συμβιβᾷ αὐτόν	τίς γὰρ ἔγνω νοῦν κυρίου; ἢ τίς σύμβουλος αὐτοῦ ἐγένετο;
	Who has measured the Spirit of the LORD, or what man shows him his counsel?	Who has known the mind of the Lord, and who has been his counselor to instruct him?	"For who has known the mind of the Lord, or who has been his counselor?"
Job 41:3 & Rom 11:35	מִי הִקְדִּימַנִי וַאֲשַׁלֵּם תַּחַת כָּל־הַשָּׁמַיִם לִי־הוּא	ἢ τίς ἀντιστήσεταί μοι καὶ ὑπομενεῖ εἰ πᾶσα ἡ ὑπ'οὐρανὸν ἐμή ἐστιν	ἢ τίς προέδωκεν αὐτῷ, καὶ ἀνταποδοθήσεται αὐτῷ;
	Who has first given to me, that I should repay him? Whatever is under the whole heaven is mine.	Or who will withstand me and survive, if the entire earth beneath the sky is mine?	"Or who has given a gift to him that he might be repaid?"

1. RESEARCH PROBLEM

This book examines Paul's use of Isa 40:13 and Job 41:3a in Rom 11:34-35.³ The primary justification for this study is to fill a notable void in a section of Romans otherwise crowded with studies.⁴

It has been said that the Bible is like a deep, broad body of water, shallow enough for a lamb to wade but deep enough for an elephant to

---

3. I am presenting a "research problem" rather than a thesis because it reflects the way I researched and wrote this book; it unfolds inductively. Although I began this project with a sense of where it was headed, I was not confident enough to express and test a clear thesis. I am glad I took that approach because I reached some significant conclusions that I did not ancitipate.

4. This book contributes to the study of the use of the OT in the NT by providing the most thorough treatment available on the use of the OT in Rom 11:34-35. (Consequently, it contributes to NT exegesis by thoroughly studying Rom 11:33-36.) For a chronological review of the literature that highlights sixteen significant articles or sections from monographs on Rom 11:34-35, see Naselli, "Paul's Use," 9-14.

swim.⁵ Some parts are simple and straightforward, and others require the highest level of historical and theological integration. Romans 9–11 is a prime example of the latter category. It is logically dense and theologically weighty, and it has been the subject of hundreds of technical studies. Since nearly one-third of all Paul's OT quotations occur in Rom 9–11 (Paul directly quotes the OT over twenty-five times in these chapters), technical studies on Rom 9–11 are preoccupied with his use of the OT.

Most studies on Rom 9–11, however, effectively marginalize the use of the OT in Rom 11:34–35 by not examining it in sufficient detail and by failing to make important historical and theological connections with Isa 40:13 and Job 41:3a. This is especially evident in commentaries on Romans, which almost universally skim over the use of the OT in Rom 11:34–35. Perhaps this is related to factors such as word-count restrictions from publishers and from a tendency to concentrate on what is most controversial. It is further understandable since interpreting Rom 11:33–36 initially seems like a "breather" compared to the intense intellectual workout required to understand the rest of Rom 9–11.

This tendency extends beyond Romans commentaries to the rest of the literature, perhaps because the use of the OT in Rom 11:34–35 is not deemed significant enough to warrant such a study. These quotations, however, occur in Rom 11:33–36, which forms the climactic capstone of Paul's argument in Rom 9–11. By exploring the use of Isa 40:13 and Job 41:3a in Rom 11:34–35, this book explains significant historical and theological connections that enrich our understanding of Rom 11:33–36 in particular and Rom 9–11 as a whole.

2. METHODOLOGY

Four methodological clarifications are noteworthy:

1. This book is an extension of the proliferating studies already written on the use of the OT in the NT, not a comprehensive guide to that massive issue. It does, however, make connections with larger issues on the use of the OT in the NT.⁶

---

5. The source of this famous illustration appears to be Gregory the Great's commentary on Job: "Quasi quidam quippe est fluvius ut ita dixerim planus et altus in quo et agnus ambulet, et elephas natet" (*Moral.* inscr. 4 [CCL 143:6]).

6. See especially chs. 7–8.

2. This book avoids a fallacy that could undermine the argument. If this book's understanding of Rom 11:33–36 is tied to only one very narrow reading of Rom 9–11, then this will limit the study's usefulness. This requires clarity regarding what is necessary to the overall argument.

3. The term "salvation history" occurs repeatedly in this book, but the term begs for qualification since biblical scholars and theologians use it in different senses.[7] "We are using the phrase [salvation history] in a rather untechnical fashion to denote a conceptual framework that Paul uses to describe what has taken place in Christ."[8] This conceptual framework differs from the Jewish apocalyptic movement, which sharply divided the sin-dominated present age from the age to come when the Messiah conquers sin and eradicates its presence. Paul, in contrast, significantly tweaks this framework by overlapping those two ages. That is, the coming of Jesus inaugurated the age to come but did not eradicate sin's presence; that will happen in future when Jesus returns. Thus, to use Oscar Cullmann's analogy from World War II, Christians today are living in between D-Day (i.e., Jesus' life, cross-work, resurrection, and ascension) and V-E-Day (i.e., Jesus' return to earth to consummate his victory).[9] So "salvation history" refers to this divine scheme, namely, God's multi-stage historical plan to save his people from their sins. Or stated another way, "'Salvation history' denotes the personal redemptive activity of God within human history to effect his eternal saving intentions."[10]

4. Structurally, the study generally follows the six-part approach used in Beale and Carson's *Commentary on the New Testament Use of the Old Testament*.[11]

> (1) *NT context*. This establishes "the topic of discussion, the flow of thought, and . . . the literary structure, genre, and rhetoric of the passage."[12] Unlike Beale and Carson's *Commentary*, which does this

---

7. Cf. §1.9 of ch. 7.
8. Moo, *Epistle*, 25; see also 26–27.
9. Cullmann, *Christ and Time*, 141–42, 145–46.
10. Yarbrough, "Paul," 297. Cf. idem, *Salvation*.
11. Beale and Carson, "Introduction," xxiv–xxvi. Except for noting relevant uses of the OT passage in Jewish literature, S. Lewis Johnson approaches six NT passages that use the OT by following this same sequence in *Old Testament in the New*.
12. Beale and Carson, "Introduction," xxiv.

"without (yet) going into the details of the exegesis,"[13] this book performs detailed exegesis at this first stage.

(2) *OT context*. This repeats step one in the corresponding OT passages. Sometimes reflection on the use of the OT in the OT itself is necessary at this stage (e.g., the use of Deuteronomy in Isaiah).

(3) *Textual issues*. This may involve textual criticism on two levels, first within the MT, LXX, and Greek NT, and then comparing the MT, LXX, and Greek NT with each other. Sometimes it is controversial whether the NT explicitly quotes the OT (as is the case with Isa 40:13 and Job 41:3a in Rom 11:34–35). Beale and Carson list this as the fourth step rather than the third step, but this book treats it as step three instead of four. It could just as easily occur as steps one, two, or four; what is important, however, is that steps one through four all occur before steps five and six, where the "cream" of the study surfaces.

(4) *Relevant uses of the OT passage in Jewish literature*. "How is the OT quotation or source handled in the literature of Second Temple Judaism or (more broadly yet) of early Judaism?"[14] It may be significant for NT interpretation to consider how approximately contemporaneous Jewish literature interpreted certain OT texts.

(5) *The NT author's hermeneutical warrant for using the OT in the NT*. The NT authors use the OT in a variety of ways, ranging from simple linguistic connections to complex biblical theological connections such as typological fulfillment. "One of the distinctive differences one sometimes finds between the way NT writers read the OT and the way that their non-Christian Jewish contemporaries read it is the salvation-historical grid that is often accompanied by the former."[15] Further, does Paul cite the OT as what some today might regard as irresponsible "prooftexts" (i.e., selective quotations abstracted from their original contexts), or does he carry over the OT context? If the latter, to what degree?[16]

---

13. Ibid.

14. Ibid.

15. Ibid., xxvi. Reflecting on Paul's "salvation-historical grid" is crucial to understanding his use of the OT in Rom 11:34–35.

16. In Rom 11:34–35, Paul carries over the OT contexts to a degree significantly larger than the majority of Romans commentaries suggest.

(6) *The NT author's theological use of the OT in the NT.* "In one sense, this question is wrapped up in all the others, but it is worth asking separately as it highlights things that may otherwise be overlooked."[17] For example (and not irrelevant to Paul's use of Isa 40:13 in Rom 11:34), "NT writers happily apply to the church, that is, to the new covenant people of God, many texts that originally referred to the Israelites, the old covenant people of God."[18]

3. PROCEDURE

What follows is a chapter-by-chapter account of the book.

1. Introduction
2. Step 1: Rom 11:34–35 in Context. Chapters 2–4 follow a similar approach. They start with the theological message of the book (Romans, Isaiah, and Job) and then funnel down to the argument of the larger sections (Rom 9–11; Isa 40; Job 38:1—42:6) and smaller section (Rom 11:33–36; Isa 40:12–14; Job 41:3–4).
3. Step 2: Isa 40:13 in Context
4. Step 2 (continued): Job 41:3a in Context
5. Step 3: Textual Issues
6. Step 4: Relevant Uses of Isa 40:13 and Job 41:3a in Jewish Literature. This includes Paul's use of Isa 40:13 in 1 Cor 2:16, which Paul wrote prior to Romans.
7. Step 5: Paul's Hermeneutical Warrant for Using Isa 40:13 and Job 41:3a in Rom 11:34–35
8. Step 6: Paul's Theological Use of Isa 40:13 and Job 41:3a in Rom 11:34–35
9. Conclusion

4. CONCLUSION

Now the table is set for an inductive study of Paul's use of the OT in Rom 11:34–35. We begin with step 1: studying the NT passage in its context.

---

17. Beale and Carson, "Introduction," xxv.
18. Ibid., xxvi.

2

Romans 11:34–35 in Context

UNDERSTANDING ROM 11:34–35 REQUIRES studying the text in relation to its immediate context (11:33–36), the section in which it occurs (chs. 9–11), and the letter in which it occurs (Romans as a whole). This chapter situates Rom 11:34–35 by surveying its larger literary and theological context before funneling down to those two verses.[1]

1. THE THEME OF ROMANS

A brief summary of Paul's grand letter sets the scene for analyzing suggested themes.

1.1. Synopsis of Romans

Paul obviously does not write with an explicit, formal outline, complete with section headings preceded by Roman numerals, capital letters, and numbers. But although it risks illegitimately imposing a reductionistic grid through which to read Romans, it is possible and profitable to trace Paul's argument in an orderly manner.[2]

Romans 1:16–17 is a transitional statement that most likely encapsulates the letter's theme: the gospel reveals God's righteousness, which people can experience only by faith. Or as Stott memorably puts it, the gospel reveals "God's righteous way of 'righteoussing'

---

1. On NT introduction issues for Romans, see Carson and Moo, *Introduction*, 391–414. Cf. Guthrie, *NT Introduction*, 403–31; Brown, *Introduction*, 559–84; Köstenberger, Kellum, and Quarles, *Cradle*, 510–57.

2. This outline generally follows Moo, *Epistle*, 33–35; Carson and Moo, *Introduction*, 391–93.

the unrighteous."³ Besides its introduction (1:1–17) and conclusion (15:14—16:27), the letter divides into four major parts:

1. People need God's righteousness because of universal condemnation for their sin (1:18—3:20), and they may be declared righteous only by faith in Jesus (3:21—4:25). This is the heart of the gospel.

2. The results of obtaining this righteousness include reconciliation and a secure hope for vindication (5:1-21), liberation from sin's dominating power (6:1-23), freedom from the law (7:1-25), and assurance and security (8:1-39).

3. The relationship between the gospel and Israel calls the reliability of God's word into question, so Paul vindicates God's righteousness (9:1—11:36).⁴

4. The gospel transforms how people live (12:1—15:13).

1.2. Suggested Themes for Romans

Since Romans is arguably the greatest theological letter ever written, it is not surprising that countless people have studied it and suggested a wide variety of themes for it. "Theme" in this sense refers to what Moo calls "the overarching topic that is able to stand as the heading" of that book of the Bible "as a whole."⁵ While it is possible that Romans discusses multiple topics but does not have one overarching, unifying topic (many occasional letters do not), it seems most appropriate to ascribe a theme to Romans because it is an unusually robust and organized letter. So what is the theme of Romans? There are at least six possibilities, and the first four focus on the different sections of the letter.⁶

1. *Justification by Faith (Rom 1–4)*. Martin Luther and the Reformers popularized this view.⁷

---

3. Stott, *Romans*, 37.
4. §2 below traces the argument of Rom 9–11 in more detail.
5. Moo, *Epistle*, 24.
6. Cf. ibid., 22–30, 22–30; Carson and Moo, *Introduction*, 408–11.
7. In the introduction to Luther, *Romans*, the editor, Hilton C. Oswald, observes, "The one chief topic of Romans for Luther is 'the righteousness of God,' that is, the righteousness by which God makes sinners righteous through faith in Jesus Christ" (xi).

Justification by faith is indeed a major and essential component of Paul's presentation of the gospel in Romans. One datum that supports this is that the δίκη word group occurs seventy-two times from 1:17 to 10:10. But although justification by faith is a critical motif of Romans, it is not large enough to function as the letter's overall theme because its prominence disappears in chapters 11–16.

2. *Union with Christ and the Work of God's Spirit (Rom 6–8)*. Others argue that the theme is Paul's teaching about the "mystical union" concept in chapter 6–8. Justification by faith, according to this view, is merely a "battle doctrine" for Paul's fight against the Judaizers.[8]

This view, like the first, takes a legitimate motif and exalts it without sufficient warrant as the entire letter's theme. Union with Christ and the work of God's Spirit is not prominent in chapters 1–5 or 9–16.

3. *The Place of Israelites and Gentiles in Salvation History (Rom 9–11)*. Stendahl challenged individualistic approaches to Romans by arguing that Paul was not concerned with how individuals may become right with a wrathful God but with how Israelites and Gentiles can constitute the one people of God.[9]

Gentile inclusion into the people of God is a major motif, but it is an unwarranted leap to emphasize this corporate aspect in a way that deemphasizes, neglects, or even denies individualistic aspects of the letter. Paul, who writes to both Jewish and Gentile Christians (cf. 1:7, 13; 11:13; 16:1–16),[10] presents a gospel with important implications for Jew-Gentile relations, but this same gospel targets individual human beings who are under God's wrath because of their sin and thus desperately need Jesus' salvation (chs. 1–8). The relationship between Israelites and Gentiles is an important background component to Romans, but the relationship between God and individual humans is the foreground.

---

8. Wrede, *Paul*, 123–25; Schweitzer, *Mysticism*, 205–26. Cf. Sanders, *Paul and Palestinian Judaism*, 434–42; idem, *Paul, the Law*, 30.

9. Stendahl, "Apostle," 199–215. Cf. Dunn, *Romans 1–8*, lxii–lxiii.

10. Contra Das, *Solving*, who argues that Paul's audience is exclusively Gentile. Karl P. Donfried, editor of *Romans Debate*, calls Das's study "vague, speculative, and ambiguous" and asserts, "The burden is on [Das] to demonstrate in a compelling and systematic manner the methodological and exegetical accuracy of his proposal; this, however, will require far more elaborate analysis of the complex situation in Rome and far greater historical and textual evidence than we are given here" (Review of *Solving*, 190).

Elevating Jew-Gentile relations as the overarching, unifying topic of Romans is reductionistic because it foregrounds the background and backgrounds the foreground.[11]

4. Practical Exhortation to Unity (Rom 14:1—15:13). Romans 14:1—15:13 rebukes two groups for not tolerating each other: the "weak in faith" (probably mainly Israelite Christians) and the "strong in faith" (probably mainly Gentile Christians). Some argue that the theme of Romans is this practical exhortation to unity that focuses on the Gentile Christians, who are becoming arrogant toward the shrinking minority of Israelite Christians.[12]

Paul's exhortation to unity in 14:1—15:13 underscores that one of his purposes is to heal the Jew-Gentile division in the Christian community in Rome, but this is not Paul's *primary* purpose for at least three reasons: (1) the issue is prominent only in 11:11–32 and 14:1—15:7; (2) much of the most theological part of the letter (chs. 1–11) is not demonstrably a basis for 14:1—15:13; and (3) Paul does not necessarily address the specific needs of the Roman church exactly as he addresses local congregations in other letters.[13]

5. God. Others suggest that the theme of Romans is God. For example, Leon Morris argues that since θεός occurs statistically more frequently in Romans than anywhere else in the NT (except for 1 John) and since θεός "occurs more often than any other theme in that book," therefore, "in Romans the one great theme is God. Paul writes on a number of topics, but everything is related to God."[14]

Statistics, however, are not paramount, and while Morris's use of them is helpful for collating linguistic data, it is ultimately unconvincing. The theme certainly must include God, but stating the theme as "God" is simply too broad.

---

11. Moo, *Epistle*, 28, 551–52. Relegating Jew-Gentile relations to the background, however, does not mean that they are unimportant. Paul was a Jew who became the apostle to the Gentiles, and he repeatedly experienced intense Jew-Gentile hatred on multiple levels. This Jew-Gentile dimension is part of what makes God so praiseworthy in Rom 11:33-36 (cf. Eph 2:11—4:16).

12. Donfried, "Short," 44–52.

13. Carson and Moo, *Introduction*, 406–7.

14. Morris, "Theme," 249–63; idem, *Romans*, 20.

6. *The Gospel in Its Salvation-Historical Context for Jews and Gentiles.* The five suggestions above are at least partially correct because each recognizes key motifs in Romans that other views tend to neglect or deemphasize. Each suggestion, however, ultimately falls short of being both broad enough to encompass the entire letter and specific enough to be useful.

The most satisfying theme of Romans is the gospel in its salvation-historical context for Jews and Gentiles.[15] At least five reasons support this:[16] (1) Εὐαγγέλλιον and εὐαγγελίζω are prominent in the introduction and conclusion (1:1, 2, 9, 15; 15:16, 19), a literary inclusio consistent with the idea that the gospel is the overarching topic. (2) Εὐαγγέλλιον is central to 1:16–17, which most likely states the letter's theme.[17] (3) Romans focuses on the gospel because it grows out of Paul's missionary situation. Multiple circumstances "led Paul to write a letter in which he carefully set forth his understanding of the gospel, particularly as it related to the salvation-historical question of Jew and Gentile, law and gospel, continuity and discontinuity between the old and new."[18] (4) Romans is "a tractate letter" that formally and systematically presents a theological argument that Paul "develops according to the inner logic of the gospel . . . Not once in chapters 1–13 does Paul allude to a specific circumstance or individual within the Roman Christian community."[19] (5) Romans 9–11 vindicates God with reference to salvation history, an issue that Rom 1–8 forces to the surface.

The theme of Romans is foundational for making hermeneutical and theological connections between Rom 11:34–35 and the two OT

---

15. Moo, *Epistle*, 25–30; idem, *Encountering*, 49; Carson and Moo, *Introduction*, 407–11; Wilckens, *Römer*, 1:91. Cf. Stuhlmacher, "Theme," 333–45; idem, *Romans*, 10–12.

16. Moo, *Epistle*, 29–30; Carson and Moo, *Introduction*, 407–10.

17. Moo, *Epistle*, 63–79.

18. Carson and Moo, *Introduction*, 407. Carson and Moo note five of these circumstances (*Introduction*, 407): (1) "the past battles in Galatia and Corinth"; (2) "the coming crisis in Jerusalem" (15:30–33); (3) "the need to secure a missionary base for the work in Spain" (15:24–29); (4) "the importance of unifying the divided Christian community in Rome around the gospel" (14:1—15:13); and (5) misguided attacks against Paul's theology "as being anti-law, and perhaps anti-Jewish" (3:8).

19. Ibid., 402.

passages quoted there. But even more significant is the theme and function of chapters 9–11.[20]

2. THE ARGUMENT OF ROM 9:1—11:32

There are at least three major views on the role of Rom 9–11 in the letter.[21] (1) Some bracket it off as an excursus, noting that the end of chapter 8 connects seamlessly with 12:1.[22] (2) Others highlight it as the heart or climax of Romans.[23] (3) From a literary standpoint, the most reasonable view sees Rom 9–11 as a critical but not central step in the argument of Romans.[24]

But what exactly is Rom 9–11 about? Some think that it is primarily about predestination or the righteousness of God, motifs illustrated by God's dealings with Israel.[25] God's dealings with Israel, however, are part of the main theme itself, not merely an illustration of a theological doctrine like predestination. So some argue that in light of the prominence of God's dealings with Israel in this section, the theme of Rom 9–11 is the need for unity between Israelites and Gentiles.[26] Narrowing the theme to such a specific application (which is indeed one of Paul's primary

---

20. Of all the secondary literature on Romans that I have consulted, §2 agrees most with Moo, *Epistle*, 547–744; idem, "Theology," 240–58; idem, "Israel," 185–216.

21. Cf. Müller, *Gottes*, 49–57; Lübking, *Paulus*, 27–50; Johnson, *Function*, 110–23; Reichert, *Römerbrief*, 149–66; Abasciano, "Paul's Use," 80–87.

22. Most famously, Dodd, *Romans*, 148–50. Cf. Bultmann, *Theology*, 2:132; Kuss, *Römerbrief*, 3:644–45; McClain, *Romans*, 22–23, 172.

23. Munck, *Christ*; Stendahl, *Paul*, 4, 28, 85; Beker, *Paul*, 87; idem, "Faithfulness," 327–32; Dunn, *Romans 1–8*, lxii; Abasciano, *Paul's Use*, 34–36.

24. Schlier, *Römerbrief*, 282; Walter, "Interpretation," 172; Moo, *Epistle*, 547–54.

25. "Israelites" and "Jews" are synonyms that Paul uses with significant distinctions. Thus, when discussing God's dealings with ethnic Israelites or Jews in Rom 9–11, this book follows Moo (*Epistle*, 560–61) by referring to those people as "Israel" or "Israelites" rather than "Jews." The title "Jew" is a "colorless, politically and nationally oriented title" generally used by those with a Gentile-perspective; this explains why Paul uses the title so many times in Romans 1–8. The title "'Israelite' connotes the special religious position of members of the Jewish people" viewed "from the perspective of salvation history and in their relationship to God and his promises to them," that is, it "is no mere political or nationalistic designation but a religiously significant and honorific title." This explains why Paul uses the title so many times in Rom 9–11. Cf. also Kuhn, "Ἰσραήλ," 3:359–69; Gadenz, *Called*, 2, 64–78.

26. Cf. Wright, "Letter," 626.

pastoral purposes for writing chs. 9–11) does not adequately capture the argument of the entire section either.

The overarching theme of Rom 9–11 is the vindication of God's righteousness, faithfulness, and integrity, namely, that God has kept and will keep his covenantal promises to Israel.[27] By explaining aspects of both the continuity and discontinuity of God's salvation-historical plan with special reference to Israelites and Gentiles,[28] Paul addresses some pressing questions regarding God himself. Were God's promises to Israel ineffectual? If so, this would inevitably call into question God's promises in general (e.g., Rom 8:28–39). Is God unfaithful and unreliable (cf. 3:1–8)? Has the church (now composed largely of Gentiles) replaced Israel as the recipient of God's covenantal promises? Since Gentiles accepted the gospel and Israelites have rejected it, is not God's integrity questionable? In short, the relationship between the gospel and Israel raises an issue that requires vindicating God's integrity. Romans 9:6a succinctly expresses this theme that Paul develops in a linear manner throughout the theodicy in Rom 9–11: "But it is not as though the word of God has failed."[29]

2.1. Introduction: God's Covenantal Promises and Israel's Predicament (Rom 9:1–6a)

Paul addresses the salvation-historical tension with which Israelites are wrestling. He is grieved (9:2) that so many of his fellow Israelites are rejecting the gospel. Israelites may have questioned the genuineness of Paul's grief since they viewed him as a Gentile-sympathizer, but Paul

---

27. Moo, *Romans*, 547–54; Morris, "Theme," 260; Wilckens, *Römer*, 2:181–83; Schmitt, *Gottesgerechtigkeit*, 72–75; Hübner, *Gottes*, 16; Walter, "Interpretation," 172; Hafemann, "Salvation," 43–44; Piper, *Justification*, 19; Schreiner, *Romans*, 469–72; Westerholm, *Understanding*, 135–49; Abasciano, *Paul's Use*, 32–33. Contra Seifrid, *Christ*, 152: "Israel's rejection of the gospel is part of the course which the promise of God must follow in coming to its fulfillment. All other construals of chapters 9–11 must be rejected. Paul is not wrestling with a cognitive dissonance brought about by an unexpected course of events. Nor is he assuring his largely Gentile audience of the faithfulness of God in the face of apparent failure. His intent is to discomfort and warn them . . . Paul's topic in these chapters is not the trustworthiness of Scripture, but the God who hides himself in Israel's failure in order that he might redeem and save." Seifrid presents a false dichotomy since Paul is comforting *and* warning in Rom 9–11.

28. See Moo, *Epistle*, 27–28, 549–53.

29. Piper, *Justification*, 19; Moo, *Epistle*, 553–54; idem, "Theology," 246–47; Schreiner, *Romans*, 472; Gadenz, *Called*, 9, 30–33, 83, 88.

emphasizes his honesty (9:1) and adds that he is willing to be ἀνάθεμα in place of his fellow Israelites whom he implies are not saved (9:3–4a; cf. Exod 32:32). Paul names eight unique privileges they have as God's covenant people (Rom 9:4b–5a). How then can it be that the Gentiles are experiencing God's blessing in a greater measure than the Israelites? This situation of Israelites and Gentiles in salvation history provokes a thorny theological question: Has God reneged on his promises to Israel (9:6a)? The argument of 9:6b–11:32 masterfully answers that single question in the negative. Paul constructs his argument in four steps, each progressively unfolding out of the previous section or sections and moving from the past to the present to the future: 9:6b–29; 9:30–10:21; 11:1–10; and 11:11–32.

2.2. God's Covenantal Promises and Israel's Past Unconditional Election (Rom 9:6b–29)

God's covenantal promises to Israel do not guarantee that every ethnic Israelite will automatically be saved. Paul's argument in this section breaks down into three parts.

1. *God unconditionally elects only some Israelites (9:6b–13)*. Paul opens by succinctly stating the thesis of 9:6b–13: "not all who are descended from Israel belong to Israel" (9:6b). The first "Israel" (i.e., Abraham's σπέρμα, τὰ τέκνα τῆς σαρκός) refers to *all* physical Israelites, and the second (i.e., Abraham's τέκνα, τέκνα τοῦ θεοῦ, τὰ τέκνα τῆς ἐπαγγελίας, σπέρμα) to a subdivision within that larger group, namely, *specific* physical Israelites (i.e., the "spiritual" Israel or remnant *within* physical Israel) whom God has chosen and called without any preconditions.[30] Why? Paul states the purpose explicitly: in order that God's electing purpose might stand (9:11). Thus, God's covenantal promises have not failed because they have been fulfilled with reference to individual election; God never promised to save every single physical Israelite. Nor has God ever chosen his spiritual people on the basis of ethnicity; the basis is always his sovereign grace. So God is entirely sovereign and righteous

---

30. Spiritual Israel is thus a subset of physical Israel. In this context, spiritual Israel is not synonymous with the church (an identification perhaps justifiable from other texts, e.g., Gal 6:16); in which case, spiritual Israel would overlap with physical Israel, but not be a subset of it. See the diagram in Moo, *Encountering*, 149; cf. idem, *Epistle*, 573–74. Contra Wright, "Romans," 634–37.

in electing specific Israelites to salvation.[31] Paul's explanation in 9:6b–13 provokes objections about whether God is right to act this way, so Paul pauses to answer them in 9:14–23 before resuming his argument in 9:24.

2. *God has the right to do whatever he wants with his creatures (9:14–23).* Paul addresses two objections—the two most common objections that people have to God's unconditional election of individuals: "But that's not fair!" and "But how can God justly blame people?" The first objection is that it is not fair for God to select individuals for salvation without any preconditions (9:14). But God alone has the prerogative to show mercy and compassion to whomever he desires; furthermore, God alone has the prerogative to harden whomever he desires (9:15–18). This explanation to the first objection raises a second objection: God is not fair to treat humans as morally responsible and culpable since they cannot resist his sovereign will (9:19). Instead of giving a philosophical answer to this apparent dilemma, Paul thunders a rebuke to anyone who would dare question God on this count since God himself *is* the standard of fairness; like a potter with his clay, God has the right to do whatever he desires with his creatures (9:20–23).

3. *God has effectually called both Israelites and Gentiles (9:24–29).* Resuming the argument in 9:6b–13, Paul explains that God has called both Israelites (9:24, 27–29) and Gentiles (9:24–26). The OT itself confirms that both Gentiles and a remnant of Israelites are "vessels of mercy."

This is the first step in Paul's vindication of God regarding his covenantal promises to Israel. Yet a lingering question remains: Why exactly are *so many* Israelites not part of "spiritual" Israel? One might assume that Paul's reply would simply be "because God did not elect them." Although that is theologically correct, it is only part of the picture and, perhaps surprisingly, not what Paul emphasizes in 9:30–10:21.

---

31. This is integral to a longstanding theological debate about whether God's election in Rom 9 is corporate or individual (among other issues—see Brand, *Perspectives*). For the view that election is corporate, see Klein, *New*; Witherington, *Romans*, 246–49, 253–55. For the view that God elects individuals to be saved, see Piper, *Justification*; Moo, *Epistle*, 570–88 (esp. Moo's theological conclusion on 587–88). See also this exchange: Schreiner, "Does Romans 9," 25–40; Abasciano, "Corporate," 351–71; Schreiner, "Corporate," 373–86.

2.3. Excursus: God's Covenantal Promises and Israel's Present Culpability (Rom 9:30–10:21)

Israelites are accountable to God for their unbelief. They are culpable because they failed to embrace God's righteousness in Christ. This excursus in Paul's argument has two parts.

1. *Many Israelites are seeking to establish their own righteousness (9:30–10:13).* Why have so many Gentiles attained δικαιοσύνη but so many Israelites have not? Paul emphasizes the human reason: faith. Generally speaking, the Gentiles pursued δικαιοσύνη by faith, but the Israelites "have stumbled over the stumbling stone" while pursuing a νόμον δικαιοσύνης ("a law that would lead to righteousness") by works (9:30–33). Paul repeats his genuine desire for his fellow Israelites to be saved (10:1; cf. 9:1–4a) because their religious zealotry is misinformed (10:2) since they are not submitting to God's righteousness (10:3). In the sweep of salvation history, Christ is the culmination of the Mosaic law εἰς δικαιοσύνην for everyone who exercises faith (10:4). The γάρ that begins 10:5 connects the paragraph (10:5–13) to the last phrase in 10:4: "to everyone who believes." Righteousness based on the Mosaic law is impossible, but righteousness based on faith is accessible to everyone—Israelite and Gentile alike.

2. *Israel's failure to believe in Christ (i.e., their rejection of God's righteousness based on faith) is inexcusable (10:14–21).* Paul lists four conditions that are necessary for someone to be saved by calling on the name of the Lord (10:14–15a, 17): (1) preachers must be sent; (2) preachers must preach; (3) people must hear the preaching; and (4) people must believe in Christ. God had met the first three conditions for the Israelites (10:15b, 18), but he is now showing himself to the Gentiles because the obstinately disobedient Israelites failed to meet the fourth condition (10:16, 19–21). The Israelites—not God—are to blame for their current predicament.

That is the second step vindicating God regarding his covenantal promises to Israel. The third step builds on the first two and directly addresses how God can be faithful to Israel in light of their current predicament.

2.4. God's Covenantal Promises and Israel's Present Predicament (Rom 11:1–10)

Even though the majority of Israelites are rejecting Christ, God's covenantal promises to Israel are still being fulfilled in some Israelites who are being saved (11:1–10). God has not totally rejected his people, whom he has corporately foreknown (11:1a, 3). Paul justifies this assertion with two examples of a remnant (cf. 9:27–29): himself (11:1b) and Elijah (11:2b–4). This grace-elected remnant continued to exist as Paul wrote Romans (11:5–6).[32] So to summarize God's dealings with corporate Israel, God saved ἡ ἐκλογή (the remnant) and hardened οἱ λοιποί (the majority of Israelites) (11:7–10). Paul thus vindicates God for his actions in the past and present by demonstrating that Israel's rejection is partial, not total. One question remains: What about Israel's future? Is Israel's rejection final? Will the beneficiaries of God's covenantal promises to Israel permanently be merely a remnant within Israel?

2.5. God's Covenantal Promises and Israel's Future (Rom 11:11–32)

Israel's fall is temporal, not final (11:11a). God has brought salvation to Gentiles *through* Israel (so Gentiles should not be arrogant), and God will completely fulfill his covenantal promises to Israel when "all Israel will be saved" (11:11–32). So God's election will ultimately prevail over Israel's unbelief. The pervasive motif in this passage is that the rejection of Israel resulted in the inclusion of Gentiles, which will in turn result in the inclusion of Israel.[33] Or stated another way, God set aside Israel in order to save more Gentiles and thus provoke Israel to jealousy and then save more Israelites (see table 2).[34]

---

32. Cf. Clements, "Remnant," 106–21.

33. For a responsible handling of this theme in Rom 11:11–32 in its sweeping biblical-theological context, see Wood, "Regathering," 299–300, 339–42, 593–99, 695–97, 700–702. See also Aletti, "Romains 11," 197–223.

34. Contra Wright, "Romans," 672–95.

TABLE 2. Salvation-Historical Twists in Rom 11:11–32: Israel → Gentiles → Israel[35]

vv.	Rejection of Israel →	Inclusion of Gentiles →	Inclusion of Israel
11	through their trespass	salvation has come to the Gentiles,	so as to make Israel jealous
12	if their trespass means	riches for the world,	how much more will their full inclusion [lit., fullness] mean!
12	if their failure means	riches for the Gentiles,	
15	if their rejection means	the reconciliation of the world,	what will their acceptance mean but life from the dead?
17	if some of the branches were broken off,	and you, although a wild olive shoot, were grafted in among the others and now share in the nourishing root of the olive tree,	
19	"Branches were broken off	so that I might be grafted in."	
20	They were broken off because of their unbelief,	but you stand fast through faith.	
21	God did not spare the natural branches		
22	the severity of God: severity toward those who have fallen	the kindness . . . of God: . . . God's kindness to you	
23			even they, if they do not continue in their unbelief, will be grafted in, for God has the power to graft them in again.
24		if you were cut from what is by nature a wild olive tree, and grafted, contrary to nature, into a cultivated olive tree,	how much more will these, the natural branches, be grafted back into their own olive tree.
25–26	a partial hardening has come upon Israel,	until the fullness of the Gentiles has come in.	And in this way all Israel will be saved

35. Cf. Moo, *Epistle*, 684.

vv.	Rejection of Israel →	Inclusion of Gentiles →	Inclusion of Israel
28	As regards the gospel, they are enemies of God	for your sake.	But as regards election, they are beloved for the sake of their forefathers.
30	because of their disobedience	you were at one time disobedient to God but now have received mercy,	
31	so they too have now been disobedient	in order that by the mercy shown to you	they also may now receive mercy.
32	For God has consigned all to disobedience,	that he may have mercy on all.	

This is comforting news, especially since election in chapter 9 may have appeared to be a discomforting doctrine. Paul's argument in this final section is threefold.

1. *God is saving Gentiles to make Israel jealous (11:11–15).* "Salvation has come to the Gentiles" by means of Israel's trespass and for the purpose of making Israel jealous (11:11b). In other words, an explicit purpose that God included Gentiles in his soteriological plan was to provoke Israel to jealousy.[36] If this sort of blessing (i.e., the salvation of Gentiles) accompanies Israel's fall, then one can only imagine what sort of blessing will accompany Israel's future restoration (11:12)! Paul restates 11:11b from the perspective of his own ministry (11:13–14) and then restates 11:12 (11:15).

2. *Gentiles must not be arrogant (11:16–24).* Verse 13 begins, "Now I am speaking to you Gentiles," denoting that Paul is directly addressing the Gentiles in the church at Rome. The rest of the passage directly and pointedly addresses Gentiles, viewing God's salvation-historical plan from their perspective (11:13–32). In the church at Rome (and elsewhere in the Roman Empire), Gentile Christians (the majority) were tempted to disparage Israelite Christians (the minority). So Paul's pastoral concern in this passage is at least twofold: on the one hand, Paul assures Israelite Christians that neither he nor God has abandoned Israel, and on the

---

36. The most thorough examination of this theme is Bell, *Provoked*.

other hand, Paul severely warns Gentile Christians against arrogance and anti-Semitism.[37]

Paul accomplishes these pastoral objectives partly by sharing an especially practical and relevant extended metaphor of the surprising turn of events in salvation history (Rom 11:16b–24). "Metaphor," according to Soskice, "is that figure of speech whereby we speak about one thing in terms which are seen to be suggestive of another."[38] Without being guilty of adhering to what Soskice calls the Substitution or Comparison theories,[39] Osborne explains a metaphor's components: "A metaphor . . . has three parts: the topic or item illustrated by the image, the image itself and the point of similarity or comparison (the actual meaning of the metaphor or simile in the passage)."[40] Sometimes one or two of the three components may be implicit rather than explicit.[41] Table 3 displays the topics that the images in Paul's metaphor illustrate as well as the point of similarity between each topic and image.[42]

37. Cf. Yarbrough's colorful reminder ("Theology," 57): "The message of Romans is not just apostolic instruction: it is prophetic outcry and warning. The problem is that it comes dressed in such symmetry, profundity, and intellectual elegance. It has become a Rubik's Cube for erstwhile expositors instead of a fire alarm to rouse God's people from their lethargy and shallowness."

38. Soskice, *Metaphor*, 15.

39. The Substitution theory "reduces metaphor to the status of a riddle or word game and the appreciation of metaphor to the unraveling of that riddle." The Comparison theory is "a slightly more sophisticated version of the Substitution theory" in which "there is more to metaphor than the mere substitution of term for term, but is still regarded as essentially ornamental usage in which two 'like' things are compared, as in 'This house is (like) a beehive.'" Soskice rightly discredits both. (1) "It is, in fact, impossible to make sense of a Substitution theory which says that no difference to significance at all is made by the metaphor. Even a wearisome metaphor like 'He is a fox' must signify something more to us than 'He is cunning'; otherwise we would regard 'fox' (as used metaphorically) and 'cunning' as synonyms, and have as our only reason for choosing between them that 'fox' in some cases actually sounded better than 'cunning.' But clearly one says 'He is a fox' not because it is more pleasing to the ear, but because it suggests something other than 'He is cunning.'" (2) "While making the metaphorical attribution intelligible," the Comparison theory "fails to explain what is interesting about it." It "fails to mark the fact that the good metaphor does not merely compare two antecedently similar entities, but enables one to see similarities in what previously had been regarded as dissimilar" (ibid., 25–26).

40. Osborne, *Hermeneutical*, 125. See Osborne's interaction with Soskice (387–94). Cf. Beekman and Callow, *Translating*, 127–28.

41. Osborne, *Hermeneutical*, 125–26; Beekman and Callow, *Translating*, 129–30.

42. The table obviously has limitations. As Soskice rightly argues, a metaphor cannot be reduced to various components such that the point of similarity could substitute for

TABLE 3. The Components of Paul's Extended Metaphor of the Olive Tree in Rom 11:16b–24[43]

1. Image	2. Topic	3. Point of Similarity
a. One cultivated olive tree	The people of God	A living organism
b. Arboriculturist	God	Skillful cultivation
c. The root of the olive tree	Israel's patriarchs as recipients and conveyors of God's covenantal promises	Basic means of support and nourishment
d. Natural branches	Israelites	Natural extension of the living organism
e. Natural branches broken off	Non-Christian Israelites	Disconnected from the living organism
f. Wild olive shoot from an uncultivated olive tree	Gentiles	Not naturally related to the living organism
g. Wild olive shoot engrafted into the cultivated olive tree	Gentile Christians	Attached extension of the living organism

Paul's metaphor achieves at least four pastoral goals. (1) It instills fear into Gentile Christians against being arrogant and presumptuous since they enjoy God's spiritual blessings *through Israelites* and *solely on the basis of God's grace*, not because they earned them. God is under no obligation to spare them if they do not persevere in the faith.[44] Gentiles must not be proud for being engrafted, especially since the original branches could be engrafted much more easily than they. Gentile Christians are part of Israel's spiritual heritage, so they must not despise or look down on Israel. This is the primary exhortatory point of the metaphor. (2) It instills hope into Israelite Christians regarding the future of ethnic Israel because "God has the power to graft them in again" (11:23). (3) It promotes unity among the one people of God: God's people under both the old and new covenants, both Israelites and

---

the image or that the image and topic are merely compared. The image of the metaphor itself communicates distinctively. Breaking down the components of the metaphors like this is merely one way to analyze it.

43. Cf. Moo, *Epistle*, 696–710.

44. This warning is a means of grace for genuine Christians to persevere since all genuine Christians are eternally secure (cf. Rom 5:9–10; 8:29–39).

Gentiles, are part of the *same* tree rooted in the soil of God's redemptive work as related in the OT. The church has not "replaced" ethnic Israel.[45] (4) It exalts God's sovereign grace by highlighting surprising turns in God's salvation-historical plan, which is "contrary to nature" (11:24). Farmers typically did not graft branches from uncultivated olive trees into cultivated olive trees; they did just the opposite. Paul's analogy reverses it to underscore God's sovereign grace in his unexpected plan that is "contrary to nature," namely, his plan to include many Gentiles as part of the people of God.[46] Wild olive trees were characteristically unfruitful and thus had no inherent merit for being grafted into a cultivated olive tree. So neither Israelites nor Gentiles have any ground for boasting. God brought both of them low so that he might exalt them in due time solely on the basis of his sovereign grace.

3. Israel will be engrafted or restored in God's time (11:25–32). Verses 16–24 emphasize the present inclusion of Gentiles, and vv. 25–32 emphasize the future inclusion of Israel. Paul reveals a μυστήριον, namely, an unexpected salvation-historical sequence: Israel is experiencing a partial hardening until the full number of Gentiles has come in to the kingdom, and this is the manner in which "all Israel will be saved" (11:25–27).[47] Πᾶς Ἰσραὴλ σωθήσεται indicates that when Christ returns God will save a significant number of the ethnic Israelites alive at that time;[48] πᾶς Ἰσραὴλ refers neither to the entire church[49] nor to ethnic Israelites be-

---

45. "Paul could have cut the Gordian knot by claiming that the church had taken over Israel's position and leaving it at that. This Paul refuses to do; in his view, to jettison God's promises to Israel is to jettison the gospel" (Moo, "Theology," 249).

46. Moo, *Romans*, 370–71, but contra Moo's earlier NICNT volume, which claims that such a theological conclusion is unwarranted and over-exegetes Paul's metaphor (*Epistle*, 703).

47. See Carson, "Mystery," 393–436, esp. 419–22; Kramer, "Mystery," 72–95. Cf. Bockmuehl, *Revelation*, 170–75.

48. Moo, *Epistle*, 719–26. Cf. Grisanti, "Progress," 93–95; Hafemann, "Salvation," 52–53; Burns, "Future," 188–229; Johnson, "Evidence," 211–19; Vanlaningham, "Romans 11:25–27," 141–74; Harding, "Salvation," 66–67; Scott, "All Israel," 489–527; Westerholm, *Understanding*, 143–44; Das, *Solving*, 235–60. Some argue further that πᾶς Ἰσραὴλ refers to every single ethnic Israelite alive at the end of the age: Hoehner, "Israel," 155–57; Brackett, "Paul's Use," 153–55; Waymeyer, "Identity," 85–154.

49. Contra Calvin, *Romans*, 437; Wright, "Christ," 249–50; idem, "Romans," 687–93; Wood, "Regathering," 597–98.

ing saved throughout the ages.⁵⁰ This unexpected sequence in salvation history is a mystery, a God-revealed truth that was previously hidden. Israelites commonly expected that the inclusion of Gentiles would occur when Christ returns—not that the inclusion of Gentiles would occur *now* and that the inclusion of *Israel* would happen when Christ returns.

Verses 28-32 bring to a conclusion Paul's lengthy argument begun in 9:6. With reference to the gospel, Israelites are now God's enemies for the sake of the Gentiles (11:28a), but with reference to corporate election, God loves them because his gifts and calling are irreversible (11:28b-29). God has ordained the disobedience of both Israel and Gentiles in salvation history for an explicit purpose: in order that he may sovereignly show them both mercy (11:30-32). As in vv. 16-24, one of Paul's pastoral objectives in vv. 25-32 is to humble Gentiles; he wants Gentiles to understand this mystery lest they be wise in their own sight (11:25a). Gentiles presently constitute the majority of the church, but that does not mean that God has abandoned Israel and reneged on his covenantal promises to them; God has purposed to show mercy to Israel. Gentile Christians must not be arrogant toward Israelites or think that they have replaced Israel, and Israelite Christians must not despair. God's salvation-historical plan breeds humility and hope.

2.6. Summary of Rom 9:1—11:32

Thus, in Rom 9:6—11:32, Paul vindicates God's righteousness in his past, present, and future dealings with Israel. (1) God's past covenantal promises do not contradict the new twist in salvation history in which God is saving some Israelites and many Gentiles. (2) God is presently fulfilling his covenantal promises by saving some Israelites. (3) God will fulfill his covenantal promises when "all Israel will be saved" (11:26). Therefore, the word of God has not failed (9:6a).

To what degree does the below exegesis of 11:33-36 (vv. 34-35 in particular) depend on the above exegesis of chapters 9-11? Or put more bluntly: Would mistaken exegesis of chapters 9-11 invalidate the exegesis of 11:33-36? The majority of the exegesis of chapters 9-11 is

---

50. Contra Refoulé, *Tout Israël*, summarized on 181-82; Merkle, "Romans 11," 709-21; Fung, "Israel's Salvation"; Zoccali, "All Israel," 289-318. Cf. Gadenz (*Called*, 275-80), who interprets πᾶς Ἰσραήλ as every individual Israelite Christian throughout history plus a significant number of the non-Christian Israelites who are alive at the time Christ returns.

foundational for the exegesis of 11:33–36. Some interpretational decisions are not crucial, such as the specific views that God unconditionally elects individuals for salvation or that God will save a significant number of the ethnic Israelites alive at the time of Christ's return. But the theme and argument of chapters 9–11 is crucially connected to 11:33–36. The nature of that connection is what next merits our attention.

3. THE ARGUMENT OF ROM 11:33–36

How does Rom 11:33–36 logically connect to what precedes it? And what is the meaning of this passage in which 11:34–35 is inserted?

3.1. The Logical Connection of Rom 11:33–36 to What Precedes It

There is some debate on about how Rom 11:33–36 connects to what precedes it. We may address three related levels of this debate by posing three different questions.

3.1.1. To Which Section of Romans Does 11:33–36 Primarily Connect?

There are three major options regarding the section of Romans to which 11:33–36 primarily connects. Romans 11:33–36 connects primarily to either (1) the immediate context as encapsulated in 11:32 ("God has consigned all to disobedience, that he may have mercy on all");[51] (2) 9:1—11:32, namely, the vindication of God's integrity in his past, present, and future dealings with Israel;[52] or (3) all that precedes in chapters 1–11.[53]

Its connection to the immediate context (esp. 11:32) is undeniably important, but that limitation is too restrictive. Its connection to chapters 1–11 is also important, but that is not its *primary* connection; rather, that is more of an indirect connection by virtue of how the four major sections in Romans up to this point (1:18–3:20; 3:21–4:25; 5–8; 9–11) relate to each other and combine to form a unified theological discourse.

---

51. Luther, *Romans*, 103n29. Cf. Ridderbos, *Paul*, 360; Schreiner, *Romans*, 632: "More likely, they conclude Rom. 9–11, in particular 11:32."

52. Cullmann, *Salvation*, 252; Cranfield, *Romans*, 2:589; Käsemann, *Romans*, 318; Schlier, *Römerbrief*, 348; Moo, *Epistle*, 740n1; Kim, *God*, 141. Cf. Murray, *Romans*, 2:104–5.

53. Edwards, *Writings*, 280–81; Bruce, *Romans*, 211; Fitzmyer, *Romans*, 633.

From a literary standpoint, 11:33–36 is most directly connected to chapters 9–11. At least three factors support this:

1. Both Romans 5–8 and 9–11 end with celebratory outbursts, suggesting that 8:31–39 concludes chapters 5–8 and that 11:33–36 concludes chapters 9–11. Romans 8:31–39 celebrates that nothing can separate Christians from God's secure love in Christ, and 11:33–36 celebrates God's spectacular salvation-historical plan.

2. The emphases in 11:33–36 correspond with the emphases in chapters 9–11, namely, the focus on God the Father and his ways with people.[54]

3. The doxologies in 9:5b and 11:36b form a doxological inclusio, suggesting that the doxology in 11:36b does not directly connect to sections before chapter 9.[55]

3.1.2. What, More Precisely, Is the Connection Between Rom 9:1—11:32 and 11:33–36?

The contrast between 9:1–5 and 11:33–36 is striking. Paul could not begin chapters 9–11 on a more tragic note: he is so distressed about his fellow Israelites who are not saved that he is willing to be ἀνάθεμα in their place. Yet after addressing this problem and its implications head-on, Paul ends with the soul-thrilling last four verses of Rom 11. On what basis can Paul express such contrasting sentiments as bookends to the same division of his letter?

§2.5 argues that Gentile Christians must not be arrogant toward Israelites or think that they have replaced Israel and that Israelite Christians must not despair. God's salvation-historical plan breeds humility for Gentile Christians and hope for Israelite Christians. But God's salvation-historical plan in 9:6—11:32, arguably the most demanding and difficult extended theological argument in Paul's letters, breeds more than humility and hope. It breeds in both Gentile and Israelite Christians deep, uncontainable adoration for God. That is why after Paul vindicates God's righteousness in 9:6—11:32, he erupts with praise to God for his marvelous soteriological plan. Godet compares 11:33–36 to Paul reaching the top of a mountain, surging with an endorphin rush as he surveys the panorama:

---

54. Moo, *Epistle*, 740n1.
55. Käsemann, *Romans*, 318.

> Like a traveler who has reached the summit of an Alpine ascent, the apostle turns and contemplates. Depths are at his feet; but waves of light illumine them, and there spreads all around an immense horizon which his eye commands. The plan of God in the government of mankind spreads out before him, and he expresses the feelings of admiration and gratitude with which the prospect fills his heart.[56]

Doxology is exactly the right response for Christians who have carefully traced Paul's argument in chapters 9–11. The following story by John Piper illustrates this well:

> One of the highest points in my short, six-year teaching career in the Biblical Studies department at Bethel College was in the spring of 1977. I had spent the entire semester on Romans 9–11 leading about a dozen advanced Greek students through the rigorous exegesis of these three chapters. It was the final class of the year, and I was drawing the final "arcs" on the board to sum up all the relationships between all the units. I drew one last arc over all three chapters, from one side of the board to the other, and underlined Rom 11:36 as the ultimate point of the entire section: "From him, though him, and to him are all things. To him be glory forever." Before I could turn around, these twelve students—some of the brightest I ever had (including Tom Steller)—began to sing the doxology.
>
> I didn't ask them to. I didn't plan it. It just came out. And that's the way it was for Paul when he wrote this. He comes to the end of these three chapters on the ultimate purposes of God to show the riches of his glory on the vessels of mercy, and he breaks into doxology as he closes. All theology, rightly grasped, leads the mind and the heart to doxology. The story of God is about the glory of God. All revelation of the ways of God leads to exultation over the wonders of God.[57]

3.1.3. What Motivates Rom 11:33–36: God's Hidden Ways or Revealed Ways?

There is some debate about what motivates Rom 11:33–36. Is it motivated primarily by God's *hiding* his ways from us?[58] Or is it motivated

---

56. Godet, *Romans*, 265.
57. Piper, "Deep Riches," para. 1–2.
58. Morris, *Romans*, 427: "[I]t is prompted by what we do not know about God (even what he has revealed we do not fully comprehend) rather than by what we do

primarily by God's *revealing* his ways to us?[59] The latter is probably the case, although there is some overlap.

> Paul, after all, claims to have received revelation into a "mystery" concerning the future of Israel that gives us access to the mind of God. Throughout Rom. 9–11, while certain points remain hard to understand, Paul is claiming to be transmitting truth to which his readers are to respond.[60]

In Rom 9–11, God's ways are hidden from us, but that does not mean that 11:33–36 is an emotional outburst after Paul has hit an intellectual brick wall. It does not express exasperated frustration, as if to say, "I give up. I just don't get it. How do God's sovereignty and human responsibility coexist? How can Israel really have a future in light of what has happened in salvation history? I can't explain this. We can't fully understand this because of our severe limitations, so let's just dump it all under the category of mystery."[61]

Several points in that statement are true: we cannot exhaustively understand God's ways; we are severely limited noetically because we are finite and fallen; we are short-sighted; we cannot fully resolve the tension we feel between God's sovereignty and human responsibility; we cannot comprehensively explain the manner, means, and purposes of God's dealings with Israel. So in one sense God's ways as described in Rom 9–11 are extremely difficult to understand and explain. We may legitimately ask hard questions, but God is not obligated to give us exhaustive answers that logically and philosophically satisfy our intellect. Ultimately, however, we must recognize some basic truths: God has an absolute right as God to reveal and conceal whatever he would like; God is completely independent and does not need us in any way, so he does not need to consult with us regarding his salvation-historical plan; since God is infinite and we are finite, we are incapable of exhaustively understanding his mind; we have no right to criticize God's ways in salvation history, endlessly pelt God with questions, or demand

---

know... He has certainly given some of the answers, but to some very important questions the answer is still not revealed."

59. Moo, *Epistle*, 740; Schreiner, *Romans*, 636. Cf. Murray, *Romans*, 2:104; Johnson, *Romans 9–11*, 173.

60. Moo, *Epistle*, 740.

61. I.e., "mystery" in the sense of "something that is difficult or impossible to understand or explain," not in the sense that Paul uses the term μυστήριον.

answers; God exists not merely to be analyzed but to be worshipped and treasured, so our logical and philosophical tension, theological gridlock, and unanswered questions must give way to unreserved trust and wholehearted worship; we may not be able to understand God's ways, but we are able to give God praise.

All this is true. But is that all there is to 11:33–36? Does this completely capture the *primary* focus of 11:33–36? And is Paul expressing *frustration*? The answer to those questions is No.

In Rom 9–11, God's ways are revealed to us. This is what Paul emphasizes. Yes, chapters 9–11 are filled with concepts that are hard to understand, but Paul is doing much more than highlighting irresolvable tensions. He is revealing God's mind-boggling ways, and this revelation is uniquely panoramic, detailed (but not exhaustive), and pastoral. Like any skilled preacher, Paul is communicating intense, profound, confounding truths[62] in a way that his audience can understand and to which they can then knowledgably respond. The right response to what God reveals in chapters 9–11 is 11:33–36, where Paul bursts forth from meditation on God's revealed plan for salvation history.

---

62. E.g., 11:32: "God has consigned all to disobedience, that he may have mercy on all."

3.2. The Content and Triadic Structure of Rom 11:33–36

Romans 11:33–36 has a triadic structure. (See table 4.)

TABLE 4. A Propositional Display of Rom 11:33–36[63]

Strophe	v.	NA[27]	Summary
1	33a	Ὢ βάθος πλούτου [θεοῦ]	Exclamation 1: God's riches, wisdom, and knowledge are deep!
	33b	καὶ σοφίας [θεοῦ]	
	33c	καὶ γνώσεως θεοῦ·	
	33d	ὡς ἀνεξεραύνητα τὰ κρίματα αὐτοῦ	Exclamation 2: God's judgments are unsearchable!
	33e	καὶ ἀνεξιχνίαστοι αἱ ὁδοὶ αὐτοῦ.	Exclamation 3: God's ways are unfathomable!
2	34a	τίς γὰρ ἔγνω νοῦν κυρίου;	Question 1 (proof 1): God is incomprehensible (Isa 40:13a).
	34b	ἢ τίς σύμβουλος αὐτοῦ ἐγένετο;	Question 2 (proof 2): God does not have any counselors (Isa 40:13b).
	35a	ἢ τίς προέδωκεν αὐτῷ,	Question 3 (proof 3): God does not have any creditors (Job 41:3a).
	35b	καὶ ἀνταποδοθήσεται αὐτῷ;	
3	36a	ὅτι	Argumentation for 11:33–35: God is supreme.
	36b	ἐξ αὐτοῦ [τὰ πάντα]	Prep. phrase 1: God is the source of all things.
	36c	καὶ δι' αὐτοῦ [τὰ πάντα]	Prep. phrase 2: God is the means of all things.
	36d	καὶ εἰς αὐτὸν τὰ πάντα·	Prep. phrase 3: God is the goal of all things.
	36e	αὐτῷ ἡ δόξα εἰς τοὺς αἰῶνας,	Response to 33–36d: Doxology. God alone deserves glory eternally! Let it be so.
	36f	ἀμήν.	

It contains three strophes, each with a group of three components: the first strophe has three exclamations, the first of which includes three nouns that most likely modify "depth" (11:33); the second strophe has

---

63. Cf. Moo, *Epistle*, 739–44; Schreiner, *Romans*, 631–38.

three rhetorical questions beginning with τίς (11:34-35); and the third strophe has three parallel prepositional phrases (11:36).

"This arrangement of the material, the short, roughly parallel lines, and some unusual vocabulary suggests that we should treat the passage as a hymn."[64] There is no compelling evidence that anyone other than Paul authored 11:33-36,[65] which reflects Paul's judicious use of three traditions: apocalyptic literature (11:33), wisdom literature (11:34-35), and Hellenistic Judaism (11:36).[66]

3.2.1. Strophe 1 (Three Exclamations): God Is Deep (Rom 11:33)

Strophe 1 (11:33) contains three exclamations about the infinite depth of God's ways.

Exclamation 1. The emotion-stirring Ὦ introduces the first awe-filled exclamation: "Oh, the depth . . . !" Paul is using βάθος metaphorically, which BDAG describes as "someth. nonphysical perceived to be so remote that it is difficult to assess." Humans cannot penetrate such depths, for this is what God's Spirit himself searches: τὸ γὰρ πνεῦμα πάντα ἐραυνᾷ, καὶ τὰ βάθη τοῦ θεοῦ (1 Cor 2:10). Thiselton suggests translating τὰ βάθη τοῦ θεοῦ as "the depths of God's own self."[67] So in Rom 11:33, Paul exclaims (to paraphrase), "Oh, the 'inexhaustible magnitude,'[68] the infinite grandeur, the bottomless depth!"

Three genitive nouns follow the word βάθος: πλούτου, σοφίας, and γνώσεως. These are three of God's deep qualities with reference to his salvation-historical plan. Some disagree and interpret σοφίας and

---

64. Moo, *Epistle*, 740. Cf. Norden, *Agnostos Theos*, 240-50; Harder, *Paulus*, 51-55; Martin, "Aspects," 18; Bornkamm, "Praise," 105-11; Dupont, *Gnosis*, 91-93; Deichgräber, *Gotteshymnus*, 61-64; Zutphen, "Studies"; Viard, *Romains*, 253-55; Michel, *Römer*, 359-62; Schlier, *Römerbrief*, 344-48; Käsemann, *Romans*, 318-21; Harrisville, *Romans*, 187; Wilckens, *Römer*, 2:269-74; Gloer, "Homologies," 115-32; Hübner, *Gottes*, 124-26; Barth, "Theologie," 330-48; Johnson, *Romans 9-11*, 164-66; Dunn, *Romans 9-16*, 697-98; Schmithals, *Römerbrief*, 414-16; Fitzmyer, *Romans*, 632-35; Stuhlmacher, *Romans*, 174-76; Martin, "Hymns," 419-22; Ryan, "Faithfulness," 159-66; Kim, *God*, 140-41; Dumbrell, *Romans*, 115.

65. Contra Zutphen, "Studies," 31-46; Jewett, *Romans*, 713-23. Jewett argues that Paul redacted a hymn already in existence (i.e., Rom 11:33, 36) by inserting two OT quotations in the middle of it (i.e., Rom 11:34-35).

66. Bornkamm, "Praise," 105; Käsemann, *Romans*, 318-19; Barth, "Theologie," 331-32; Moo, *Epistle*, 740.

67. Thiselton, *Corinthians*, 257.

68. Moo, *Epistle*, 741.

γνώσεως as modifying πλούτου: "Oh, the depth of the riches *both* of the wisdom and knowledge of God!"[69] It seems more likely, however, that all three qualities are coordinate: "Oh, the depth of the riches *and* wisdom and knowledge of God!"[70] The latter is more likely for two reasons. First, although Paul usually qualifies πλοῦτος with a genitive of content, his two most recent uses of πλοῦτος occur in 11:12, where he uses them absolutely and does not follow them by genitives of content.[71] Second, the genre of 11:33–36 is likely a hymn, and it is filled with triads: three strophes consisting of three exclamations, three questions, and three prepositional phrases. Structurally, it fits nicely for the opening line to list three of God's deep qualities.

But to what do πλούτου, σοφίας, and γνώσεως refer? (1) Πλοῦτος generally refers to a "plentiful supply of someth., *a wealth, abundance*" (BDAG),[72] but in 11:33 it probably means something more specific than God's inexhaustible wealth. In light of the context—11:12 uses πλοῦτος twice and 10:12b uses the cognate πλουτέω—πλοῦτος in 11:33 refers to God's abundant kindness to both Israelites and Gentiles in his revealed salvation-historical plan.[73] (2) Σοφία refers to "the capacity to understand and function accordingly, *wisdom*" (BDAG), and here it refers more specifically to God's wisdom with reference to his revealed salvation-historical plan. Wisdom is a significant theme elsewhere in Paul's letters regarding God's salvation-historical plan (e.g., 1 Cor 1:17—2:16; Col 2:2–3). (3) Γνῶσις refers to "comprehension or intellectual grasp of someth., *knowledge*" (BDAG), specifically, God's omniscience with reference to his revealed salvation-historical plan.[74]

---

69. KJV; NASB; HCSB (emphasis added). Cf. NIV; TNIV; Calvin, *Romans*, 444; Godet, *Romans*, 265–66; Bruce, *Romans*, 211; Schreiner, *Romans*, 632–33.

70. ESV; NRSV; NET (emphasis added). Cf. NLT; Liddon, *Romans*, 222; Käsemann, *Romans*, 319; Wilckens, *Römer*, 2:269; idem, "σοφία," 7:518; Fitzmyer, *Romans*, 634; Moo, *Epistle*, 741; Osborne, *Romans*, 313; Jewett, *Romans*, 716.

71. Of the fifteen times Paul uses πλοῦτος, eleven are followed by genitives of content (Rom 2:4; 9:23; 2 Cor 8:2; Eph 1:7, 18; 2:7; 3:8, 16; Col 1:27; 2:2; 1 Tim 6:17), three are not (Rom 11:12 [2x]; Phil 4:19), and the one in 11:33 is debatable.

72. Cf. Jewett, *Romans*, 716: "The reference to 'riches' in the possessive seems peculiar at first glance (how can riches be deep?), but the formulation would not have seemed odd in the ancient world, in which riches were conceived as precious metal piled in mounds that are βαθύς ('deep' or 'high'), depending on one's viewing position."

73. Moo, *Epistle*, 741.

74. It seems like an unsubstantiated stretch to connect γνῶσις with its cognate προγινώσκω in 11:2 and thus conclude with Moo (*Epistle*, 741–42), "God's knowledge

Exclamations 2–3. The second and third exclamations in 11:33 (33d and 33e in table 4: ὡς ἀνεξεραύνητα τὰ κρίματα αὐτοῦ and καὶ ἀνεξιχνίαστοι αἱ ὁδοὶ αὐτοῦ) are parallel in three ways:

1. They are parallel in syntax. The single ὡς introduces both exclamations (connected by καί), and their parts of speech line up exactly (i.e., predicate adjective + an implied copulative verb + article + noun functioning as the subject + a possessive third person personal pronoun). The particle ὡς functions as "a relatively high point on a scale involving exclamation, *how!*" (BDAG).

2. They are parallel in morphology. Both predicate adjectives (ἀνεξεραύνητα and ἀνεξιχνίαστοι) have the ἀνεξ- prefix.

3. They are parallel in meaning. Their meanings are essentially identical, namely, God's salvation-historical plan is inscrutable to humans.[75] The first of the two statements, ἀνεξεραύνητα τὰ κρίματα αὐτοῦ, means that God's executive decisions or decrees[76] regarding salvation history are unfathomable (lit., unsearchable). The second, ἀνεξιχνίαστοι αἱ ὁδοὶ αὐτοῦ, means that God's ways of acting[77] in salvation history are inscrutable or incomprehensible (lit., beyond tracing out).[78] Trying to track God's ways in salvation history is like trying to track an unseen person by following their footsteps on the beach right into the water where they disappear into the shallowest part of the ocean.[79] Those who have discovered God's ways in Rom 9–11 and therefore conclude that they fully understand God's ways would be as foolish as the Vikings discovering a slice of the shoreline of what is now America and therefore concluding that they fully understand North America. "Behold, these are but

---

here [in 11:33] is that special relational 'knowing' which comes to expression in his election of individuals to salvation (and perhaps also of Israel to her corporate blessing)."

75. Moo, *Epistle*, 742.

76. Cf. BDAG, definition 2 of κρίμα: "content of a deliberative process, *decision, decree*."

77. Cf. BDAG, definitions 3 and 3b of ὁδός: "course of behavior, *way, way of life*" and "*way of life, way of acting, conduct*."

78. The standard definition for "incomprehensible" is "not able to be understood," but this is not what we mean when we say that God is incomprehensible. Rather, we mean that God is not able to be *fully* or *exhaustively* understood.

79. Cf. Ps 77:19: "Your way was through the sea, your path through the great waters; yet your footprints were unseen."

the outskirts ["outer fringe," NIV] of his ways" (Job 26:14).[80] The adjective ἀνεξιχνίαστος occurs in only one other place in the NT, Eph 3:8, where Paul uses it to modify πλοῦτος (the third word in Rom 11:33): τοῖς ἔθνεσιν εὐαγγελίσασθαι τὸ ἀνεξιχνίαστον πλοῦτος τοῦ Χριστοῦ ("to preach to the Gentiles the unsearchable riches of Christ").[81]

Commentators commonly note that 11:33 shows similarities to 2 Bar. 14:8-9 (OTP): "O Lord, my Lord, who can understand your judgment? Or who can explore the depth of your way? Or who can discern the majesty of your path? Or who can discern your incomprehensible counsel? Or who of those who are born has ever discovered the beginning and the end of your wisdom?"[82] When considered in light of 2 Bar. 75:1-5, "This text [2 Bar. 14:8-9] comes in a passage that wrestles with much the same issue that occupies Paul in Rom. 9-11: the destiny of the people of God in light of apparent calamity."[83] This demonstrates that Paul was not the first Israelite to wrestle with the issues in Rom 9-11 and then ask rhetorical questions about God's deep judgments, ways, counsel, and wisdom.

3.2.2. Strophe 2 (Three Rhetorical Questions): God Is Incomprehensible, without Counselors, and without Creditors (Rom 11:34-35)

The γάρ that begins 11:34 indicates that strophe 2 (11:34-35) supports strophe 1 (11:33) by exulting in three specific reasons that God's riches, wisdom, and knowledge are deep. Paul does this by quoting three rhetorical questions from the OT that sharply contrast God's infinite ways with finite humans. These three questions appear to be part of a chiasm with the three divine qualities in 11:33:[84]

---

80. Cf. Talbert, *Beyond*, 146.

81. Ἀνεξιχνίαστος occurs four times in the LXX: Job 5:9; 9:10; 34:24; Pr Man 6. Three of those occur in Job, which Paul quotes in Rom 11:35.

82. Cf. *2 Bar.* 20:4; 75:1-5; *1 En.* 84:2-3; 93:11-14; 1QHa 7:26-33; 10:3-7; 15:26-32; 1QS 11:15-17.

83. Moo, *Romans*, 742n17. Cf. Johnson, *Romans 9-11*, 168-71.

84. Bengel, *Gnomon*, 134; Stifler, *Romans*, 212, 214; Lund, *Chiasmus*, 222; Bornkamm, "Praise," 107; Deichgräber, *Gotteshymnus*, 62; Barth, "Theologie," 332-33; Jeremias, "Chiasmus," 150-51; Zutphen, "Studies," 47-48; Käsemann, *Romans*, 319; Pesch, *Römerbrief*, 90; Folker, *Argumentation*, 178; Fitzmyer, *Romans*, 634; Stuhlmacher, *Romans*, 175; Ryken, Wilhoit, and Longman, "Rhetorical Patterns," 720-27; Harvey, *Listening*, 203; Moo, *Epistle*, 742-43; Jewett, *Romans*, 714, 718. Others connect the two

A πλοῦτος (God's deep merciful kindness to ill-deserving Israelites and Gentiles in salvation history)[85]
   B σοφία (God's deep wisdom regarding salvation history)
      C γνῶσις (God's deep knowledge regarding salvation history)
      C' τίς γὰρ ἔγνω νοῦν κυρίου; (God is incomprehensible.)
   B' ἢ τίς σύμβουλος αὐτοῦ ἐγένετο; (God does not have any counselors.)
A' ἢ τίς προέδωκεν αὐτῷ, καὶ ἀνταποδοθήσεται αὐτῷ; (God does not have any creditors.)

Grant Osborne rejects this chiasm because it "stretches the language and fails to fit the development of thought. It is more likely that the questions build on the general idea of verse 33, namely, the unknowable mind of God."[86] In view of the possibility that 11:33–36 is a hymn, however, it seems quite natural and hardly like a "stretch" for Paul to use a common and memorable rhetorical device like chiasm.

The rhetorical effect of these three questions in 11:34–35 is to humble finite humans and exalt the infinite God. The implied answer to each rhetorical question is "no one."[87] Finite humans cannot (1) understand God's infinite ways, (2) counsel God, or (3) place God in their debt. According to 11:34, God's knowledge and wisdom with reference to salvation history are inscrutable: no one has known the mind of the Lord, and no one has been his counselor.[88] According to 11:35, God does not owe any human anything,[89] thus giving him the prerogative to dispense his rich grace in salvation history however he wants: no one has

---

statements in 11:34 to γνῶσις and σοφία respectively. For example, Meyer (*Romans*, 2:245) makes this connection and cites Theodoret, Theophylact, Wetstein, and Fritzsche.

85. Cf. Moo, *Epistle*, 741, 743.

86. Osborne, *Romans*, 315. Cf. Godet, *Romans*, 265; Schreiner, *Romans*, 633.

87. Contra Haacker, *Römer*, 247; Jewett, *Romans*, 719, who argues, "Since the mystery of God's plan has just been disclosed in vv. 25-26, the rhetorical questions in the citation are not intended to evoke the generic response 'No one!'"

88. Cf. Job 15:8; Isa 55:8–9; Jer 23:18; see also Wis 9:13. Fitzmyer (*Romans*, 633) argues, "The key verse in this passage [i.e., Rom 11:33–36] is 11:34, 'Who has known the mind of the Lord?' It sums up all of Paul's foregoing discussion about the relationship of Israel to Christ, about the relationship of Jews to Christians ever since Paul penned these lines. One has to realize that Paul has not solved 'the problem of Israel,' nor have Christian theologians since then."

89. Cf. 1 Chr 29:14; Job 35:7.

given a gift to God with the result that[90] God is obligated to repay them. In short, God is incomprehensible (i.e., unable to be understood *fully*) and has neither counselors nor creditors.

3.2.3. Strophe 3 (Three Prepositional Phrases): God Is Supreme (Rom 11:36)

Strophe 3 (11:36) begins with ὅτι, thus giving reasons that support strophes 1–2 (11:33–35).[91] It does this by summarizing the God-centeredness of the universe with three prepositional phrases that lead into the climactic doxology: ἐξ αὐτοῦ καὶ δι' αὐτοῦ καὶ εἰς αὐτὸν τὰ πάντα. God the Father is the source (ἐκ), means (διά), and goal (εἰς) of all things. He encompasses the beginning, middle, and end. Boice insightfully uses Nebuchadnezzar's question in Dan 4:30 ("Is not this great Babylon, which I have built by my mighty power as a royal residence and for the glory of my majesty?") to illustrate Rom 11:36a negatively: "Nebuchadnezzar was saying that the great city of Babylon and its empire, which he admired (and desired) more than anything else in the world, was from him (he 'built' it), through him ('by my mighty power') and for him ('for the glory of my majesty')."[92]

Some follow Origen by identifying the three prepositional phrases in 11:36a with God the Father, Son, and Holy Spirit respectively.[93] Such a view, however, is mistaken: there is not a hint in the text that Paul is making Trinitarian connections, and from a systematic theological perspective the final prepositional phrase (εἰς αὐτόν) could modify either God the Father or Christ but not the Holy Spirit. The three prepositional phrases in 11:36a are remarkably similar to other descriptions of God the Father and Christ outside of Romans (emphasis added):

---

90. The καί in 11:35 (ἤ τίς προέδωκεν αὐτῷ, καὶ ἀνταποδοθήσεται αὐτῷ;) does not coordinately connect the two clauses; it fits BDAG, definition 2d: "w. expressions that introduce cause or result."

91. It is possible that the ὅτι at the beginning of 11:36 connects solely to 11:35 (i.e., finite humans cannot place God in their debt *because* God is supreme). Cf. Meyer, *Romans*, 246; Stifler, *Romans*, 214. It also may connect to 11:34–35 (i.e., no one is God's counselor or creditor *because* God is supreme). Cf. Schreiner, *Romans*, 631, 637. It most likely connects with all of 11:33–35 given its triadic structure and the sweeping way in which final strophe concludes.

92. Boice, *Romans 9–11*, 1466.

93. Origen, *Romans*, 189–90. Cf. McClain, *Romans*, 204.

ἀλλ' ἡμῖν εἷς θεὸς ὁ πατὴρ
<u>ἐξ οὗ τὰ πάντα</u> καὶ ἡμεῖς εἰς αὐτόν,
καὶ εἷς κύριος Ἰησοῦς Χριστὸς
<u>δι' οὗ τὰ πάντα</u> καὶ ἡμεῖς δι' αὐτοῦ. (1 Cor 8:6)[94]

εἷς θεὸς καὶ πατὴρ πάντων,
ὁ <u>ἐπὶ πάντων</u> καὶ <u>διὰ πάντων</u> καὶ <u>ἐν πᾶσιν</u>. (Eph 4:6)

ὅτι <u>ἐν αὐτῷ</u> ἐκτίσθη <u>τὰ πάντα</u>
ἐν τοῖς οὐρανοῖς καὶ ἐπὶ τῆς γῆς,
τὰ ὁρατὰ καὶ τὰ ἀόρατα,
εἴτε θρόνοι εἴτε κυριότητες
εἴτε ἀρχαὶ εἴτε ἐξουσίαι·
<u>τὰ πάντα δι' αὐτοῦ</u> καὶ <u>εἰς αὐτὸν</u> ἔκτισται·
καὶ αὐτός ἐστιν πρὸ πάντων
καὶ τὰ πάντα <u>ἐν αὐτῷ</u> συνέστηκεν ... (Col 1:16–17)

<u>τὰ</u> δὲ <u>πάντα ἐκ τοῦ θεοῦ</u>. (1 Cor 11:12c)

<u>δι' ὃν τὰ πάντα</u> καὶ <u>δι' οὗ τὰ πάντα</u> ... (Heb 2:10b)

The literary context of 11:36a closely resembles the language of some Greek stoic philosophers.[95] There are two major views: (1) Romans 11:36a is rooted exclusively in OT Judaism or Scripture and does not borrow from Greek Stoic philosophers at all. (2) Romans 11:36a borrows from Greek stoic philosophers indirectly via Hellenistic Judaism, which borrowed directly from Greek Stoic philosophers. The second view is far more convincing and reasonable. Romans 11:36a is not rooted lexically in OT Judaism, nor does it borrow Stoicism's pantheistic worldview (Paul's worldview contrasts starkly with Stoicism).[96] It is, however, rooted theologically in OT Judaism, and it borrows Stoicism's words (although it changes the preposition ἐν to διά, removing any trace of Pantheism).[97] The OT heralds that God is the

---

94. Dunn (*Romans 9–16*, 704) concludes that Rom 11:36 "is probably better seen as an echo more of 1 Cor 15:27–28 despite the closer verbal links with 1 Cor 8:6."

95. E.g., Pseudo-Aristotle, *Mund.* 6; Philo, *Spec.* 1.208; idem, *Cher.* 125–26; Seneca, *Ep.* 65.8; Marcus Aurelius, *Meditations* 4.23; and *Asclepius* 34.

96. Cf. Charles, "Pagan," 756–63.

97. Cf. Norden, *Agnostos Theos*, 240–50; Bultmann, *Theology*, 229; Cranfield, *Romans*, 2:591; Schlier, *Römerbrief*, 347; Dunn, *Romans 9–16*, 701–2; Morris, *Romans*,

Creator of the entire universe[98] and emphasizes God's all-encompassing, supreme, sovereign rule.[99] Consequently, God alone deserves all the glory.[100] Thus, without using the exact language of Rom 11:36a, the OT teaches that God is the source (ἐξ αὐτοῦ), sustainer (δι' αὐτοῦ), and end (εἰς αὐτόν) of all things (τὰ πάντα). This parallels Acts 17:28 in that both verses contextualize the gospel by borrowing the *language* of pagan Greeks while not borrowing their *worldviews*.[101]

Romans 11:33–36 culminates with a triumphant doxology to God the Father in Rom 11:36b: αὐτῷ ἡ δόξα εἰς τοὺς αἰῶνας, ἀμήν. By ascribing "glory" to God, Paul praises God for his unique excellence and openly highlights his infinite worth. It is similar to other doxologies in Second Temple Judaism[102] and the NT.[103] The ringing message of Rom 11:36 is that God is supreme.

429n149; Schmithals, *Römerbrief*, 415; Johnson, *Romans 9–11*, 171; Fitzmyer, *Romans*, 633; Keener, *IVP*, 438; Byrne, *Romans*, 361; Moo, *Epistle*, 740–41, 743; Schreiner, *Romans*, 632, 637; Wright, "Romans," 695–96; Osborne, *Romans*, 316; Keck, *Romans*, 288; Jewett, *Romans*, 721–22; Seifrid, "Romans," 678.

98. E.g., Gen 1:1; Pss 19:1–6; 33:9; Prov 16:4; 26:10; Isa 44:24; Jer 10:12. Isaiah in particular proclaims that God created the heavens and earth (37:16; 40:12–28; 41:20; 42:5; 45:12, 18; 48:13; 66:1–2), including light and darkness (45:7), and God promises to create a new heaven and earth (4:5; 65:17–18). More specifically, he created humans (17:7; 27:11; 45:12; 51:13; 54:5, 16), including Israel (43:1, 15; 44:2, 21, 24), and he created his people for his glory (43:7, 21).

99. E.g., 1 Chr 16:31; Pss 47:8; 93:1; 96:10; 97:1; 99:1; Isa 52:7. God's single, comprehensive plan extends over the material universe (Ps 119:89–91), the rise and fall of rulers (Dan 4:25), the length of a human's life (Job 14:5), and the most trivial circumstances (Job 36:32; cf. Matt 10:29–30). Human responsibility is subject to God's sovereign plan (cf. Prov 16:1), which includes even the evil free acts of humans (Gen 50:20; Ps 76:10; Lam 2:17; Amos 3:16).

100. E.g., Exod 14:4, 18; 2 Sam 7:23; 12:20, 22; 2 Kings 19:34; Pss 25:11; 106:7–8; Isa 43:6–7, 25; 48:9–11; 49:3; Ezek 20:14; 36:22–23, 32; Hab 2:14.

101. Acts 17:28b ("For we are indeed his offspring") is likely a direct quotation of Aratus' *Phaenomena* 5, which in turn quotes Cleanthes' *Hymn to Zeus*. Regarding Paul's contextualizing this quotation, see Carson, "Athens," 384–98.

102. 1 Esd 4:40; 4 Macc 18:24; Pr Man 15; Sir 39:14b–16; *1 En.* 22:14; 25:7; 27:5; 36:4; 1QHa 7:26–27; 1QS 11:15–17; *m. 'Abot* 6. Cf. Matt 11:25–26; Luke 10:21.

103. Rom 1:25; 9:5; 16:27; Gal 1:5; Eph 3:21; Phil 4:20; 1 Tim 1:17; 2 Tim 4:18; 1 Pet 4:11; Jude 24–25.

4. CONCLUSION

The theme of Romans is the gospel in its salvation-historical context, and chapters 9–11 are—from a literary standpoint—a critical but not central step in unfolding Paul's argument. Romans 9:6—11:32 vindicates God's righteousness in his past, present, and future dealings with Israel. The uncontainable praise for God in 11:33–36 naturally flows out of and euphorically concludes chapters 9–11. In response primarily to the revealed nature of God's ways, Paul exults in God with carefully crafted praise for God's being deep (11:33), incomprehensible (11:34a), without counselors (11:34b), without creditors (11:35), and supreme (11:36).

3

Isaiah 40:13 in Context

STUDIES ON SPECIFIC USES of the OT in the NT may do injustice to OT passages, superficially treating them as stepping stones to advance to more controversial hermeneutical and theological issues. Examining Isa 40:13 in context, however, is essential for substantively discussing the use of the OT in Rom 11:34–35. This chapter opens by highlighting some hermeneutical issues in Isa 40:13 and then situates 40:13 in its larger literary and theological context before focusing on that verse.

1. HERMENEUTICAL ISSUES IN ISA 40:13

Isaiah 40:13 consists of only eight Hebrew words (מִי־תִכֵּן אֶת־רוּחַ יְהוָה וְאִישׁ עֲצָתוֹ יוֹדִיעֶנּוּ),[1] but explaining only those eight words does not sufficiently explain the verse. A layered interpretation recognizes the complex nature of hermeneutics and accounts for at least the following nine contextual elements: historical context, genre, lexis, grammar and syntax, immediate context, major section, book, author, and Testament.[2] Each of these levels (except "author" since the prophet Isaiah did not write other Scripture) contains hermeneutical issues that are significant for a nuanced interpretation of Isa 40:13 in context, and briefly commenting on each of them increases clarity and focus. We will establish the first two here and deal with the next six later in the chapter.

1. *Historical Context.* Controversy swirls around Isaiah's author, date, and audience. A popular view among critical scholars is that the prophet

---

1. See ch. 5 below for a discussion of textual issues in this passage.
2. Osborne, *Hermeneutical*, 40.

Isaiah wrote the majority of chapters 1–39, Deutero-Isaiah wrote chapters 40–55, and Trito-Isaiah wrote chapters 56–66.[3] Over the last two decades, OT scholars have not necessarily rejected that popular source-critical view, but the general consensus now affirms that Isaiah is a literary unity.[4] Some scholars persuasively argue that the prophet Isaiah wrote the entire book and that he wrote to Israelites toward the end of his ministry, which spanned over five decades to four kings (739–686 B.C.).[5] Based on this historical context, then, Isa 40:13 is part of a section designed to comfort Israelites in light of their impending Babylonian captivity.

2. *Genre.* In the prophecy of Isaiah, Isa 40:13 is wisdom poetry. Distinctive features of poetry include parallelism, terseness, lines of generally equal length, fewer conjunctions and particles, more figurative language, and more aesthetic language (e.g., consonance and assonance); it is "commissive" (i.e., emotive) rather "referential."[6] Parallelism is the most important structural feature to grasp in order to read biblical poetry correctly.[7] It is basically rhyme of thought rather than rhyme of sound so that the balance of thought in logical rhythm conveys the meaning. This is especially important for interpreting Isa 40:13.

The genre of wisdom literature is common in the Ancient Near East.[8] More specifically, it is common in the OT, namely, Job, Proverbs, Ecclesiastes, and some psalms. Waltke acknowledges that "it is often said" that biblical wisdom literature is "humanistic, international, non-historical, and eudaemonistic," but he asserts that each of those descriptions requires qualification.[9] This is significant for interpreting Isa 40:13

---

3. The most influential proponent of the Trito-Isaiah theory was Duhm, *Jesaia*, whose first edition was published in 1892.

4. Cf. Williamson, "Recent," 21–39.

5. See Young, *Isaiah*, 3:538–49; Payne, "Eighth Century," Parts 1–3; Harrison, *Introduction*, 764–800; Archer, *Survey*, 366–90; Oswalt, *Isaiah 40–66*, 3–16; idem, *Isaiah*, 33–41; Beale, *Erosion*, 123–59. Longman and Dillard, *Introduction*, 301–12.

6. Stein, *Basic Guide*, 68–69, 109–10. Cf. Longman, "Literary," 114–24.

7. Cf. Berlin, "Parallelism," 155–62.

8. Waltke, *Proverbs*, 28–31.

9. Ibid., 51.

because it has a linguistic connection with מִשְׁפָּט in v. 14.[10] This is wisdom language, and it is part of a theme that is central to Isaiah.[11]

More specifically, Isa 40:13 is disputation (*Disputationswort, Disputationsrede,* or *Streitgespräch*).[12] This form of argument is a subset of wisdom literature that asks rhetorical questions "from ground common to both sides to prove a disputed point."[13] Isaiah 40:12–26 disputes the viewpoint expressed in v. 27, and vv. 28–31 draw the correct conclusion.[14]

3. *Lexis.* At least four lexical issues are significant in Isa 40:13, namely, the meaning and significance of תִּכֵּן, רוּחַ, עֲצָתוֹ, and יוֹדִיעֶנּוּ. It is important to compare how each word is used elsewhere in Isaiah, the prophets, and the rest of the OT. (See §4.2.)

4. *Grammar and Syntax.* The most significant grammatical and syntactical issue in Isa 40:13 is understanding וְאִישׁ עֲצָתוֹ, which literally reads "or [as] the man of his counsel." (See §4.3.)

5–8. *Immediate Context* (see §3.3), *Major Section* (see §3.1), *Book* (see §2), *and Testament.* The immediate context of Isa 40:13 is chapter 40, which begins the second half of Isaiah. Broad, sweeping themes common to Isaiah and the rest of the OT include God's supreme greatness, covenant faithfulness and loyalty to his people, and salvation-historical acts.

---

10. Cf. Goldingay, *Message*, 39–41.

11. Cf. Morgan's survey of the wisdom tradition in Isaiah 40–55 (*Wisdom*, 114–19).

12. Begrich, *Deuterojesaja*, 48–49; Whybray, *Heavenly Counsellor*, 5–6; idem, *Isaiah 40–66*, 53; idem, *Second Isaiah*, 38, 54–56; Westermann, *Isaiah*, 48; idem, *Deuterojesajas*, 41–51, 95–96; Schoors, *I Am God*, 176–89, 245–59; Albertz, *Weltschöpfung*, 7–13; Blenkinsopp, *Isaiah*, 187–94; Melugin, *Formation*, 28–30, 90–93; Elliger, *Deuterojesaja*, 44–47; Klein, *Israel*, 104–5; Naidoff, "Rhetoric," 62; Clifford, "Isaiah," 497; Ruppert, "Disputationsworte," 317–25; Hanson, *Isaiah*, 26–28; Koole, *Isaiah*, 1:86; Childs, *Isaiah*, 309; Thompson, *Isaiah*, xxvi–xxvii, 10–11; Berges, *Jesaja*, 124–30.

13. Whybray, *Isaiah 40–66*, 53.

14. Motyer, *Prophecy*, 302. Seitz ("Isaiah," 342) asserts, however, that Isa 40:12–31 "falls short of pure disputation." Baltzer, who recognizes elements of disputation in Isa 40:12–31, argues that 40:12–17 is a hymn and that 40:21–31 in a "hymnal dialogue" ("Jes 40:13–14," 7–10; *Deutero-Isaiah*, 65–86). Smith concludes that Isa 40:12–31 "does not follow the pattern of any well-known genre of literature" (*Isaiah 40–66*, 106).

2. THE THEME OF ISAIAH

A brief summary of Isaiah's massive prophecy sets the scene for analyzing its theme.

2.1. Synopsis of Isaiah

Isaiah may be divided into two major sections: chapters 1–39 and 40–66. The first section begins by contrasting the rebellion of God's people with the future redemption that they will experience (chs. 1–5). The call of the prophet Isaiah in chapter 6 illustrates what must happen to the nation of Israel in order for them to experience God's future redemption: they must be deeply aware of their sinfulness, experience God's cleansing by fire, and receive God's commission. At the point in history when Isaiah was writing this, Israel had a poor track record in this regard; the pressure from the Assyrians revealed Israel's lack of trust in God (chs. 7–39). Ahaz trusted the nations instead of God, so God judged Israel (chs. 7–12). Israel foolishly continued to trust the nations instead of God, and God severely judged both Israel and the nations (chs. 13–35). Hezekiah trusted God, so God delivered Israel from the Assyrians; but his pride had sealed Israel's fate—the Babylonians would capture them (chs. 36–39).

Israel dreaded their impending Babylonian captivity, which would lead them to question God's power and trustworthiness, so the second section begins by responding to their despair and lack of trust in God (chs. 40–55). Isaiah exalts God's uniqueness (particularly in chs. 40–48 with reference to God's power over Babylonian gods), promises God's deliverance, and explains that they are God's elected servants. They need to be cleansed of their sins by the suffering servant's substitutionary death and resurrection (52:13—53:12). Then they must—by God's strength—live righteously and be a light to the nations (chs. 56–66).

2.2. The Theological Message of Isaiah: Why People Should Trust the Holy One of Israel

"There is no other book in either Testament which comprehends the whole of biblical theology so completely as does Isaiah."[15] Isaiah threatens Israel with impending judgment, exalts God's majesty, vividly describes the Servant's suffering, and promises Israel's future glory. The prophecy

---

15. Oswalt, "Isaiah," 217.

centers on Yahweh and his redemptive plan for his rebellious people. At the risk of flattening Isaiah's theological message, one way to state it succinctly is that *people should trust the Holy One of Israel because he is the incomparable King and Savior*. This risks flattening the message because it does not capture the contours of the literary masterpiece. Isaiah is like a rich symphony in which variations on interlocking themes appear, disappear, and reappear.[16] Although there are many more motifs in Isaiah,[17] what follows expands on five key themes embedded in this succinct summary statement.

2.2.1. "The Holy One of Israel": The Paradox of Transcendence and Immanence

The most striking title for God in Isaiah is קְדוֹשׁ יִשְׂרָאֵל. It occurs thirty-one times in the OT, and twenty-five of those occur in Isaiah: twelve in chapters 1–39 and thirteen in 40–66.[18] As the קָדוֹשׁ, Yahweh is transcendent (separate) in his uniqueness and sovereignty. As the Holy One of יִשְׂרָאֵל, Yahweh is immanent (near).[19]

1. *Transcendence*. Yahweh's transcendence as *the Holy One* of Israel is evident in two ways. First, he is holy. He is uniquely, supremely, and exclusively God (6:6). He has no rivals. He is in his own category as uniquely excellent, and he towers over everything that is not God. "I am God, and there is no other; I am God, and there is none like me" (46:9; cf. 40:25; 43:10–11; 44:6, 8; 45:5–6, 14, 18, 21–22). His holiness is the basis for his glory (5:16; 6:6; 57:15), and it manifests itself in צְדָקָה and מִשְׁפָּט (e.g., 5:16) as well as righteous jealousy. His uniqueness makes

---

16. Oswalt, *Isaiah*, 17, 41.

17. Other useful perspectives on Isaiah's theme(s) include the following: Barrett, "Theology," 144–51; Roberts, "Isaiah," 130–43; Chisholm, "Theology," 305–40; Gileadi, *Isaiah*, 249–70; Oswalt, "Key Themes," 13–90, 202–11; Wegner, "Isaiah," 375–79; Goldingay, "Theology," 168–90.

18. Isa 1:4; 5:19, 24; 10:20; 12:6; 17:7; 29:19; 30:11, 12, 15; 31:1; 37:23; 41:14, 16, 20; 43:3, 14; 45:11; 47:4; 48:17; 49:7; 54:5; 55:5; 60:9, 14. Cf. 29:23; 40:25; 43:15. The other seven OT occurrences are 2 Kgs 19:22; Pss 71:22; 78:41; 89:18; Jer 50:29; 51:5; Ezek 39:7.

19. Barrett ("Theology," 144–45) observes, "The title is paradoxical. It did not seem possible that a God whose essential character was separateness could be associated in this manner with His creation." See Jaeggli, "Isaiah 40–66," 183–274.

idolatry look foolish (cf. 2:8, 18, 20; 37:19; 41:24, 29 with 43:10b–13; 44:6; 45:20–22).[20]

Second, he is sovereign.[21] יְהוָה צְבָאוֹת [22] planned, created, and controls everything for his glory. No one can frustrate what Yahweh sovereignly and independently planned (יעץ: 14:24, 26–27; 19:12, 17; 23:8–9; 40:14; 41:28; 45:21; cf. 22:11; 25:1; 37:26; 46:10–11). He alone created everything (44:24). He created the heavens and earth (37:16; 40:12–28; 41:20; 42:5; 45:12, 18; 48:13; 66:1–2), including light and darkness (45:7), and he promises to create a new heaven and earth (4:5; 65:17–18). More specifically, he created humans (17:7; 27:11; 45:12; 51:13; 54:5, 16), including Israel (43:1, 15; 44:2, 21, 24); he created his people for his glory (43:7, 21).

He alone controls everything in accordance with his comprehensive plan. God controls humans like a potter controls clay (45:9). The most prominent examples of this are God's use of Assyria, Babylon (39:6–7), and King Cyrus. God calls Assyria "the rod of my anger" (10:5; cf. 5:26; 10:33), and he calls Cyrus "my shepherd" who "shall fulfill all my purpose" (44:28). Cyrus is God's "anointed" (45:1); God "stirred him up" (45:13).

These themes are especially prominent in chapters 40–48, which sharply contrast the gods of the nations with God the Creator. "The gods are a part of the cosmic system . . . [God] is the Creator of the system."[23]

2. *Immanence*. Yahweh's immanence as the Holy One *of Israel* is the other side of the separateness-nearness paradox: "I dwell in the high and holy place, and also with him who is of a contrite and lowly spirit" (57:15).[24] Several relationships describe Yahweh's intimate immanency. He is the Redeemer to his kinsmen.[25] The "Everlasting Father" (9:6) is a father to

---

20. Cf. Pao (*Acts*, 181–93) on Isaiah's "anti-idol polemic" in Isaiah 40–55.

21. Cf. Brassey, "Metaphor," 135–224.

22. The title יְהוָה צְבָאוֹת occurs fifty-eight times in Isaiah, and אֲדֹנָי יְהוָה צְבָאוֹת occurs eleven times (1:24; 3:1, 15; 10:23–24; 19:4; 22:5, 12, 14–15; 28:22). These titles emphasize God's sovereignty over everything as the almighty warrior.

23. Oswalt, "Theology," 728.

24. Jaeggli ("Isaiah 40–66," 220) explains, "This key verse forges the link between God's transcendent, exalted holiness and His immanent presence. Isaiah's designation of Yahweh as the 'high and exalted One' (רָם וְנִשָּׂא) is identical to the prophet's account of his inaugural vision of the Lord (cf. 6:1)."

25. Of the twenty-five times that גאל occurs in Isaiah, it refers to Yahweh thirteen times using the qal participle (41:14; 43:14; 44:6, 24; 47:4; 48:17; 49:7, 26; 54:5, 8; 59:20;

his children (45:11; 63:16; 64:8). Most intimate of all, he is the husband to his wife (54:5–6; 62:5). He demonstrates his personal nearness especially when his people are in crisis (7:11; 38:6; 43:1–4). He comforts (נחם) his people (40:1–2; 49:13; 51:3, 19; 61:2; 66:13; cf. 57:18).

2.2.2. King: Sovereign Judgment

As the King, Yahweh exercises his sovereignty by judging rebellious people for their wickedness.[26] Judgment, which bookends the prophecy (1:2 and 66:24), is "the most dominant theme in Isaiah,"[27] and its basis is Yahweh's holiness (5:16).

The Holy One of Israel judges two groups of rebellious people for their sin. First, he judges his enemies for their wickedness. Chapters 13–21 and 23 describe God's denunciation of the wickedness of Babylon, Assyria, Philistia, Moab, Syria, Ethiopia, Egypt, Edom, Arabia, and Tyre. While he uses nations like Assyria and Babylon to purge Israel, he nevertheless holds these nations accountable for their wickedness.

Second, he judges his own people.

> The great historical crises of Isaiah's day inevitably raised serious questions about God. How could Israel's God be the greatest God if Israel was not the greatest nation? . . . But Isaiah insists that God is not part of the cosmic system. His greatness is not to be identified with the greatness of Israel or Judah. The great empires are not coming in spite of him, but because of him. He is the Lord of all nations, not merely of Israel. And all nations, including Israel, are subject to his judgment.[28]

God denounces Judah (chs. 1–12; 29–31), Jerusalem (ch. 22), and Samaria (ch. 28) for their sin, and he judges them for turning away from him (1:2–4). He condemns specific sins, including murder (1:15, 21), oppression (1:23; 5:7–8), divination (2:6), idolatry (2:8), pride (2:12; 3:16–17), drunkenness (5:22–23), reliance on military might (22:8), reliance on pagan nations (30:1–5), religious ritualism (58:1–5), and deceit (59:3–4). This confrontation with sin culminates in chapters 59, 64,

---

60:16; 63:16), and Yahweh is the subject of גאל six times (43:1; 44:22–23; 48:20; 52:9; 63:9; cf. 52:3; 62:12).

26. Cf. Oswalt, "Key Themes," 13–30, 202–4.
27. Oswalt, "Isaiah," 219.
28. Ibid., "Theology," 728.

and 65. God also judges his people for failing to believe God's promises (8:11–15), which was a cause of Israel's failure to obey God's law.

Israel's special relationship with Yahweh made their sin against him even more abominable. They were like rebellious sons whom he reared and who then revolted against him (1:2; 30:1) and rejected his word (5:24; 24:5). So Yahweh would certainly judge his people for their sins (1:25; 5:25; 13:9–11; 29:2–3). This judgment is full of poetic justice: they worshipped false gods under desired oaks and at gardens, so God would make them like an oak whose leaf fades away and like a garden without water (1:29–30); the women were proud, so they would experience putrefaction instead of sweet perfume, a captives' rope instead of a luxurious belt, a plucked-out scalp instead of well-set hair, sackcloth instead of fine clothes, and branding instead of beauty (3:16–24); they were land-grabbers, so the Lord would make the land desolate (5:8–10); they were drunkards, so the Lord would make them parched with thirst in exile (5:11–13); and they substituted darkness for light and light for darkness, so the Lord would send them darkness and distress (5:20, 30).

In the Day of the Lord, Yahweh will abase those who are proud (2:11–12), exterminate sinners (13:9), and exercise vengeance (61:2). But Yahweh does not judge his people in order to destroy them but to purge them. In other words, God's salvation comes only *through* God's judgment.[29] This hope of salvation is another aspect of the Day of the Lord.

2.2.3. Savior: Gracious Deliverance and Restoration

As the Savior, Yahweh delivers repentant people through the suffering Servant's salvific work.[30] Israel's predicament is both physical and spiritual, and so is Yahweh's salvation. The basis for this salvation is Yahweh's holiness (57:15) and unswerving faithfulness; he is supremely trustworthy. Isaiah testifies that God is his "salvation" (12:2) and Israel's "Savior" (43:3; 45:15, 21). Yahweh in his redemption is gracious (30:18–19), loving and merciful (63:9), and lovingly loyal.[31] He continued to save at least a remnant (4:3; 10:20–22; 27:12–13; 48:10), and he accomplishes

---

29. Hamilton's *God's Glory* traces this theme not only through Isaiah, but the entire Bible.

30. Cf. Oswalt, "Key Themes," 53–71, 206–8.

31. חֶסֶד, occurs eight times in Isaiah, five of which refer to God's loving loyalty in relation to salvation (54:8, 10; 55:3; 63:7 [2x]). חֶסֶד is loving loyalty or loyal love based on a relationship that results in kind deeds. It occurs in the OT 248 times (127 times in the Psalms and from one to twelve times throughout twenty-seven other OT books).

salvation through his Anointed One, who is the King (1–39), Servant (40–55), and Conqueror (56–66).[32]

2.2.4. Incomparability

There is no one like Yahweh. This theme is inseparable from his transcendence in Isaiah (see §2.2.1), and it is especially prominent in chapters 40–48 (see §3.3).[33] Anticipating questions that Israel will have about God's uniqueness during the Babylonian captivity, chapters 40–48 exalt God's unique power.

2.2.5. Trust

Since Yahweh, the Holy One of Israel, is the incomparable King and Savior, Isaiah argues that people should trust him (cf. 12:2; 26:3–4).[34] This theme permeates the entire prophecy: Israel must not trust the nations for deliverance from oppressing nations (chs. 1–39), but instead trust God alone (chs. 40–55) and not their privileged election (chs. 56–66).[35] Isaiah warns Ahaz, "If you are not firm in faith, you will not be firm at all" (7:9).[36] God's invitation is open: "There is no other god besides me, a righteous God and a Savior; there is none besides me. Turn to me and be saved, all the ends of the earth! For I am God, and there is no other" (45:21b–22).

Isaiah assertively exposes idolatry as foolish while exalting God as supremely trustworthy. Reflecting on the first commandment, Martin

---

God's חֶסֶד is faithful covenant love. In English, "loyalty" is an attitude that can exist apart from kind deeds, but with חֶסֶד kind deeds are inseparable from loyalty.

32. See Motyer, *Isaiah*, 13. These are the three primary portraits of the Anointed One in the respective three sections, but Motyer qualifies, "Standing back from the portraits, however, we discover the same features in each, indicative of the fact that they are meant as facets of the one Messianic person" (13).

33. See Labuschagne, *Incomparability*; Klein, "Beweis," 267–73; Co, "Incomparability," 43–53; Oswalt, *Isaiah*, 49–50, 55–58; idem, "Key Themes," 73–90, 209–11.

34. Cf. Oswalt, "Key Themes," 31–51, 204–5; Johnston, "Faith," 104–21. Dorsey (*Literary*, 234–35) calls trust the "well-developed central theme" of Isaiah.

35. Oswalt, "Theology," 730.

36. Literally, "if you will not believe, you will not endure." NASB: "If you will not believe, you surely shall not last." NIV: "If you do not stand firm in your faith, you will not stand at all." NET: "If your faith does not remain firm, then you will not remain secure." Motyer (*Isaiah*, 83) comments, "Faith is the central reality of the Lord's people, not just their distinctiveness but their ground of existence. No faith, no people." Oehler (*Theology*, 459) calls 7:9 "*the thesis of prophetism.*"

Luther's *Large Catechism* shrewdly makes the same connection between idolatry and trust that Isaiah does:

> "You are to have no other gods."
>
> That is, you are to regard me alone as your God. What does this mean, and how is it to be understood? What does "to have a god" mean, or what is God?
>
> Answer: A "god" is the term for that to which we are to look for all good and in which we are to find refuge in all need. Therefore, to have a god is nothing else than to trust and believe in that one with your whole heart. As I have often said, it is the trust and faith of the heart alone that make both God and an idol. If your faith and trust are right, then your God is the true one. Conversely, where your trust is false and wrong, there you do not have the true God. For these two belong together, faith and God. Anything on which your heart relies and depends, I say, that is really your God.[37]

3. THE ARGUMENT OF ISA 40

The literature on Isa 40 is immense because the chapter is so important.[38] Before tracing the argument of chapter 40, it is helpful to locate its function in the book as a whole.

3.1. The Relation of Isa 40 to the Book of Isaiah: The Hinge from Judgment to Comfort

Isaiah 40 is the hinge between chapters 1–39 and 40–66 that transitions from the dominant theme of judgment to comfort.[39] The first half of Isaiah is heavily weighted with judgment, but the second is dominated

---

37. Kolb and Wengert, *Book of Concord*, 386. Luther proceeds to elaborate further on the relationship between idolatry and trust (386–92), a connection he highlights hundreds of times in his works. See, e.g., Luther, *Sermons*, 138–41.

38. Grogan ("Isaiah," 718) remarks, "To move from ch. 39 to ch. 40 is to enter a part of the book (chs. 40–66) that has produced more scholarly literature than any other part of the OT. The number of different views as to authorship, structure, and other related matters of introduction is bewildering."

39. Waltke, *OT Theology*, 844; Wagner, "Isaiah 40–66," 268–70; Walker, "Isaiah," 168; Merrill, *Everlasting Dominion*, 506.

by comfort and salvation.[40] The theme of chapters 40–55 is Yahweh's superiority, and its main point is restoration.[41]

Isaiah prophesies Israel's forthcoming Babylonian captivity in 39:5-8, and the second division of Isaiah's prophecy is designed to comfort Israel in light of that. Israel's temptation—especially during this captivity—would be to question God for allowing them to be in that predicament (40:27; 41:17; 49:14). Israel would feel like singing Psalm 137. They would be wrestling with two implied questions: (1) "Has not God been defeated by the gods of Babylon?" and (2) "Has not our sin separated us from God forever?"[42] No, God is greater than both the Babylonian gods and his own people's sin. Isaiah directly addresses the first question by comforting God's people with revelation about God's unique greatness (esp. in ch. 40), and he answers the second question by affirming their special relationship to God and God's faithfulness to his people (41:10). Isaiah continues through chapter 55 to emphasize Israel's restoration and God's unique greatness, and chapters 49–55 (esp. 52:13—53:12) enhances this theme with a further dimension: the solution to their sin is redemption through atonement.

3.2. The Argument of Isa 40:1-11: Comfort

Isaiah 40 consists of two parts: vv. 1–11 and 12–31. The first part is the prologue to chapters 40–66, and it contains an introduction (vv. 1–2) followed by messages from three voices (vv. 3–5, 6–8, 9–11). It may be summarized with one word: comfort.[43] It comforts God's people by promising that God will vindicate them and bring them home from their captivity. D. A. Carson sets the stage for the prologue:

---

40. Young, *Isaiah*, 3:17; Oswalt, *Isaiah 40-66*, 47; Walker, "Isaiah," 168.

41. Oswalt (*Isaiah: 40-66*, 5, 8) exclaims, "Without doubt, the theme of chs. 40–55 is the superiority of Israel's God over the idols of the nations as proved in three ways: his ability to explain the past (41:22), tell the future (41:23), and do things that are radically new (43:18–19). That is, he alone transcends the bounds of the cosmos . . . The fundamental point that chs. 40–55 address is the possibility of restoration. That possibility is called into question by two factors. First, ability: *can* God restore? Second, intention: does he *want* to restore? Note that both questions relate to God. More than anything else, the exile would raise questions about the character of the God whom Isaiah and the preexilic prophets had been proclaiming." Cf. idem, *Isaiah*, 443, 446; Fohrer, *Jesaja*, 24.

42. Oswalt, *Isaiah*, 443.

43. Berges, *Jesaja*, 125.

> The prophet envisages the Israelite exiles under the Babylonian superpower and knows full well that they have sunk into massive discouragement. This proclamation is characterized by comfort, hope, and promise of deliverance and is addressed to a discouraged covenant community exiled in the Diaspora and uncertain about the validity of God's promises.[44]

God specifically commissions Isaiah in chapters 6 and 40, and the prologue in chapter 40 is "a reapplication of Isaiah's call" in chapter 6.[45]

God commands unidentified heralds to comfort his exiled people, who have received complete retribution for their sins (40:1-2). Three voices explicate this comfort. Voice 1 commands Israel to prepare a way for Yahweh, whose glory will replace their misery (40:3-5).[46] Voice 2 contrasts transitory humans with God's eternally reliable word (40:6-8). 40:6 (כָּל־הַבָּשָׂר חָצִיר). By calling "all flesh" grass, Isaiah calls both Israelites *and* Babylonians ephemeral grass. Voice 3 announces that Yahweh will return as a warrior-shepherd like David (40:9-11). On the one hand, he is a mighty warrior: "the Lord God comes with might" (40:10). On the other hand, he is a tender shepherd: "He will tend his flock like a shepherd; he will gather the lambs in his arms; he will carry them in his bosom, and gently lead those that are with young" (40:11).[47]

The eleven-verse prologue leaves no doubt that God wants to deliver his people. But can he? He may have the desire, but does he have the ability? Isaiah's answer is 40:12-31.

3.3. The Argument of Isa 40:12-31: God's Incomparability

Verses 12-31 glory in God's incomparability. Isaiah does this because he anticipates that Israel might doubt God's power after Babylon con-

---

44. Carson, "1 Peter," 1020.

45. Childs (*Isaiah*, 295-96, 302) writes, "The prologue signals that the old age is passing away and a new day is dawning . . . The primary role of the prologue (40:1-11) is to announce God's new purpose for Israel in bringing forth totally new redemptive events on its behalf, which serve as evidence for the faithfulness of God's word standing forever." Cf. Seitz, "Divine Council," 238-43; Oswalt, *Isaiah 40-66*, 48.

46. Cf. Lim, "Way," 118-63.

47. Brettler ("Incompatible," 118-19) highlights Isa 40:10-11 as an example of a "'contradictory' metaphor": "These verses present YHWH on the one hand as a powerful warrior (v. 10a), but temper this with touching imagery stressing the concern of the shepherd (v. 11). In this case, shepherd does not seem to be a sub-metaphor of YHWH as king. Yet, shepherd and warrior combine in an interesting way, to evoke an image of a powerful, but caring deity, an image which either metaphor alone could not depict."

quered them. Isaiah removes all doubt that God has the ability to deliver his people.

Isaiah conveys God's incomparable grandeur in several literary ways. He uses rhetorical questions (40:12–14, 18, 21, 25–28), metaphors and similes (40:15, 22, 24, 31), synecdoche that argues from the lesser to the greater (40:16), hyperbole (40:17), assertions (40:17, 23, 26, 28–31), satire (40:19–20), commands (40:26), and the titles "the Holy One" (40:25) and "Creator" (40:28).[48]

The passage breaks down into three parts: vv. 12–20, 21–26, and 27–31.[49]

1. *God is incomparably powerful, wise, immense, and superior to idols (40:12–20).* First, God is incomparably powerful and wise (40:12–14).[50] The formidable series of rhetorical questions in 40:12–14 can be distilled to two basic questions: Who can measure the universe (40:12)? And who gives God advice (40:13–14)?[51] The implied answer to the first is no one but God, and the implied answer to the second is no one at all.

The first question emphasizes God's incomparable power (40:12; cf. Ps 104:1–9).[52] No one but God can (1) measure the waters of the earth in the hollow of his hand, (2) measure the sky with his outstretched hands, (3) carefully weigh the dust of the earth, (4) weigh the mountains in scales, or (5) weigh the hills in a balance.

---

48. On the relationship between rhetorical questions and metaphors in Isa 40:12–31, see Brassey, "Metaphor," 36–45. On the use of rhetorical questions to express incomparability (esp. with reference to Isa 40:12–31), see Labuschagne, *Incomparability*, 16–28 (esp. 19, 27). Labuschagne explains, "Rhetorical questions are frequently used in the Old Testament to express the absolute power, uniqueness, singularity and incomparability of a person. The rhetorical question is one of the most forceful and effectual ways employed in speech for driving home some idea or conviction. Because of its impressive and persuasive effect the hearer is not merely listener: he is forced to frame the expected answer in his mind, and by doing so he actually becomes a co-expressor of the speaker's conviction" (ibid, 23).

49. Oswalt (*Isaiah*, 446) observes that 40:12–20 and 40:21–26 are parallel: (1) rhetorical questions assert that Yahweh is the only Creator (40:12–14, 21); (2) Yahweh sovereignly rules over all nations and rulers (40:15–17, 22–24); (3) rhetorical questions assert that Yahweh is incomparable (40:18a, 25); (4) Yahweh is absolutely superior to other gods (40:18b–20, 26).

50. Isaiah 40 is about *God*, but not Jesus in particular. Contra the christological interpretation of Lupieri, *Il cielo*, 79–96.

51. Cf. Bonnard, *Second Isaïe*, 98.

52. Ridderbos, *Isaiah*, 345: "If, then, creation is of such mind-boggling magnitude, how infinitely great must be its Maker!" Cf. Couroyer, "Isaïe," 186–96.

The universe is in view here since Isaiah uses polarities that serve as *inclusiones*: waters vs. heavens; heavens vs. earth; dust of the earth vs. mountains and hills.[53] Isaiah depicts God "as a craftsman making the tiny universe at his bench: he needs only a handful of water and of dust carefully measured and weighed out."[54]

The second question emphasizes God's incomparable wisdom (40:13–14). Verse 14 asks five rhetorical questions, and the answer to each of them is "no one." (1) God does not consult anyone for advice.[55] (2) No one makes him understand—as if he did not already understand while they did. (3) No one taught him the right way to do things. (4) No one imparts knowledge to him. (5) No one shows him the way of understanding. In short, no one gives God advice because he does not need it. His plans proceed without directions from counselors because his understanding in unsearchable (cf. 40:28). In short: "keines Beraters bedürftig."[56]

Second, God is incomparably immense (40:15–17). Although mighty nations like Assyria and Babylon have plagued Israel and may seem impressive, daunting, and insurmountable (especially during the Babylonian captivity), Isaiah reminds God's people that all the nations are nothing compared to God. "The nations are like a drop from a bucket," "the dust on the scales," "nothing," and even "less than nothing and emptiness" (40:15, 17). "Emptiness" translates תֹּהוּ, rendered "without form" in Gen 1:2. God is so big that the grand forest of Lebanon—filled with cedars and animals—is not sufficient for making a worthy sacrifice to him (40:16).[57] The three similes in 40:15 strikingly correspond with 40:12: (1) In 40:12a, God can measure all the waters in the world in the hollow of his hand. In 40:15a, the powerful nations are merely a drop in a bucket. (2) In 40:12d–e, God can measure the mountains and hills on a scale, and he can gather up all the dust in the world in a basket. In 40:15b, the powerful nations are merely like a bit of dust on a

---

53. Cf. Motyer, *Isaiah*, 303.

54. Whybray, *Isaiah 40–66*, 53. Oswalt (*Isaiah 40–66*, 59) is probably overcritical of Whybray here since Whybray agrees with "the point": "This interpretation is probably overliteral. The point seems to be simply that God is infinitely greater than the created world."

55. Grimm, *Deuterojesaja*, 67.

56. Köhler, *Deuterojesaja*, 123.

57. Oswalt, *Isaiah 40–66*, 61: "The smallness of Lebanon stands for the smallness of the whole world compared to God."

scale. (3) In 40:12c–e, God can weigh the earth's dust, mountains, and hills. In 40:15c, God weighs or lifts up islands or coastlands like they are fine dust.

Third, God is incomparably superior to idols (40:18–20; cf. 2:20–21; 19:1; 31:6–7; 41:7; 42:17; 44:9–20; 46:5–7; 48:5).[58] Verses 12–17 show how God views his creation, but how do many of God's creatures view him? They create idols (40:19–20). So Isaiah asks, "To whom then will you liken God, or what likeness compare with him?" (40:18). No physical image or likeness can represent the God of 40:12–17, so Isaiah becomes even more intense and aggressive by using satire to ridicule idols in 40:19–20.[59] He gives four humorous reasons that comparing God to an idol is ludicrous: (1) "a metal worker casts it" (TNIV); (2) "a goldsmith overlays it with gold and casts for it silver chains"; (3) a person selects "wood that will not rot"; (4) and he then tries to find a skilled craftsman to ensure that it will not wobble over! It is folly that God's creatures (e.g., craftsmen) create their own gods with God's creation (e.g., wood and precious metal)—and the ideal idols are ones that do not rot or fall over!

2. *God is incomparably sovereign and powerful (40:21–26).* In contrast to idols, God is incomparably sovereign (40:21–24). Again Isaiah leads with a series of rhetorical questions, this time designed to frame what follows as the most elementary common knowledge (40:21). God is in a category of his own; he is transcendent, and he towers over his creation (40:22). The earth and the sky seem massive to us, but they are just a little anthill or tent to God. "The mighty heavens are to the true God as cobwebs are to steel."[60] He effortlessly governs the heavens and the earth, including human rulers, whom he reduces to nothing (40:22–23). The

---

58. Childs (*Isaiah*, 310) explains, "The utter incomparability of God lies at the base of the Old Testament's uncompromising rejection of every attempt to represent the God of Israel by means of an image (cf. Ex. 20:3ff.)."

59. Childs (*Isaiah*, 310) asserts that vv. 19–20 lack "the high level of sarcasm and ridicule" contained in 44:9ff. or 46:5ff., but there is nevertheless a significant level of satire in 40:19–20. Young (*Isaiah*, 3:55) exclaims, "There were actually those who bowed down to this rather than to the eternal and immutable God. Here the temporal would create the eternal, the weak the strong, the finite the infinite, the changeable the unchangeable. Man seeks to create God—and all in the image of man! Isaiah could not more clearly have placed in the open the utter folly and pointlessness of idolatry." Cf. Goldingay, *Message*, 51.

60. Oswalt, *Isaiah 40–66*, 67.

most imposing, powerful human rulers in the history of the world are like mere chaff that the wind blows away (40:24; cf. 40:6–8).

God is also incomparably powerful (40:25–26). He powerfully created the stars, which he calls by name and sustains by his absolute power and awesome strength. Isaiah conveys this by quoting a rhetorical question from the קָדוֹשׁ himself: "To whom then will you compare me, that I should be like him?" (40:25). It is folly to speak of God being like someone else because God is unique. There is no one like him, and he is like no one else. He is in a class all by himself. A case in point is 40:26: Isaiah gives a basic theological astronomy lesson. He commands his audience to look up at the sky (where God is enthroned) to observe the stars. He asks one question: "Who created these?" The answer is obvious: God did. The lesson continues. Not only did God create the stars, he calls each one of them by name, and not a single one is missing. How can God do this? "By the greatness of his might, and because he is strong in power." Once again Isaiah underscores God's supreme power.

3. *Therefore, God's people should trust him (40:27–31).* Next Isaiah pastorally applies God's incomparable greatness to the sort of fears Israel would have during the Babylonian captivity. Verse 27 is key to understanding the chapter, although "Israel's expression of doubt is not the center of the passage."[61] If 40:27 was not in this passage, then 40:12–31 could be copied and pasted into all sorts of other places in the Bible. But 40:27 gives this passage historical particularity as a follow-up to chapter 39. The whole point of this passage is to respond to complaints and fears among the Israelites about whether God will actually deliver them from their impending exile in Babylon. They were tempted to question God's power to save them from mighty Babylon.

Isaiah argues from the greater to the lesser: If God is incomparably great, why then should God's people continually complain that he is unaware of the injustice they are enduring, uncaring, or unable to deliver them (40:27)? Their complaints are utterly foolish because of who their God is. Yahweh was well aware of what was happening to them, and he planned to vindicate them. God calls every single star by name and can always account for each one (40:26); it is certainly not too hard for him to remember and account for his people.

---

61. Childs, *Isaiah*, 307.

Again Isaiah asks, "Have you not known? Have you not heard?" (40:28). He proceeds to list five characteristics of the incomparable God, each of which is relevant for the Israelites as they contemplate their Babylonian exile. The first four are from 40:28 and the fifth is from 40:29-31. (1) Yahweh is the eternal God. He has always been there, and he will always be there. "Yahweh is a God of the long view."[62] (2) Yahweh is the Creator of the entire earth. (3) Yahweh does not get tired. (4) Yahweh is omniscient. His understanding is infinite, inscrutable, unsearchable, incomprehensible (cf. Rom 11:33). (5) Yahweh empowers the weak, namely, those who wait for him. He renews their strength. So God is incomparably eternal, powerful, and wise; he is not limited in time, power, or wisdom (40:28). And he strengthens his people (40:29-31).

The implied application of 40:12-31 is that because God's power, wisdom, immensity, sovereignty, and eternity are incomparable, God's people should wait on him (i.e., trust him; cf. 8:17; 25:9; 26:8; 33:2; 49:23; 64:4) rather than question his ways with them.[63] God has his own timetable (cf. 2 Pet 3:3-10). Because there is no one like God, his people should trust him, standing in awe of his unfathomable wisdom "in stunned admiration."[64]

4. THE ARGUMENT OF ISA 40:13: NO ONE GIVES GOD ADVICE

Now we may focus on the verse that Paul quotes in Rom 11:34.

---

62. So translates Watts, *Isaiah*, 95.

63. Oswalt's application of 40:27-31 is forceful (*Isaiah 40-66*, 71-72): "In these five verses the prophet reverts to his opening question and, in the light of vv. 12-26, concludes the entire discussion. He puts in the mouths of his people the perennial question of all who suffer: Why doesn't God take action to right this situation? While this question would certainly be appropriate for the Babylonian exiles, it is by no means limited to them. In Isaiah's own day the question was forced on him (5:19), and it remains with us today. One may put forward two reasons for God's perceived slowness: he does not wish to act (vv. 1-11), or he is unable to act (vv. 12-26). Thus Isaiah seems to say, 'In the light of what I have said, how can you believe God is ignoring you? Don't you understand? God is utterly other than we. He does not work on our timetable, and he has none of our limitations. But he is at work and you can depend on him.'" Cf. idem, *Isaiah*, 447.

64. Childs, *Isaiah*, 307.

4.1. Historical Context: Contrasting Yahweh with Babylonian Deities and Human Rulers

No one gives God advice (40:13-14).[65] In general, this contrasts with all major rulers such as pharaohs and kings, who rely on counsel and intelligence from experts in different fields (e.g., Esth 1:13).[66] R. N. Whybray, in his penetrating monograph on 40:13-14, observes, "The scene depicted in these verses is primarily one in which Yahweh is represented as a king consulting his professional advisers before embarking upon some course of action."[67] Whybray argues that the questions in 40:13-14 "gain the greatest significance," however, "if their purpose is to elicit the reply that Yahweh alone created the universe without assistance from other gods."[68] The gods typically made decisions by consulting with others in the divine council,[69] but Yahweh is unique. Yahweh's absolute independence in creating the universe strikingly contrasts with the creator-god Marduk, who, according to Babylonian mythology, could not create the world independently; rather, he required the advice of his father Ea.[70] Further, Marduk's liturgy describes him as measuring the waters (cf. 40:12).[71] Whybray concludes that the implication of 40:13-14 is that "the idea of a counsellor god, in the sense of one without whose counsel Yahweh could not have created the world, is unthinkable for believers in Yahweh: Yahweh is God in an absolute sense unknown to the Babylonians."[72]

---

65. Oswalt (*Isaiah 40-66*, 60) summarizes, "The answer to the rhetorical questions in both vv. 13 and 14 is that no one has advised God either in the creation or in the administration of the world."

66. Cf. Young, *Isaiah*, 3:45: "In ancient times it was the duty of citizens to counsel the king."

67. Whybray, *Heavenly Counsellor*, 30.

68. Ibid., *Isaiah 40-66*, 53.

69. Mullen, *Divine Council*; idem, "Divine Assembly," 214-17; Seitz, "Divine Council," 229-47.

70. See Whybray, *Heavenly Counsellor*, 31-84, who convincingly argues that the object of Isaiah's polemic here is Babylonian mythology. Cf. idem, *Isaiah 40-66*, 53-54; *ANET* 64, 68; Herbert, *Isaiah*, 2:22; Merrill, "Language," 64-65; idem, "Unfading," 147-48; Motyer, *Isaiah*, 303; Brueggemann, *Isaiah*, 23; Walton, Matthews, and Chavalas, *IVP*, 626; Blenkinsopp, *Isaiah 40-55*, 105-10, 191; Oswalt, *Isaiah*, 447; Goldingay, *Message*, 40-41; Koole, *Isaiah*, 92.

71. Young, *Isaiah*, 3:43n49; Merrill, "Unfading Word," 147-48.

72. Whybray, *Heavenly Counsellor*, 81-82.

Verses 13–14 are not limited, however, to God's creation of the universe. It extends to his providence, which includes his sovereignty even over politics. וְאִישׁ עֲצָתוֹ "recalls Isaiah's emphasis on Yahweh's capacity to effect a purpose in historical events," and מִשְׁפָּט is "usually translated justice." Thus, to Isaiah, "Creation is the first of God's great acts in history. Creation and history belong to the same activity. So God's sovereignty in creation is one with and establishes God's sovereignty in politics."[73] Childs concludes that in 40:12–14, "God's omnipotence in creation and his supreme wisdom in history are viewed as fully complementary," and "both are directed toward the fulfillment of his sovereign will."[74]

4.2. *Lexis:* תכן *and* רוּחַ

1. תִּכֵּן. In this context the meaning of the piel of תכן is uncertain. *HALOT* lists 40:13 as a "special" instance that could be translated as (1) mete out or assess, (2) determine, (3) set out in readiness, or (4) guide or direct.[75] Isaiah uses the piel of תכן in both vv. 12 and 13. The object of תכן in v. 12 is שָׁמַיִם, and the object in v. 13 is אֶת־רוּחַ יְהוָה. The meaning of תכן in v. 12 is straightforward, namely, measuring or marking off the sky with a span or hand-breadth (the distance between the tips of one's outstretched thumb and little finger). Verse 13 repeats the same verb, but its object cannot be measured in the same sense as the sky.[76] So the two most likely meanings

---

73. Goldingay, *Isaiah*, 226.

74. Childs, *Isaiah*, 309. Cf. Oswalt (*Isaiah 40–66*, 60): "The answer to the rhetorical questions in both vv. 13 and 14 is that no one has advised God either in the creation or in the administration of the world."

75. *HALOT* 4:1734.

76. Young (*Isaiah*, 3:44) insists with a little less nuance than desirable, "The first verb, *tikken*, has the same significance as in the previous verse, and indicates the measuring or meting out of something. God alone has measured the waters in the hollow of His hand, but He Himself is unmeasurable. He who has measured the creation cannot be measured by the creation." Goldingay and Payne (*Isaiah*, 1:101) more carefully note that if תכן shares the same meaning in vv. 12–13, then in v. 13 it "has a metaphorical sense, and suggests an *a fortiori* movement between v. 12 and v. 13: 'no-one has measured creation, so no-one has measured the creator.' . . . 'Directed,' however, yields a better parallelism with v. 13b, suggesting not merely 'who ever gets the measure of Yhwh' (which would lead on from v. 12 in one way) but 'who ever causes Yhwh to act in the world' (which leads on from v. 12 in another way)." Cf. Knight, *Isaiah*, 19: "The word *directed* is identical with the word rendered *marked off* in v. 12. Thus does DI with both wit and sarcasm force his readers to take seriously the blasphemy of man. Man in DI's day was just as apt to imagine, as any astronomical scientist today is tempted to do, that humanity may one day measure the mind of God."

of תכן in v. 13 are (1) measure, mark off, or determine as a metaphor for comprehend, fathom, or plumb (cf. ESV, NET, NIV, TNIV, Tanakh)[77] or (2) direct or advise (cf. NASB, KJV, NKJV, HCSB, NRSV, NLT).[78] These two senses are not mutually exclusive. Rather, the former may carry the sense of the latter by metonymy given v. 13b (cf. conceptually 45:9–12).[79] In other words, who can comprehend (metaphorically expressed by measure) Yahweh's mind with the result that he can advise him?

2. רוּחַ. *HALOT* lists fifteen senses of רוּחַ, which may refer to the Spirit, spirit, breath, wind, or mind. English translations do not uniformly translate the fifty-two occurrences of רוּחַ in Isaiah,[80] and translators are divided among three options on how to translate it in 40:13: Spirit (NASB, KJV, NKJV, ESV, RSV, HCSB, TNIV, NLT), spirit (NRSV),[81] and mind (LXX, NET, NIV, Tanakh). The translation "mind" seems contextually superior to Yahweh's personal Spirit/spirit for six reasons.[82] (1) This passage is about God's incomprehensibility and is not singling out the Holy Spirit.

---

77. Childs (*Isaiah*, 304) translates 40:13, "Who has plumbed the mind of the Lord, or with whom has he shared his plan?" He explains, "The verb *tikkēn* in v. 12 appears to have a concrete meaning such as 'determine' or 'gauge,' but in v. 13 there is a slight shift of meaning to suit the content, best translated to '*plumb* the spirit of Yahweh'" (309). Whybray (*Heavenly Counsellor*, 13–18) prefers the gloss "gauge" or "estimate," and he translates 40:13, "Who has understood the mind of Yahweh, or who was his counsellor, who instructed him?"

78. Goldingay and Payne (*Isaiah*, 1:101) argue that direct or advise "yields a better parallelism with v. 13b, suggesting not merely 'who ever gets the measure of Yhwh' (which would lead on from v. 12 in one way) but 'who ever causes Yhwh to act in the world' (which leads on from v. 12 in another way)."

79. Cf. Merendino, *Erste*, 76. Compare Koole, *Isaiah*, 91: "Ridderbos, who reads תכן as 'to measure' in v. 12, renders the word 'to limit' in v. 13. But this shift in meaning is unnecessary if תכן is already taken to mean 'to limit' in v. 12. The train of thought is that God has determined the measurements of the universe, but no man measures up so far as to determine God to a certain plan. Small people cannot impose their wills on the supreme God. He is the sovereign ruler over all events in nature and history."

80. For example, the NASB, ESV, TNIV, and NET translate רוּחַ the same way in only sixteen of its fifty-two occurrences in Isaiah.

81. Oswalt (*Isaiah 40–66*, 59) defines רוּחַ here as "the sum total of the interior life, including the volitional, affective, and cognitive aspects. Who can accurately comprehend that aspect of God and so tell him what to do?"

82. Cf. Calvin, *Isaiah*, 219; BDB 925; Skinner, *Isaiah* (2nd ed.; Cambridge Bible for Schools and Colleges; Cambridge: Cambridge University Press, 1917), 9; Pieper, *Isaiah*, 114–15; Whybray, *Heavenly Counsellor*, 10–13; Goldingay, "Breath," 15; idem, *Message*, 37–38; Smith, *Isaiah 40–66*, 110n91.

(2) It is unlikely that רוּחַ refers to the Holy Spirit because otherwise תכן would refer to "measuring" God himself in 40:13 (e.g., "Who has measured the Spirit, namely, Yahweh?") instead of an aspect of God (e.g., his mind). (3) Isaiah 40:13a is parallel to 40:13b, which focuses on the mind (i.e., showing God counsel). (4) Isaiah 40:13a is tied to 40:14, which focuses on the mind ("understand," "taught," "taught him knowledge," "showed him the way of understanding"). (5) The LXX translates רוּחַ as νοῦς. (6) Paul twice quotes Isa 40:13 and both times translates רוּחַ as νοῦς (Rom 11:34; 1 Cor 2:16). The difference, however, between the translations Spirit, spirit, and mind is not terribly significant with reference to the point of the clause: no one can comprehend Yahweh's mind nor advise him. Some who advocate the translation "spirit" argue that spirit includes the mind.[83]

The next two lexical items, עֵצָה and ידע, are subsumed under grammar and syntax in §4.3.

4.3. Grammar and Syntax: וְאִישׁ עֲצָתוֹ יוֹדִיעֶנּוּ

Isaiah 40:13b (וְאִישׁ עֲצָתוֹ יוֹדִיעֶנּוּ) literally reads "or [who as] the man of his counsel causes him to know." This may be rendered in one of three basic ways: (1) [who] gives him instruction as his counselor? (NET; cf. NASB, RSV, NRSV, NIV, TNIV); (2) what man shows him his counsel? (ESV; cf. HCSB, NLT, Tanakh);[84] or (3) with whom has he shared his plan?[85] The first rendering is preferable, though it differs only slightly from the second.[86] עֵצָה occurs ninety-two times in the OT, nineteen of which are in Isaiah,[87] and Goldingay's theological reflection on אִישׁ עֲצָתוֹ is particularly instructive:

---

83. E.g., Watts writes, "'spirit' is a literal translation. It includes mind, purpose, and plans, but moves beyond them to include motivation and implementation" (*Isaiah 34–66*, 90–91). Elliger likewise argues that spirit includes motives and intentions (*Deuterojesaja*, 50–51).

84. Cf. Koole, *Isaiah*, 92–93.

85. Cf. Elliger, *Deuterojesaja*, 51–52; Merendino, *Erste*, 76; Childs, *Isaiah*, 304, 309. Childs's argument for this third translation consists of but one sentence that seems to miss the point: "While there are other references in Isaiah by 'a man of God's counsel' (e.g., 46:11) nowhere does a counsellor ever inform God" (*Isaiah*, 309).

86. Young (*Isaiah*, 3:45) rightly notes, "The man of God's counsel is the man who gives God counsel. No one, the prophet is declaring, can serve as a counsellor of God to cause Him to know what is necessary, inasmuch as He is omniscient."

87. Isa 5:19; 8:10; 11:2; 14:26; 16:3; 19:3, 11, 17; 25:1; 28:29; 29:15; 30:1; 36:5; 40:13; 44:26; 46:10, 11 (2x); 47:13.

> The noun and verb "counsel" [עֵצָה] have had a significant place and a distinctive prominence in the book called Isaiah so far. They will recur in 40.14; 41.28; 44.26; 45.21; 46.10, 11; 47.13. They are used both for the advice or counsel that someone receives and for the purpose or plan that they formulate on its basis. In chs 1–39 Yhwh's [עֵצָה] has suggested the purpose Yhwh formulates for the destiny of the nations, and of Israel in particular (5.19; 9.6; 14.24, 26, 27; 19.12; 23.8, 9; 25.1; 28.29). This parallels the plans a monarch and others formulate for a nation, or the deliberations they undertake (1.26; 3.3; 11.2; 16.3; 19.17; 32.7, 8; 36.5). Yhwh's plans may well take unexpected forms, but unlike an earthly monarch's plans, they will definitely be effective in shaping events; rival plans will be frustrated (7.5; 8.10; 19.3, 11; 29.15; 30.1).
>
> The occurrences of the terms in chs 40–47 take further those in chs 1–39. Here, v. 13 dares anyone to deny that Yhwh is the great strategist. In 46.10 Yhwh's counsel denotes Yhwh's purpose at work in history, while in 46.11 "the man of his counsel" is Cyrus as the one through whom that purpose is being fulfilled. In 44.26 the term denotes predictions uttered by Yhwh's messengers (cf. "counsellor" in 41.28). These predictions no doubt embody Yhwh's "counsel," in the same sense as the predictions of earthly prognosticators embody theirs (47.13; cf. the related verb in 45.21).[88]

Goldingay then draws a theological conclusion about this passage with reference to its use of רוּחַ and עֵצָה:

> The occurrence of two such ambitious yet theologically freighted expressions in v. 13 opens up the possibility that the verse should be read at two levels. It needs to be read in the context of vv. 12–14 on its own, and also in the context of the significance these expressions will come to have later in the chapters. Given that chs 40–48 are so allusive in the way they open up the theme of Yhwh's intent with regard to Jacob-Israel's deliverance (cf. 41.1), an oblique reference to Cyrus here would be a nice introduction to him. As he will turn out to be a surprising, indeed scandalous, referent of the term "Yhwh's anointed" (45.1), so he will turn out to be a surprising and scandalous embodiment of the term "Yhwh's consultant," "the person through whom Yhwh's purpose is executed." An implication would be that the appropriate reading of the colon's construction is the more open one that makes

---

88. Goldingay, *Message*, 38. Cf. Goldingay and Payne, *Isaiah*, 1:103; Koole, *Isaiah*, 91–92.

the "consultant," whether heavenly or earthly, the means of executing Yhwh's plan rather than its author.[89]

4.4. Genre: Wisdom Poetry

The parallelism of 40:13 has a remarkable cumulative effective: no one is able to give Yahweh advice.[90] The poetry in vv. 12–14 strengthens the passage's emotive effect with rich consonance and assonance,[91] and both vv. 13 and 14 use wisdom language: עֵצָה (counsel), ידע (know), מִשְׁפָּט (justice), אֹרַח (way), דֶּרֶךְ (way) and תְּבוּנָה (understanding).[92] This seems to indicate that this passage is part of the wisdom tradition.[93] Isaiah connects God's wisdom with creation and his involvement in the human arena with the result that he is the sovereign, incomparable King over all kings. He alone will hold all humans accountable, and consequently no one can serve as his counselor.

5. CONCLUSION

In order to understand how Paul uses Isa 40:13 in Rom 11:34, one must first understand how the prophet Isaiah uses it. This chapter's understanding of Isa 40:13 is rooted in its understanding of chapter 40 and

---

89. Goldingay, *Message*, 39.

90. Young (*Isaiah*, 3:45) probes, "The second half of the verse stands in chiastic relation to the first. Thus, the object comes first and is emphasized, and the verb and suffix conclude the first half of the verse. These words are probably to be construed as follows: 'And a man of His counsel, will He cause Him to know?' The thought then is that no one can act as a counsellor and cause God to know the things that He should know. On this construction, the latter half of the verse really continues the question introduced by the first interrogative pronoun." Cf. Dahood, "Breakup," 537–38.

91. Cf. Gitay, *Prophecy*, 88–90.

92. Cf. Muilenberg, "Isaiah," 437; Whybray, *Heavenly Counsellor*, 19, 26–27; Leclerc, "*Mišpāṭ*," 179–93; Goldingay, *Message*, 39–41.

93. Whybray (*Heavenly Counsellor*, 27) is more cautious: "But in spite of the use of these verbs [i.e., the three verbs meaning "teach"], the primary reference of the verse is not to the wisdom schools . . . In the absence of any clear agreement at present on what is meant by 'wisdom influence,' it would be hazardous to assert the existence of such influence here except in a very general sense." The primary picture of Isa 40:13–14 is Yahweh as king consulting professional advisers, and "the similarities to the style and vocabulary of the wisdom literature are secondary to this, and do not suggest the direct influence of the wisdom schools, but rather show how far 'wisdom' and court usage coincided" (30). In a book published three years later, however, Whybray classifies Isa 40:13–14 as "'wisdom' as intelligence" (*Intellectual*, 10).

the book as a whole. (We will see in due course that Paul presupposes all this by quoting Isa 40:13.) Isaiah's theological message is that people should trust the Holy One of Israel because he is the incomparable King and Savior. Chapters 40–66 emphasize God's comfort and restoration of his people, and chapter 40 exalts God's incomparability to demonstrate that he can easily restore his people. Isaiah 40:13 exclaims that no one gives God advice, evoking God's unrivaled wisdom and incomparable greatness.

4

Job 41:3a in Context

EXAMINING JOB 41:3A (ENG. 41:11a) in context is essential for substantively discussing the use of the OT in Rom 11:34–35. This chapter traces the argument of Job in more depth than the previous two chapters trace the arguments of Romans and Isaiah, but it follows the basic organization of the previous two chapters by situating Job 41:3a in its larger literary and theological context before focusing on that verse.[1]

1. SYNOPSIS OF JOB

Understanding the entire book of Job is essential for understanding Job 41:3a—even more so than understanding the entire book of Romans or Isaiah is essential for understanding Rom 11:34–35 and Isa 40:13, respectively. The reason is that Job 41:3a occurs near the end of a carefully crafted wisdom story, so the weight of 41:3a is felt most significantly when one reads it in light of all that precedes it as well as how the story concludes.

This book assumes that the book of Job is a coherent, literary unity.[2] The book's genre is difficult to identify because it is *sui generis*. There is nothing like it in the rest of the OT, and its similarities to Ancient Near Eastern literature are limited. Most OT scholars agree that the book may be categorized broadly as wisdom literature, but it is wisdom literature

---

1. The formats of this chapter and the ones on Rom 11:34–35 and Isa 40:13 slightly differ from each other because the chapters analyze different genres. Thus, it is less useful to analyze each passage through exactly the same grid.

2. Contra, e.g., Maag, *Hiob*. On this and related introductory issues, see Harrison, *Introduction*, 1022–46; Hartley, *Job*, 3–63; Archer, *Survey*, 503–15; Longman and Dillard, *Introduction*, 224–36; Carson, *How Long*, 137–39, 154–56.

distinct from the books of Proverbs and Ecclesiastes, for example, because it "is both an epic and a wisdom disputation" that "has drawn on numerous genres."[3] The drama unfolds in five parts; the first and last are prose, and the middle three are poetry.

1. Prologue (chs. 1–2)
2. Job's lament and three cycles of debates between Job and Eliphaz, Bildad, and Zophar (chs. 3–31)
3. Elihu's discourse (chs. 32–37)
4. God's interrogation of Job (38:1—42:6)
5. Epilogue (42:7–17)

What follows summarizes the prose frame (i.e., the prologue and epilogue) and paraphrases the poetic dialogue (3:1—42:6). Each paraphrase expresses the kernel of the speech in order to track the interaction between the speakers and to follow the progression of the dialogue. It conveys the characters' emotions to a greater degree by unconventionally employing an informal writing style.[4]

1.1. Prologue (Job 1–2)

The prologue sets the scene by introducing the patriarch Job and the problem with which the rest of the book wrestles. Job is a "blameless and upright," God-fearing, evil-hating man (1:1; cf. 1:8; 2:3). He is the richest person in the East and unusually devout: he regularly offers pre-emptive burnt offerings to God on behalf of his seven sons and three daughters (1:2–5).

Meanwhile, unknown to Job, Satan joins the sons of God (apparently God's angels) when they present themselves before God, and God initiates a discussion with Satan about Job (1:6–8). Satan accuses Job of serving God merely because God has blessed Job, and God gives Satan permission to test Job but not touch him (1:9–12). Satan strikes acutely by synchronizing a series of calamities like a terrorist mastermind: he destroys Job's livestock and murders all ten of his children and nearly all of his servants (1:13–19). Without any knowledge of God's interaction

---

3. Hartley, *Job*, 38.

4. Kidner similarly paraphrases the twenty-seven stanzas in the Babylonian Theodicy (*Wisdom*, 135–38). Cf. the occasional paraphrases of Job's dialogue in Talbert, *Beyond Suffering*.

with Satan, Job responds with remarkable integrity, worshipping and praising Yahweh (1:20–22).

Again Satan joins God's angels when they present themselves before God, and again God initiates a discussion with Satan about Job (2:1–3). Satan accuses Job of serving God merely because God blessed him with health, and God gives Satan permission to touch Job but not murder him (2:4–6). Satan strikes severely by inflicting Job with painful sores over his entire body (2:7–8). Even Job's wife urges him to curse God, but he again, without any knowledge of God's interaction with Satan, responds with remarkable integrity (2:9–10).

When three of Job's friends—Eliphaz, Bildad, and Zophar—hear about Job's suffering, they come to sympathize with him and comfort him (2:11). They stay with him for a full week without saying a word because his suffering is so severe (2:12–13), but they soon confirm several proverbs about keeping silent (e.g., Prov 10:19; 17:28; 21:23).

1.2. Paraphrase of Job's Lament and Three Cycles of Debates between Job and Eliphaz, Bildad, and Zophar (Job 3–31)

1.2.1. Paraphrase of Job's Lament (Job 3)

I wish I had never been born (3:3–10)! I would be better off if I had been stillborn or just starved to death right after birth (3:11–19). I wish God would let me die (3:20–24)! My worst nightmare has come true, and I'm in turmoil and despair (3:25–26).

1.2.2. Paraphrase of Round One (Job 4–14)

Eliphaz's Response (Job 4–5). I must speak (4:2). It looks like Mr. Advice-giver is actually a hypocrite in need of advice himself (4:3–5). If you really are blameless, would you be suffering like this or be so discouraged (4:6)? God destroys the wicked—not the upright (4:7–9). I heard in a vision that mortals can't be more righteous than God, so stop pretending that you are (4:12–21). If I were you, I would humbly and repentantly submit to God's chastisement and not despise it; then you can experience his blessings (5:8, 17–27).

Job's Response (Job 6–7). My misery is immeasurably heavy (6:2–3). God has afflicted me (6:4), and I'd rather die than deny his words (6:8–10). I've lost hope that God might restore me (6:11–13). What compassionate friends you are (6:14–23)! I'm willing to listen to you if you actually teach me, but show me what I've done wrong instead of wrongly assuming that I deserve this because I sinned (6:24–30). This is my hopeless lot: life is hard and then you die (7:1–10). Have pity on me, God (7:7). I'd rather be strangled to death than continue my meaningless life; I hate my life (7:15–16). Why are you picking on me, God (7:17–21)?

Bildad's Response (Job 8). You windbag (8:2)! Do you dare to question God's justice (8:3)? Your children must have deserved to die because they sinned against God (8:4). If you seek God and if you are pure and upright, God will lavishly restore you (8:5–7), but he hasn't because you are godless (8:13). Just ask the previous generations, and you'll see that what we're telling you is right (8:8). God neither rejects blameless people nor blesses evildoers (8:20).

Job's Response (Job 9–10). I agree that God is just, but how can I prove to him that I'm suffering innocently so that he will vindicate me (9:2)? No one can win a legal dispute with God because he is wise and powerful (9:3–24). I'm blameless! I hate my life (9:21). What's the point? God destroys both the innocent and the guilty (9:22). And you're actually increasing my suffering by condemning an innocent man (9:28). I am presumed guilty until proven innocent, so why should I even try defending myself (9:29)? Even if I were sparkling clean, you would ignore the evidence and plunge me into a slime pit to prove that I'm dirty (9:29–31). I need a mediator to arbitrate between God and me, but that's not going to happen (9:32–33). I hate my life, so I'm going to complain about it (10:1). God, don't condemn me; please explain why you're doing this to me (10:2). Are you sadistic? Do you get pleasure from torturing me while beaming at the schemes of the wicked (10:3)? You know I'm not guilty (10:7). Why did you create me and then do this to me (10:8–19)? Go away, and let me die (10:20–22)!

Zophar's Response (Job 11). Will no one rebuke your mocking (11:2–3)? How dare you claim to be pure in God's sight (11:4)? I wish God would openly rebuke you; he's exacting less punishment from you than you deserve (11:5–6). You can't fathom the deep things of God, you idiot; God is so powerful and wise that he can see right through your deception, so he must punish you (11:7–12). Repent and experience God's blessing, or perish (11:13–20).

Job's Response (Job 12–14). Wisdom will doubtless die with you (12:2)! I know as much as you do about God's greatness; I'm not inferior to you (12:3; 13:2). Even animals are smarter than you because at least they know that Yahweh has done this (12:7–10). Wisdom and power belong to God (12:13–25), and I wish I could argue my case with him (13:3). You worthless quacks are smearing me with lies (13:4). The best way you could demonstrate wisdom is to shut up (13:5). You're defending God with lies (13:7). I am innocent and don't deserve this (13:13–19), but even if God kills me, I'll hope in him because I know he will vindicate me (13:15). Why are you doing this, God (13:23–25)? You have ordained our lives to be short and full of trouble (14:1–5). Give us a break (14:6)! My death is inevitable and irreversible, so I wish you would just kill me and get it over with (14:7–13). Then I'd eagerly await my resurrection (14:14–17). Meanwhile, you unremittingly grind down my hope with impending death (14:18–22).

1.2.2. Paraphrase of Round Two (Job 15–21)

Eliphaz's Response (Job 15). You're not a wise man, you windbag (15:2–3)! Your own words testify against you (15:5–6). Don't ignore the wisdom of your elders (15:7–11). You claim to be righteous, but mortals are corrupt (15:12–16). The wicked always suffer eventually, so your extreme suffering is irrefutable evidence that you have been extremely wicked (15:20–35).

Job's Response (Job 16–17). You miserable comforters are endlessly blowing hot air (16:2–3). If I were in your place, I would edify and comfort with my words (16:4–5). God has crushed me even though I am innocent (16:7–22). I'm surrounded by taunting mockers; there's not a single wise man among you (17:2–10). I just want to die (17:11–16).

Bildad's Response (Job 18). Do you think we're stupid (18:2–4)? God severely punishes the wicked: he snuffs out his lamp, weakens his steps, traps him, terrifies him, destroys him, burns him, dries up his roots, perishes the memory of him from the earth, and cuts off his descendents (18:5–20). Therefore, you are wicked and don't even know God (18:21).

Job's Response (Job 19). How long will you shamelessly torture me with your insulting words (19:2–3)? Even if I have sinned, it's none of your business (19:4). God has wronged me; I don't deserve this (19:6–12). My own family and friends have abandoned me, and even little boys scorn me (19:13–20). Have pity on me (19:21)! Why do you persecute me like God does (19:22)? But I know that my Redeemer lives, and in my body I will see God; he will vindicate me and punish you for persecuting me (19:25–29).

Zophar's Response (Job 20). You're insulting me, Job (20:2–3). God always judges the wicked like this (20:4–29).

Job's Response (Job 21). Just hear me out, and then you may mock on (21:2–3). Why do the wicked prosper (21:7–21)? Who can teach God knowledge (21:22)? Some people experience a vigorous, prosperous, secure life, and others never enjoy a single good thing; but both die (21:23–26). Open your eyes, and look around: wicked people prosper all the time (21:27–33). How can your futile words comfort me? Your so-called answers are nothing but lies (21:34).

1.2.3. Paraphrase of Round Three (Job 22–31)

Eliphaz's Response (Job 22). Is God punishing you because you're so righteous (22:4)? It's obvious to everyone that your wickedness is great: you've ruthlessly robbed your own poor relatives, refused to feed the poor, mistreated widows, and crushed orphans (22:5–9). That's why you're suffering (22:10–11). Do you think that God is so far away that he can't see us and judge us accurately (22:12–14)? Will you continue on the path with wicked people (22:15)? Repent and experience God's blessing (22:21–30).

Job's Response (Job 23–24). I wish I knew where God is so that I could present my case to him; then he would answer me and establish my innocence (23:3–9). I am innocent (23:10–12), but God sovereignly does whatever he wants (23:13–14). He terrifies me (23:15–17). Why doesn't the Almighty punish the wicked now (24:1–17)? He will punish them in due course (24:18–24). If this is not so, then who can prove me a liar (24:25)?

Bildad's Response (Job 25). God is awesome (25:2–3). How can mortals be righteous before God (24:4)? They are maggots and worms (25:5–6).

Job's Response (Job 25–31). Thank you so much for helping me when I'm powerless and for giving such wise advice to me when I'm without wisdom (26:2-4)! God sovereignly controls death, the heavens, the weather, animals, and what we perceive as chaos—and that's just scratching the surface (26:5-14). God has unjustly denied me justice; I'm innocent (27:2-6). Nevertheless, God will bring the wicked to justice, if not in this life then certainly in the next (27:7-23). Only God has all the answers because people don't even know where to find wisdom (28:1-27). Wisdom, for us, means fearing the Lord and turning away from evil (28:28).[5] I used to be blessed and esteemed (29:2-25), but now contemptible wretches mock me (30:1-15). I'm in the grip of suffering as God ruthlessly attacks me (30:16-31) even though I have been righteous: I have not lusted after women, lied, committed adultery, treated my servants unfairly, refused to help the poor, mistreated widows, refused to care for orphans, trusted or boasted in my wealth, worshiped the sun or moon, rejoiced over the misfortune of my enemies, cursed anyone, turned away strangers, nor hid my sins (31:1-34). If only I could plead my case to the Almighty (31:35-37)! I have neither stolen nor murdered to obtain my land (31:38-40).

1.3. Paraphrase of Elihu's Discourse (Job 32–37)

(Elihu, who waits to speak because he is much younger than the others, is furious with both Job and his three friends: "He burned with anger at Job because he justified himself rather than God. He burned with anger also at Job's three friends because they had found no answer, although they had declared Job to be in the wrong" [32:2-3].)[6]

---

5. Many commentators are convinced that ch. 28 does not record the words of Job, but instead is a reflective interlude inserted as a parenthesis and composed by the narrator. But this issue does not merit our attention here because it makes little difference to the overall message of the book whether ch. 28 records the words of Job or the narrator. For a recent analysis of Job 28 that sees it as central to the book of Job, see Lo, *Job 28*.

6. Elihu's role in Job is debated. There are two primary views among those who consider the book to be a literary unity. (1) Elihu is an arrogant whippersnapper, a pompous young know-it-all who merely recycles the retribution theology of Job's three friends. Luther, for example, calls Elihu "the good-for-nothing chatterer" who is "greedy and anxious" to teach (*Zechariah*, 234). Cf. Good, *Turns*, 321; Dumbrell, "Job," 91, 101; Wilson, *Job*, 13, 420; Longman and Dillard, *Introduction*, 229-30. (2) More convincing is the view that Elihu speaks accurately and transitionally as a precursor and foil to God. "Elihu is right to defend the justice of God, and he has advanced the discussion by suggesting that Job's greatest sin may not be in something he said or did *before* the suffering started, but the rebellion he is displaying *in* the suffering (Carson, *How Long*, 150-51, emphasis in original). "The three counselors had claimed that Job was suffering because he was sinning, but Elihu explained that he was sinning because

I know I'm young, but I've listened to you guys long enough; listen to me (32:6-11). Not one of you three refuted Job's arguments, so I must speak (32:15-22). Listen carefully to me, Job (33:1-7). You claim to be innocent and thus charge God with injustice, but you're wrong to charge God with injustice; God is just and can do whatever he wants (33:8-13). God is not as remote as you think: sometimes he reveals himself by dreams, and other times the language he uses to communicate to us is pain (33:14-22).[7] Repent and experience God's blessing (33:25-30). I've got more wisdom to share, so keep listening (33:31-33).

Job claims that he is just and that God is unjust (34:5-9). But God can't be unjust (34:10-30)! Job deserves God's severest judgment for answering like wicked men (34:36-37). Job, do you think it's right to claim, on the one hand, that you're more righteous than God and, on the other hand, that living a righteous life doesn't pay off (35:2-3)? God is not listening to your pathetic pleas to plead your case before him; you're foolish to think that God is obligated to answer you (35:13-16). Job is speaking without knowledge (35:16).

I've got more to say on God's behalf, and be assured that I am "perfect in knowledge" (36:2-4). God is just (36:3). He is mighty and gives justice to the afflicted (36:5-7). He tells them how they have sinned and then restores them if they repent or punishes them if they don't (36:8-15). God is ready to restore you, Job, so don't turn to evil (36:16-21). God is incomparably great and beyond our understanding (36:22-26); you don't even understand how he controls thunderstorms (36:27-37:18). We're too ignorant to argue our case before the majestic, merciful, almighty, righteous God (37:19-23). That's why people fear him (37:24).

---

he was suffering!" (Zuck, *Job*, 141). Some who hold this view also consider Elihu to be arrogant and bumptious to some degree. Cf. Hartley, *Job*, 427-86; Carson, *How Long*, 148-50; Konkel, "Job," 191-95, 218-19; cf. also Wilson, "Role," 81-94; McCabe, "Elihu's Contribution," 47-80; Waters, "Elihu's Theology," 143-59. Others who hold this view argue that Elihu is not arrogant. Cf. Calvin, *Job*, 558-88; Talbert, *Beyond Suffering*, 163-94, 339-54.

7. Cf. Lewis, *Problem*, 90-91: "Pain is unmasked, unmistakable evil; every man knows something is wrong when he is being hurt . . . Pain insists upon being attended to. God whispers to us in our pleasures, speaks in our conscience, but shouts in our pains: it is His megaphone to rouse a deaf world."

1.4. Paraphrase of God's Interrogation of Job (Job 38:1—42:6)

God's First Interrogation (Job 38:1—40:2). Who is this who questions my wisdom and justice with words without knowledge (38:2)? Get ready to defend yourself, Job, because now *I* will question *you*, and you will inform me (38:3)! Where were you when I created the universe (38:4–7)? Can you providentially control every detail of my creation: the sea, the morning daylight, the springs that fill the sea, death, the vast expanses of the earth, light, darkness, snow, hail, the east wind, rain, thunderbolts, dew, ice, frost, the stars, the laws of the universe, clouds, lightning, wisdom, lions, and ravens (38:8–41)? Surely you know these things, for you were already born and have lived so many years (38:21)! Do you know everything about my animals: the mountain goat, deer, wild donkey, wild ox, ostrich, horse, hawk, and eagle (39:1–30)? Will you contend with, accuse, and correct the Almighty? Now is your chance to speak up (40:2).

Job's First Response (Job 40:3-5). I am not worthy. How could I answer you? I am speechless. I have said far too much and will say no more (40:4–5).

God's Second Interrogation (Job 40:6—41:26 [Eng. 40:6—41:34]). Get ready to defend yourself, Job, because now I will question you, and you will inform me (40:7)! Will you defend your own righteousness at the expense of my righteousness (40:8)? Are you as strong as God? Prove it by punishing everyone who is proud, and then I'll acknowledge your superiority (40:9–14). Can you control the untamable, invincible Behemoth (40:15-24) and Leviathan (40:25—41:26 [Eng. 41:1–34])? You would never pick a fight with them, so why are you picking a fight with me? Why do you think you can stand against me—that you have a claim against me that I must pay? I own everything and owe nothing to anyone (41:2–3 [Eng. 41:10–11])!

Job's Second Response (Job 42:1-6). You are supremely sovereign, so you do whatever you want (42:2). I questioned your wisdom with words that lacked knowledge; I didn't know what I was talking about (42:3–4). Now that I understand you far more clearly than before, I repent (42:5–6).[8]

---

8. Some disagree that Job repented of sin, insisting that God's commendation of Job's words in 42:7-8 implies that Job did not have anything for which to repent. In support of the above paraphrase, see §3 below.

1.5. Epilogue (Job 42:7–17)

God then rebukes Job's three friends because they spoke wrongly about God in a way that Job did not (42:7–9).[9] Further, God blesses Job with twice as much wealth as before, family and friends who are sympathetic and comforting, seven more sons, and three more daughters (42:10–17).

God allows Satan to afflict Job, but he does not *merely* allow it. The epilogue describes Job's Satan-inflicted calamities as "all the evil that the LORD had brought upon him" (42:11). This is consistent with the prologue where God twice initiates discussions with Satan about Job (1:8; 2:3). The end of God's statement in 2:3 implies that God himself is the ultimate cause of the calamity since he, not Satan, is the one who destroys Job: "you incited me against him to destroy him without reason."

2. THE THEME OF JOB

Some argue that it is fruitless to seek a single overarching theme for the book of Job.[10] Many such themes have been suggested. Some are not only unconvincing as the overarching theme of the book; they are not even motifs in the book. For example, some people argue that the book's theme is that doubting orthodoxy is a sign of mature faith.[11] Many of God's people, while mature in their faith, have expressed doubts to God (cf. many of the psalms), but the book of Job does not commend questioning and rejecting orthodoxy as a sign of mature faith. Job rightly questions whether retribution theology, the traditional theology of his day, can explain everything, but he is rebuked—not commended—for questioning God's justice.

2.1. Eight Motifs in Job

Each of the following eight motifs is textually rooted and thus contributes to the book's theme, but none adequately encapsulates the book as a whole.[12] §2.2 shows how these various motifs cohere as part of one overarching theme, but first it is worth describing these motifs.

---

9. See Porter, "Job," 291–304.
10. E.g., Dell, *Job*.
11. Di Lella, "Job," 54.
12. Some have suggested these motifs as the overall theme of the book, but authors referenced below under various motifs do not necessarily consider that motif as Job's

1. *The problem of innocent, unexplained suffering.*[13] All humans are sinful and thus deserve God's eternal righteous wrath, but there is a sense in which some humans suffer more than they deserve. Job does not claim to be sinless, but he does claim to be innocent with reference to this particular suffering (10:7; 13:13–19; 16:7–22; 19:6–12; 23:10–12; 27:2–6; 31:1–40). Job deserves this suffering about as much as an eight-year-old girl deserves to be raped by her uncle. His suffering is evil, horrific, painful, disorienting, disillusioning. It seems irrational to him. He cannot figure out what he did to deserve losing his children, his servants, his wealth, his health, support from family and friends, and his reputation. The narrator and reader know that Job's innocence itself is the catalyst for his suffering, but Job is left in the dark. God never explains to Job why he is suffering, and his suffering never makes sense to him.

2. *Maintaining faith during innocent, unexplained suffering.*[14] Job never learns the answer to his "Why?" question (7:20–21; 10:8–19; 13:23–25), but he learns something more important. He learns that God is immensely great, absolutely sovereign, and unfailingly trustworthy. Although his questions about why he is suffering remain unanswered, Job learns to trust God and not demand answers as if God owes them to him. This does not mean that in the end Job trusts God ignorantly or blindly. Rather, Job trusts God on the basis of God's character and revelation. Job's faith is a reasonable, informed faith. Even though Job is burning to prove himself innocent before God, he learns that God is more concerned that Job trust him.

3. *Mystery.*[15] Even worse than abusing Job with their retribution theology, Job's friends do not speak rightly about God. They think they know more about God than they really do. But none of the human characters in the book of Job understand why God treats Job the way he does. They do not have all the information. Nor do we. The only person not limited

---

overarching theme. Sometimes authors may describe the book of Job with one of these motifs while subsuming other motifs under it.

13. Cf. Hengstenberg, "Job," 91; Tsevat, "Job," 96; Archer, *Job*, 17–19; idem, *Survey*, 503–4; Clines, "Job," 459; Brueggemann, *Theology* 386–87; Good, "Problem," 50–69, 236–38. See also Waters, "Reflections," 436–51; Carson, *How Long*, 140, 146–48.

14. Cf. Steinmann, "Job," 89–91, 99–100. Wilson (*Job*, 2) argues that Job's "core message" is "that it is necessary to endure faithfully in the face of extreme loss and suffering."

15. Thomas argues that John Calvin understood this to be the theme of Job (*Proclaiming*, 373 et al.).

by perspective is God, so everyone except God lacks sufficient information to understand God and his ways completely.

Job learns to live with tension on one level, but the reader is faced with tension on another level. Even though the narrator gives the reader a glimpse into God's heavenly throne room to learn about God's interaction with Satan (information never disclosed to Job), the reader does not learn the full reason that God brought all this evil upon Job (42:11). We do not know all the reasons that God ordained that Job experience undeserved suffering. It is a "mystery" in the sense of "something that is difficult or impossible to understand or explain" (not in the sense that Paul uses the term μυστήριον). We know about God's interaction with Satan, but this may strike some readers as cruel: Why should Job have to endure excruciating innocent suffering merely so that God can win a bet with Satan? That is a crass way to put it because it assumes that Job is suffering *merely* for that reason, but we do not know all of the reasons for God's inscrutable ways.[16] We know only what he has revealed, and he has not revealed everything (cf. Deut 29:29). We may not know all of God's reasons, but we must conclude based on God's character and revelation that his reasons must be good ones: "The solemnity and majesty of God's response to Job not only mask God's purposes in mystery, but presuppose they are serious and deep, not flighty or frivolous."[17]

Because Job calls God's justice into question, some describe the book of Job as a theodicy.[18] But the book is not a typical theodicy because it does not directly answer Job's charge that God is unjust for his innocent suffering—or at least it does not answer the question the way many people would expect. In his interrogation of Job, God defends his right to do whatever he wants to whomever he wants and insists that he is always righteous in doing so. And Job humbly affirms it.[19]

---

16. We can, however, reasonably deduce at least some of these reasons. For example, God has used Job's suffering to teach millions of humans over some three millennia about himself and his ways. We can also eliminate possible reasons, such as this one proposed by Patton ("Beauty," 167): "We know God is speaking truth when God says chaos is created for divine amusement, because we know Job suffers because God was amused by Satan's wager."

17. Carson, *How Long*, 156.

18. E.g., Bullock, *Introduction*, 69–71.

19. Cf. Lévêque, *Job*, 2:532; Nicholson, "Limits," 71–82.

4. *Comfort.*[20] Job's three friends "come to show him sympathy and comfort him" (2:11). It would comfort Job for him not to deny God's words (6:10). He cannot seem to find comfort anywhere else (7:13). Eliphaz rebukes Job for spurning "the comforts of God" (15:11), and Job replies, "Miserable comforters are you all" (16:2). Job pleads with them to comfort him by at least hearing him out (21:2) rather than comfort him "with empty nothings" (21:34). Job used to comfort mourners, but now he is a mourner in need of comfort (29:25). The narrator records in the epilogue that Job's family and friends "showed him sympathy and comforted him" (42:11). Some argue that Job remarks in 42:6 that he is "comforted in dust and ashes."[21]

5. *Refuting retribution theology.*[22] Job's insensitive friends so glibly and inflexibly cling to a proverbial truth that they merit God's rebuke (42:7–9). Appealing to their venerable tradition (8:8–20), they insist that you reap what you sow (cf. Prov 22:8; Gal 6:7), that God blesses the righteous and curses the wicked (cf. Prov 3:9–10; 10:27–32). That is generally true, but it is not always true. You reap what you sow, but you do not reap only what you sow. Conversely, it is wrong to conclude that those whom God blesses are righteous and that those whom God curses are wicked. Because Job's condescending friends have no category for guiltless suffering, they mechanically conclude that because Job is suffering, he must have sinned (cf. Job 4:7–9; 11:13–20). But the law of retribution does not explain everything because it is a general principle, not an inviolable rule (cf. John 9:1–3, 34). Thus, their error is at least threefold:

> The basic error of Job's friends is that they [1] overestimate their grasp of truth, [2] misapply the truth they know, and [3] close their mind to any facts that contradict what they assume. . . . The book shows (by its context, the opening scene in heaven) [1] how small a part of any situation is the fragment that we see; [2] how much of what we do see we ignore or distort through preconceptions; and [3] how unwise it is to extrapolate from our elementary grasp of truth.[23]

---

20. Cf. Mickel, *Hiobbuch*.

21. See further discussion on 42:6 in §3 below.

22. Cf. Dhorme, *Job*, cxxviii–cli; Dumbrell, "Job," 91–105. Burrell (*Deconstructing*, 16), who denies that the book is about theodicy at all, unconvincingly argues that its primary role is "to correct that characteristic misapprehension of the revelation [from God] displayed by Job's friends."

23. Kidner, *Wisdom*, 61.

Consequently, the three friends cruelly abuse Job by unbendingly adhering to a general rule and then rigidly and heartlessly applying that rule to him.

6. *Putting humans in their place.*[24] People sinfully tend to view God's universe through a self-centered lens. They tend to think too highly of themselves and too lowly of God. In few places is this evident more clearly than when people suffer and then demand answers from God as if God owes them an explanation, as if they have the authority to call God into account, as if God must defend himself to them, as if they are qualified to judge God. It is hard to think of a better illustration of self-idolatry. This mindset domesticates the omnipotent and omnibenevolent God.

7. *Wisdom.*[25] Who is wise? That is, who has wisdom to diagnose Job's situation most accurately? The book of Job is, after all, wisdom literature.[26] The book's first verse and the prologue's leading question are about a prominent unifying theme of wisdom literature, the fear of the Lord: the narrator comments that Job "feared God" like a wise man (1:1; cf. Prov 3:7; 14:16; 16:6), and Satan asks, "Does Job fear God for no reason?" (Job 1:9).[27] All of the characters in the dialogue—Job, Eliphaz, Bildad, Zophar, Elihu, and God himself—analyze Job's situation in a way that claims they have wisdom (cf. 11:12; 12:2–3, 12–16; 13:2–12; 15:2–13; 17:10; 26:3; 28:12–28; 32:7–13; 33:33; 34:2; 37:24; 38:36–37; 39:17). Chapter 28, which is devoted to wisdom, is integral to the book,[28] and God's argument in chapters 38–41 "is essentially that what is inexplicable from human understanding is explicable within the context of divine wisdom."[29]

---

24. Cf. Carson, *How Long*, 152–53.

25. Cf. Longman and Dillard, *Introduction*, 232–34. See also Zerafa, *Wisdom*, 96–184; Habel, "Of Things," 142–54; Perdue, "Wisdom," 73–98; Berry, *Introduction*, 11–12, 141–56.

26. Cf. G. Wilson, *Job*, 3–5.

27. L. Wilson ("Book of Job," 59–79) traces this theme through Job and rightly concludes that it is not the answer to Job's dilemma.

28. Lo, *Job 28*.

29. Hartley, "Theology," 790.

8. *Emotional and spiritual maturity.*[30] God does not waste suffering. Job's suffering is a catalyst that helps all of the human characters in the book to mature emotionally and spiritually. The clearest example, of course, is Job himself because his raw honesty gives the reader a window into his emotional and spiritual condition. Job's view of God and his ways is enhanced significantly by the end of the story. This maturity motif is related to the wisdom motif because God commends Job as a wise man (42:7–9). Brown argues that the central issue of Job is not God, theodicy, or anything other than Job himself, namely, the transformation of his moral character.[31]

2.2. The Theological Message of Job: Why People Should Trust God

The suggested themes above are motifs in the book of Job, but no one of them standing alone sufficiently summarizes the book's theme, that is, its holistic, overarching topic. The theme of Job is "the nature and basis of the relationship between God and man."[32] Stated pastorally and rhetorically, Job's theological message is that *people should respond to innocent, unexplained suffering by trusting God because he is supremely wise, sovereign, just, and good.* Job's suffering precipitates discussion about the book's main focus: God. The book is not consumed with answering why the righteous suffer innocently but how they should relate to God in the midst of that suffering. "Suffering clarifies and isolates the central issue of faith."[33] Talbert usefully distinguishes between the book's subject, theme, function, and thesis:

> The primary *subject* under discussion throughout the book of Job is God. The concept of suffering is only a secondary subject, the catalyst for the discussion. The *theme* of Job is the nature and basis of the relationship between God and man—founded on faith in God's self-revelation as ultimate reality and God's Person as supremely worthy. The *function* of the book is to display the dynamics of the relationship between God and man—honesty, trust, and submission to a sovereign, wise, and good God. The *thesis* of the book is two-sided: (1) God is unquestionably sovereign, sometimes inscrutable, but always righteous, aware, com-

---

30. Cf. Harrison, *Introduction*, 1043–46.
31. Brown, *Character*, 51, 115–19.
32. Talbert, *Beyond Suffering*, 22.
33. Wilson, "Job, Book of," 386. Cf. Terrien, "Job," 897; Barrett, "Job," 25.

passionate, and good in all He does or allows. (2) Man has the privilege and responsibility to know and to trust this one true God in an intimate and infinitely rewarding relationship.[34]

3. THE ARGUMENT OF JOB 38:1—42:6

God's interrogation of Job in 38:1—42:6 is "the literary and theological climax of the book,"[35] and understanding it is crucial for understanding 41:3a. The unit is a disputation speech dominated by the motif of praise.[36] The genre in which God addresses Job in chapters 38–41 is unique:

> The Yahweh speeches, being a blend of multiple genres—theophany, hymn of praise, dispute, interrogation of a defendant, myths of the divine battle with primordial monsters—create a unique form. The essential nature of these speeches is a hymn of praise, but the list of natural phenomena and the series of rhetorical questions dominate their structure.[37]

3.1. The Setup for God's Interrogation of Job (Job 38:1—42:6)

Job persistently maintains his innocence in his suffering—and rightly so—but he is wrong on at least two counts. First, he is determined to prove his innocence before God even at the expense of God's justice. He concludes that God is unjust for allowing his innocent suffering (cf. 27:2-6). Second and more fundamentally, he presumes that God owes him an explanation.

Job repeatedly wishes to appeal directly to God and get a hearing with him (13:13-23; 23:3-9; 31:35-37; cf. 9:32-33). All will be well, he thinks, if only he gets an interview with God. The exasperated Job finally gets his wish, but the interview is not what he had in mind. After thirty-

---

34. Talbert, *Beyond Suffering*, 22. This agrees with the thesis of Parsons' dissertation ("Job 38:1—42:6," 1 of abstract): "The major purpose of Job was not to explain human suffering but to demonstrate that the proper relationship of man to God (whether in suffering or otherwise) is based solely upon the sovereign grace of God and man's response of faith and submissive trust" ("Job 38:1—42:6," ThD diss., Dallas Theological Seminary, 1980). Cf. idem, "Structure," 142-51; idem, "Job, Theology of," 415-19; Viberg, "Job," 202-3.

35. Rowold, "Theology," 1.

36. Westermann, *Hiob*, 108-24 (see also 30, 40-51, 84-92); Murphy, *Wisdom*, 44; Perdue, *Wisdom*, 76-80, 201-2, 218.

37. Hartley, *Job*, 488.

five chapters of human dialogue, God responds to Job, but only on his own terms. Instead of Job questioning God, God questions Job. He does not informally pull up a chair and ask Job to have a seat on the couch over a cup of coffee. Nor does he take Job to a courtroom to let Job plead his case for God's vindication. He answers Job by thundering out of the whirlwind, an appropriate vehicle to convey the gravitas and authority of his words (cf. 2 Kgs 2:1; Ezek 1:4; Nah 1:3; Zech 9:14). His very presence evokes a response of humility.

3.2. God's First Interrogation of Job (Job 38:1–40:5)

No one would want to be Job when the first words come from God's mouth (38:2). He immediately puts Job in his place by asking, "Who is this . . . ?" In other words, "Who is this peon? Who does he think he is?" Then comes a piercing rebuke: "Who is this that darkens counsel by words without knowledge?" God rebukes Job for foolishly questioning his wisdom and justice.

It is important to qualify God's rebuke of Job, again presuming the book's literary unity and coherence.[38] First, the narrator and God commend Job in the prologue (1:1, 8, 20–22; 2:3, 10), and the rest of the book never rescinds that commendation. Second, God firmly expresses his anger at Job's three friends and firmly rebukes them while again commending Job. He explains to Eliphaz, "My anger burns against you and against your two friends, for you have not spoken of me what is right, as my servant Job has" (42:7). Third, God will not deal with Job's three friends according to their folly only if they offer sacrifices and then Job intercedes to God on their behalf (42:8-9). God states the reason, repeating, "For you have not spoken of me what is right, as my servant Job has" (42:8). Fourth, the book ends with God restoring and bountifully blessing Job (42:10-17). Thus, despite his missteps, Job maintains his integrity and trust in God throughout the book. So in the book as a whole, God vindicates Job but not his three friends.[39]

---

38. Some who examine the book of Job as a literary whole argue that the description of Job in prose frame and Job's words in the poetic core contradict each other. E.g., Cheney, *Dust*.

39. See Porter's probing essay "Job," which concludes that in Job 42:7b God commends Job "both for his protesting and questioning and for his repenting" (303), even though "the ambiguity is unsettling" (304).

God asks Job a series of stunning, humbling questions about creation (38:2—40:2).[40] God's point is that only he controls every aspect of his creation and that Job cannot control any of them. The way God talks about his animals also offers a glimpse of his compassion.[41]

These are not the sorts of questions Job wants to consider because they do not directly address the justice of his innocent suffering. But these are exactly the sorts of questions Job needs to hear because they reframe the issue in such a way that shows Job how myopic, self-centered, presumptuous, arrogant, and idolatrous his worldview and its corresponding assumptions are. Job wrongly presumes that he has the ability and the right to accuse God of injustice, stand before God, and learn the answer to his questions.

God's interrogation exalts his unique greatness and goodness, and the result is that Job is humbled. He recognizes, "I am of small account" and then shuts his mouth (40:4–5).[42] But God is not done yet. His second round of questions is even more intense.

3.3. God's Second Interrogation of Job (Job 40:6—42:6)

Some argue that various portions of God's speeches to Job are interpolations,[43] but the unified testimony of the Hebrew manuscripts affirms the book's unity with the result that positing interpolations is highly subjective.[44] Consequently, it is not uncommon for biblical scholars to treat God's speeches as a literary unity even if they are not necessarily convinced that it is.[45]

If God's first speech emphasizes his justice, then his second speech emphasizes his supreme sovereignty, namely, his authority and power.[46] He asks a second series of stunning, humbling questions. The key verse of this interrogation is 40:8, where God rebukes Job for discrediting

---

40. Cf. Crenshaw, "When Form," 70–84.

41. Talbert, *Beyond Suffering*, 206.

42. Contra Dailey ("Wisdom," 105–19), who argues that Job's response "is actually a sophisticated epistemological ploy."

43. Westermann (*Hiob*, 124) postulates that 39:9–12, 13–30; 40:15–24; and 41:4–26 (Eng. 41:12–34) are secondary additions. Cf. Rowley, *Job*, 254; Vermeylen, *Job*, 25–27.

44. For defenses of the second speech's literary integrity, see Kubina, *Hiob*, 115–23; Hartley, *Job*, 31–33; Perdue, *Wisdom in Revolt*, 199–201.

45. E.g., Gradl, "Ijobs," 66–67.

46. Cf. Hartley, *Job*, 522.

God's justice at the expense of Job's innocence. Job questions how God governs his universe, and God retorts by questioning whether Job is as strong as God (40:9–14).

> Here [in 40:8–14], if we have rightly found the heart of the theology of the whole book, is a very great depth. There is a rebuke in it for any person who, by complaining about particular events in his life, implies that he could propose to God better ways of running the universe than those God currently uses.[47]

God reinforces the message of 40:8–14 with two formidable illustrations: Behemoth (40:15–24) and Leviathan (40:25—41:26 [Eng. 41:1–34]). This second interrogation intensifies God's unique grandeur, sovereignty, and independence.

There are four major views on the identification of Behemoth and Leviathan.

1. Behemoth and Leviathan refer to prehistoric dinosaurs.[48] Some of the descriptions of Behemoth and Leviathan do not seem to correspond literally with any known animal living today, but could correspond with dinosaurs (e.g. 41:10–12 [Eng. 41:18–21]).

2. Behemoth and Leviathan refer to known animals living today, namely, the hippopotamus and crocodile, respectively.[49] Most of the descriptions of Behemoth and Leviathan seem to correspond with these animals, and the few apparent discrepancies are poetic hyperbole (e.g., 41:10–13, 23 [Eng. 41:18–21, 31]), a device that God uses frequently in chapters 38–41, which are laced with figures of speech.[50]

---

47. Andersen, *Job*, 287.

48. Udd, "Evaluation," 72–199; Morris, *Job*, 115–22. Cf. Maarten, "לִוְיָתָן," 2:780.

49. Delitzsch, *Job*, 687–99; Dhorme, *Job*, 619; *BDB* 97, 531; Kroeze, *Job*, 445–66; Gordis, *Book of God*, 119–20; idem, *Book of Job*, 569–72; Rowley, *Job*, 255–64; Andersen, *Job*, 288–89; Archer, *Job*, 107–8; Rude, "God's Answer," 40; Bullock, *Introduction*, 84–85.

50. E.g., God shut up the sea behind doors "when it burst out from the womb" and "made clouds its garment" (38:8–10); God makes the dawn know its place (38:12); light lives in a home (38:19–20); lightning talks to God (38:35); God keeps snow and hail in storehouses (38:22); rain and ice were conceived and birthed (38:28–29); rain falls from tipped water jars in the sky (38:37); young ravens cry out to God for food (38:41); the ostrich laughs at the horse and its rider (39:18); the horse laughs at fear, swallows the ground, and says "Aha!" when it hears the trumpet (39:22, 24–25); Behemoth's bones are made of bronze (40:18); Leviathan's "back is made of rows of shields" (41:7 [Eng.

The second most common suggestion for Behemoth is the elephant since "tail" in 40:17 could be translated as "trunk." Couroyer argues that Behemoth is a buffalo.[51] A less common suggestion for Leviathan is the whale.

3. Behemoth and Leviathan refer to mythological creatures that represent evil, primordial, cosmic, chaotic forces (cf. the other four OT references to Leviathan: Job 3:8; Pss 74:14; 104:26; Isa 27:1).[52] Smick holds a variation of this view, namely, Behemoth and Leviathan are not "mythological creatures," but God uses "mythological terminology . . . to present graphic descriptions of the powers of evil such as the Satan in the Prologue."[53] Waltke calls Behemoth and Leviathan "mythological creatures, quintessential representations of evil's power" that "show that humanity cannot subdue evil."[54] Leviathan may be a mythical sea monster who represents chaos and evil and whom God crushes (cf. Job 3:8; Ps 74:13–14; Isa 27:1). This leads some to identify Leviathan with Satan, a serpent and dragon who embodies evil and whom God will crush (Gen 3; Rom 16:20; Rev 12:9; 20:2–3, 7–10).[55]

4. Behemoth and Leviathan refer to a combination of views 2 and 3 (or possibly views 1 and 3): God describes two real creatures that secondarily symbolize larger cosmic realities.[56] This is not a *tertium quid* view

---

41:15]); Leviathan "laughs at the rattle of javelins" (41:21 [Eng. 41:29]). Cf. 41:12–13 (Eng. 41:20–21) with Ps 18:8.

51. Couroyer, "Qui," 418–43; idem, "Glaive," 59–79; idem, "Behemoth," 214–21.

52. Gordon, "Leviathan," 1–9; Terrien, "Yahweh," 503–4; Pope, *Job*, 320–46; Habel, *Job* (1975), 221–22; Rowold, "Theology," 121–60; Payne, "לוה," in *TWOT*, 472; Day, *God's Conflict*, 62–87, 180–82; idem, "Leviathan," 296; Gibson, *Job*, 250–51; idem, "On Evil," 402–9; Caquot, "Léviathan," 40–69; Mettinger, "God of Job," 45–47; idem, "Enigma of Job," 11–14; Clifford, *Wisdom Literature*, 92–94; Viberg, "Job," 202; Patton, "Beauty," 149–53; Scobie, *Ways*, 241–42, 671; Fyall, *Now*; Dempster, *Dominion*, 204; Waltke, *OT Theology*, 939, 943; Schifferdecker, *Whirlwind*, 63–64 et al.; Cornelius, "Job," 298–99. Cf. Good, *Job*, 358–70; Lévêque, "L'interprétation," 212–16; Yeager and Dailey, "Job's World," 184.

53. Smick, "Job," 1049; see also 1047–51. Cf. idem, "Mythology," 106; idem, "Another," 226–28; idem, "Architectonics," 99–101.

54. Waltke, *OT Theology*, 939.

55. The most persuasive argument for this is Fyall, *Now*, whose thesis is that Behemoth and Leviathan represent death and Satan, respectively (see esp. 101–74).

56. Keel, *Jahwes*, 126–56; Parsons, "Job 38:1—42:6," 199–207, 215–28, 336–48; Martens, "בְּהֵמוֹת," 93; Zuck, "Job," 772–73; Alter, "Truth," 85–86; Hartley, *Job*, 521–22,

that identifies Behemoth and Leviathan as liminal creatures that are neither earthly nor supernatural or mythical.[57] Rather, this view affirms that Behemoth and Leviathan are actual animals with which Job is familiar while also affirming that these animals have additional significance because of their connection to cosmic realities. This is the most convincing view. The evidence for larger cosmic realities is too strong to dismiss, but Behemoth and Leviathan cannot refer exclusively to evil forces because God says that he created Behemoth (and, by implication, Leviathan) just as he created Job (40:15).

Far more important than identifying what Behemoth and Leviathan refer to is understanding why God speaks about them the way he does to Job. The four views above do not significantly alter the main point of 41:2-3 (Eng. 41:10-11) since various adherents of all four views agree on the theological significance for God's mentioning Behemoth and Leviathan: God created these powerful, fear-inducing creatures, and only God can control them. God is God; Job is not. Therefore, Job's respectful fear of God should surpass his respectful fear of Behemoth and Leviathan.[58]

Adhering to view 4 above enhances the application further: God controls not only the earthly dimensions of Job's suffering but also the cosmic ones, namely, the role of Satan himself. Once again, God's questions make Job recognize that God has the ability and right to do many things that Job does not and that, therefore, Job should think twice before demanding a hearing with God or accusing him of injustice.

Job's response is commendable. He recognizes God's omnipotence, sovereignty, and omniscience, and he repents (42:1-6). Suggested translations of 42:6 that depict Job as merely changing his mind about himself (dust and ashes are taken to represent the injustice of human

---

530, 534; idem, "Theology," 791; Clines, *Job 1-20*, xlvi; Perdue, *Wisdom in Revolt*, 221-32; Kaiser et al., *Hard*, 261-62; Maarten, "לִוְיָתָן," 779-80; Uehlinger, "Leviathan," 514; Goldingay, *OT Theology*, 723; Carson, *How Long*, 151-52; Talbert, *Beyond Suffering*, 269-82, 371-75.

57. Proponents of that view include Newsom, "Job," 615; Balentine, *Job*, 683.

58. Contra Gammie ("Behemoth," 226), who reverses the passage's meaning by arguing that God's second interrogation is ironic; i.e., it merely seems to humble Job and accentuate his inferior strength compared to Behemoth and Leviathan, but it actually portrays "the divine pride in human triumph over oppression" while "the beasts themselves celebrate instead Job's triumph."

life)⁵⁹ are unpersuasive because Job repents of sin, namely, misinformed presumption.⁶⁰

3.4. The Significance of God's Interrogation of Job (Job 38:1—42:6)

Parsons shrewdly summarizes 38:1—42:6 with this "thesis statement":

> Because of his omnipotent work of creating and sustaining the order of the cosmos, YHWH alone is its sovereign and benevolent lord who relates to finite man only on the basis of his own sovereign grace and man's joyous trust in him.⁶¹

God's questioning of Job is the book's climax and turning point, and its significance is at least fourfold.⁶²

1. God is too small in Job's eyes. Prior to God's interrogation of Job, Job's perception of God is too soft, too tame, too domesticated. But God's questions underscore his unshakable trustworthiness as uniquely and infinitely wise, sovereign, just, and good.⁶³ God is not someone whom Job can drag into court so that he and God can argue their case before an impartial judge. The Almighty God is without peer. He himself is the judge, jury, executioner, and standard of justice.

2. Correspondingly, Job is too large in his own eyes.⁶⁴ God gives Job a theocentric view of the universe because Job cannot help viewing God's world with himself at its center.⁶⁵ Job actually discredits God's justice at the expense of his own innocence. So an effect of God's piercing ques-

---

59. Gutiérrez, *Job*, 86–87; Engseth, "Role," 128–30; Dailey, "Job 42,6," 205–9; idem, "Aesthetics," 64–70; Wolde, "Job 42,1–6," 223–50; Brown, *Character*, 108–11; Habel, "Verdict," 33–34; Wilson, *Job*, 14–15, 420–21, 468; Krüger, "Did Job," 217–29.

60. Cf. §3.1 above and §3.4 below. See also Newell, "Job," 298–316, who concludes, "Job recognized that he had sinned and he repented of that sin. This sin was not committed prior to his suffering—it was not the cause of his suffering. Rather, his sin was in the words he spoke, accusing and condemning God, though in measure unconsciously, as he justified himself. He also sinned in thus exalting himself as a 'rival god'" (315).

61. Parsons, "38:1—42:6," 231.

62. Cf. Kidner, *Wisdom*, 70–72.

63. Cf. Pury, *Hiob*, 32–35.

64. See Parsons, "Job 38:1—42:6," 208–9.

65. See Schifferdecker, *Whirlwind*, whose thesis is that God's speeches in Job 38–41 sufficiently answer Job's situation by showing people their place in God's "radically non-anthropocentric" creation. Cf. Fohrer, "Gottes," 1–24.

tions is that Job repents by humbling himself before God as insignifcant, ceasing to question God's ways with him, and submitting to God's unthwartable sovereignty (40:4–5; 42:1–6). Job does not claim to understand why he is suffering, nor does he insist on his right to know why. Instead, he repents. But he does not repent of sins that he committed prior to his innocent suffering. Rather, he repents of his conceited perspective about God's justice that he expressed in the midst of his suffering.[66] Job's maturity grows as he himself becomes smaller.

3. God is not obligated to give Job anything, not even answers to his questions. So he changes the subject. He does not answer the main question that Job repeatedly asks: "Why am I suffering?" The closest God comes to answering it is rebuking Job for defending his own righteousness at the expense of God's righteousness (40:8). God does not answer Job's "Why?" question because Job's question, though sincere, is misguided. The narrator and reader know that God challenges Satan about Job's integrity and gives Satan permission to make Job suffer, but Job never learns this. The point for Job—and the point that the narrator is making for the reader—is that God is not obligated to answer Job's question. The reason is simple: God is infinite, and Job is finite. God himself is the answer.[67] God as the Creator of the universe owns everything and owes nothing to anyone; a finite person cannot understand the inscrutable ways of the infinite God.

> That a discourse which began with the cosmos should end in praise of two aquatic monsters, however fearsome, may strike us as eccentric; and that it should ignore our burning questions altogether may be a bitter disappointment.
>
> But there is no mistaking the thrust of it, congenial or not. It cuts us down to size, treating us not as philosophers but as children—limited in mind, puny in body—whose first and fundamental grasp of truth must be to know the difference between our place and God's, and to accept it. We may reflect that if, instead of this, we were offered a defense of our Creator's ways for

---

66. Contra Wilson, "Job, Book of," 387: "The Hebrew permits, and the context demands, a translation [of 42:6] such as 'therefore I reject and turn from the way of dust and ashes' (lamenting as a social outcast)." Wilson argues elsewhere that Job does not repent of sin, but merely retracts his litigation ("Protest," 137–47). But Job does more than simply retract his litigation; he turns from the sinful assumptions behind his litigation.

67. Preuß, "Jahwes," 342.

our approval, it would imply that he was accountable to us, not we to him. And if, not being offered this, we were to demand it, we should be guilty of the arrogance of Adam.[68]

This is why some alternative interpretations of Job 38:1—42:6 fail.[69] They are based on the errant assumption that Job deserves to know the whole story, that it is his right to learn the answer to his "Why?" question, that God really does owe him an explanation regarding his suffering. For example, some mock God's "answer" to Job as an inadequate reply: Job calls God's bluff, but God dodges Job's "Why?" question and instead boasts about creating and controlling various aspects of the universe like the weather and animals. In other words, they claim that a fallible God gives Job a proud, abusive, rude, intimidating, impertinent, irrelevant non-argument that adds fog to the situation instead of clearing up his confusion. Brueggemann, for example, concedes that God's answer "takes Job seriously," but not in a way that helps Job:

> It is not, however, a user-friendly answer, and it concedes nothing to Job. . . . Yahweh is lordly, haughty, condescending, dismissive, reprimanding, refusing to entertain Job's profound question, refusing to answer the probe of 21:7, and refusing to enter into any discussion about justice, sanctions, moral reliability, or covenantal symmetry. . . . The lyrical, self-congratulatory assertions of Yahweh about the wonder of Behemoth (40:15–24) and Leviathan (41:1–34) open the assertion of power to the claim of artistry. But the whole statement is one of overwhelmingness, not engagement.[70]

Some criticize God's address to Job more brazenly than Brueggemann.[71]

Other views are not quite so impudent yet are equally misguided. For example, some argue that God's talk about the weather and animals

---

68. Kidner, *Wisdom*, 72.

69. Cf. the refutation of some of these by Andersen, *Job*, 270–71; Carson, *How Long*, 152–53.

70. Brueggemann, *Theology*, 390. Similarly, Wilson, surpassing the audacity of Job's questioning God, depicts God's speeches as "bombastic" (*Job*, 8, 13, 359, 421). Cf. Rad, *Wisdom*, 224–25; Gibson, "On Evil," 399.

71. Shaw, *Adventures*, 11–13; Robertson, "Job," 446–69; Curtis, "Job's Response," 511; Brenner, "God's Answer," 129, 134–35; Penchansky, *Betrayal*, 48–53; Williams, "Victims," 208, 221–22; Morriston, "God's Answer," 345–51, 355–56.

is medicine to dull Job's pain.[72] But God's creation, as inspiring and breathtaking as it is, looks different to people who view it through the lens of excruciating innocent suffering. It may even make their suffering worse rather than minimize it.

4. Only God is all-wise. By asking two series of imposing questions, God answers the question "Who is wise?" The answer is that God alone is wise.[73] So rather than accusing God and doubting his integrity, the right response for Job is to trust God, who is supremely wise, sovereign, just, and good. God demonstrates that he sovereignly controls his universe and that he is not unjust and capriciously cruel. To the contrary, τὸ τέλος κυρίου with Job is to show "how the Lord is compassionate and merciful" (Jas 5:11).[74]

4. THE ARGUMENT OF JOB 41:2–3

Quoting Job 41:3a, as Paul does in Rom 11:35, recalls to mind the entire context of the book of Job since that framework is necessary to make sense of the brief quotation. The part makes the most sense in light of the whole. Now that we have surveyed the contours of the book of Job, we may examine the argument of Job 41:3a with significantly more profit.

In Job 40:25—41: 26 (Eng. 41:1–34), God highlights Leviathan, one of his most fearsome creatures. Of the thirty-four verses devoted to Leviathan, two most concisely explain why God asks Job about Leviathan: verses 2–3 (Eng. vv. 10–11).

לֹא־אַכְזָר כִּי יְעוּרֶנּוּ וּמִי הוּא לְפָנַי יִתְיַצָּב׃
מִי הִקְדִּימַנִי וַאֲשַׁלֵּם תַּחַת כָּל־הַשָּׁמַיִם לִי־הוּא׃

No one is so fierce that he dares to stir him up.
Who then is he who can stand before me?
Who has first given to me, that I should repay him?
Whatever is under the whole heaven is mine.[75]

---

72. E.g., Gordis, *Book of God*, 133: "When man steeps himself in the beauty of the world his troubles grow petty, not because they are unreal, but because they dissolve within the larger plan, like the tiny dabs and scales of oil in a painting. The beauty of the world becomes an anodyne to man's suffering—and the key to truth."

73. Cf. Lévêque, *Job*, 2:528.

74. Cf. Moo, *James*, 228–30.

75. See ch. 5 below for a discussion of textual issues in this passage.

God makes two basic arguments in these two verses by using simple logic. The first is a lesson on humility, and the second a lesson on ownership.

4.1. A Lesson on Humility:
An Argument from the Lesser to the Greater (Job 41:2)

The word translated "stand" in 41:2 (Eng. 41:10) is the hithpael stem of יָצַב, a legal term that Elihu uses when challenging Job: "Answer me, if you can; set your words in order before me; take your stand [הִתְיַצְּבָה]" (33:5). God demonstrates that Job's actions are logically absurd. On the one hand, he confidently demands to plead his case before God so that he can contend with him. But on the other hand, he would never demand to contend either with Leviathan or the evil, primordial, cosmic powers that Leviathan symbolizes. God argues that if Job could not contend with Leviathan, why was he contending with God, who created and controls Leviathan? If Job would be terrified to stand before Leviathan, why is he not terrified to demand a trial with God and stand before him? Compare how Carson summarizes the argument of 40:15–41:26 (Eng. 40:15—41:34):

> If Job is to charge God with injustice, he must do so from the secure stance of his own superior justice; and if he cannot subdue these beasts [Behemoth and Leivathan], let alone the cosmic forces they represent, he does not enjoy such a stance, and is therefore displaying extraordinary arrogance to call God's justice into question....
>
> If there are so many things that Job does not understand, why should he so petulantly and persistently demand that he understand his own suffering? *There are some things you will not understand, for you are not God.*[76]

While this seems like a non-answer to some skeptics, Job's response to God indicates that God's answer is indeed satisfying. With his characteristic wit, G. K. Chesterton observes,

> God comes in at the end, not to answer riddles, but to propound them.... Verbally speaking the enigmas of Jehovah seem darker and more desolate than the enigmas of Job; yet Job was com-

---

76. Carson, *How Long*, 152–53, emphasis in original. Cf. Parsons, "Job 38:1—42:6," 202; Fohrer, *Buch Hiob*, 529; Caquot, "Léviathan," 55–56; Lévêque, "L'interprétation," 217; Merrill, *Everlasting Dominion*, 616.

fortless before the speech of Jehovah and is comforted after it. He has been told nothing, but he feels the terrible and tingling atmosphere of something which is too good to be told. The refusal of God to explain His design is itself a burning hint of His design. The riddles of God are more satisfying than the solutions of man.[77]

4.2. A Lesson on Ownership: An Argument from the Greater to the Lesser (Job 41:3)

The axiom of this logical lesson is that a creator owns his creation. He is not in debt to his creation. He does not owe his creation anything. Rather, the creation owes its very existence to the creator.

More specifically, God is the Creator of the universe, that is, he created everything that is not God. Therefore, he owns the universe. He is not in debt to the universe in any way. He does not owe the universe anything. Rather, the universe owes its very existence to God. God is not anyone's debtor because he owns the universe. God is without creditors.

Even more specifically, God created Job. Therefore, he owns Job. He is not in debt to Job in any way. He does not owe Job anything. Rather, Job owes his very existence to God. God is not Job's debtor because he owns Job. Job is not God's creditor.[78]

As Job recognizes earlier, God is free to give what he desires, and he is free to take away what he desires (1:21; 2:10). God has given Job everything: his life, health, family, wealth, position, and reputation. So God owes Job nothing. God's words in 41:3 reinforce Elihu's earlier rebuke to Job in 35:7: "If you are righteous, what do you give to him? Or what does he receive from your hand?"

5. CONCLUSION

In order to understand how Paul uses Job 41:3a in Rom 11:35, one must first understand its context in the book of Job. This chapter's understanding of Job 41:3a is rooted in its understanding of 38:1—42:6 and the book as a whole. (We will see in due course that Paul presupposes all this by quoting Job 41:3a.) Job's theological message is that people

---

77. G. K. Chesterton, "Job," para. 10.

78. "The pagan religions" held "that God was obligated (by a business contract or a judicial claim) to reward man if he was obedient" (Parsons, "Job 38:1—42:6," 203).

should respond to innocent, unexplained suffering by trusting God because he is supremely wise, sovereign, just, and good. The significance of God's interrogation of Job in 38:1—42:6 is at least fourfold: God is too small in Job's eyes; Job is too large in his own eyes; God is not obligated to give Job anything, not even answers to his questions; and only God is all-wise.

God's argument in 41:2–3 is twofold. First, he argues from the lesser to the greater to teach Job a lesson on humility. If Job would be terrified to stand before Leviathan, he should be even more terrified to demand a trial with God and stand before him. Second, God argues from the greater to the lesser to teach Job a lesson on ownership. Because God created Job, God owns Job, and because God owns Job, God does not owe Job anything.

5

Textual Issues

THIS BOOK HAS SIX steps:
1. the NT context of Rom 11:34–35 (ch. 2)
2. the OT context of Isa 40:13 and Job 41:3a (chs. 3–4)
3. textual issues in Isa 40:13, Job 41:3, and Rom 11:34–35 (ch. 5)
4. relevant uses of Isa 40:13 and Job 41:3a in Jewish literature (ch. 6)
5. Paul's hermeneutical warrant for using Isa 40:13 and Job 41:3a in Rom 11:34–35 (ch. 7)
6. Paul's theological use of Isa 40:13 and Job 41:3a in Rom 11:34–35 (ch. 8)

Step three could just as easily occur as step one, two, or four. What is important is that steps one through four all occur before steps five and six.[1]

Step three involves textual criticism on two levels. The first level analyzes any textual issues within the MT, LXX, and Greek NT. The purpose of this exercise is to discern whether any textual variants are significant for understanding how Rom 11:34–35 uses Isa 40:13 and Job 41:3. The second level compares the MT, LXX, and Greek NT with each other. The purpose of this second exercise is to discern whether any differences are significant for understanding of how Rom 11:34–35 uses Isa 40:13 and Job 41:3. The second level is particularly important because there is some controversy whether Rom 11:34–35 actually quotes Isa 40:13 and Job 41:3.

---

1. On the form of NT quotations of the OT, see Nicole, "NT Use," 142–48; Silva, "NT Use," 147–65, 381–86; idem, "OT in Paul," 630–34.

1. TEXTUAL ISSUES IN THE MT, LXX, AND GREEK NT

The integrity of Isa 40:13, Job 41:3, and Rom 11:34–35 is remarkably strong since the manuscripts are nearly unanimous. Table 5 highlights words discussed below.

TABLE 5. Textual Issues in Isa 40:13, Job 41:3, and Rom 11:34–35

vv.	BHS	LXX (NETS)	NA²⁷
Isa 40:13 & Rom 11:34	מִי־תִכֵּן אֶת־רוּחַ יְהוָה וְאִישׁ עֲצָתוֹ יוֹדִיעֶנּוּ	τίς ἔγνω νοῦν κυρίου καὶ τίς αὐτοῦ σύμβουλος ἐγένετο ὃς συμβιβᾷ αὐτόν	τίς γὰρ ἔγνω νοῦν κυρίου; ἢ τίς σύμβουλος αὐτοῦ ἐγένετο;
	Who has measured the Spirit of the LORD, or what man shows him his counsel?	Who has known the mind of the Lord, and who has been his counselor to instruct him?	"For who has known the mind of the Lord, or who has been his counselor?"
Job 41:3 & Rom 11:35	מִי הִקְדִּימַנִי וַאֲשַׁלֵּם תַּחַת כָּל־הַשָּׁמַיִם לִי־הוּא	ἢ τίς ἀντιστήσεταί μοι καὶ ὑπομενεῖ εἰ πᾶσα ἡ ὑπ'οὐρανὸν ἐμή ἐστιν	ἢ τίς προέδωκεν αὐτῷ, καὶ ἀνταποδοθήσεται αὐτῷ;
	Who has first given to me, that I should repay him? Whatever is under the whole heaven is mine.	Or who will withstand me and survive, if the entire earth beneath the sky is mine?	"Or who has given a gift to him that he might be repaid?"

1.1. One Textual Variant in Isa 40:13

There is only one textual variant in Isa 40:13, and it is trivial. Isaiah 40:13b (וְאִישׁ עֲצָתוֹ יוֹדִיעֶנּוּ) literally reads "or [who as] the man of his counsel causes him to know."[2] The nets renders it well: "[who] gives him instruction as his counselor?"[3] The single textual variant is that the LXX, Latin Vulgate, and some Syriac versions add to וְאִישׁ. They smooth out the phrase by repeating the word "who," which already occurs at the beginning of the verse. The LXX, for example, reads καὶ τίς (adding the word τίς), which in Hebrew would be וּמִי אִישׁ.

---

2. Cf. Berges, *Jesaja*, 122–23.
3. See §4.3 in ch. 3 above.

1.2. One Textual Issue in Job 41:2-3

There are no textual variants in Job 41:3, but there is a significant textual issue in 41:2-3 related to two textual variants in 41:2. Since some manuscripts use third-person pronouns instead of first-person pronouns in 41:2, some commentators and translations see the referent in Job 41:2 *and* 3 as Leviathan, not God. The NRSV, for example, reads, "No one is so fierce as to dare to stir *it* up. Who can stand before *it*? Who can confront *it* and be safe?—under the whole heaven, who?" (emphasis added). Its marginal notes, however, indicate that the second and third "it" literally read "me" and "who" literally reads "to me." Rowley, Gordis, and others suggest changing (1) the pronouns in the MT to refer solely to Leviathan rather than God and (2) לִי־הוּא ("belongs to Me" [NASB]) to one of three options: לֹא הוּא ("there is no one"), אֶחָד לֹא ("there is no one"), or מִי הוּא ("who indeed?").[4] Pope similarly remarks, "MT presents a lofty thought entirely out of keeping with the context."[5] Gibson, who rejects the traditional reading of Job 41:3 MT, concludes, "Looking at this line of tradition laid out, I cannot help suspecting that Paul [in Rom 11:35] has succeeded in angling it [i.e., Job 41:3] away from the original meaning."[6] Newsom retains the first-person pronouns but creatively suggests that 40:2-3 is quoting Leviathan talking about himself.[7]

These suggested changes are inferior textually and contextually.[8] First, they do not follow the MT's best readings (e.g., the most difficult readings in 41:2) in favor of misguided internal evidence. Not a scrap of manuscript evidence supports emending the personal pronouns in 41:3 from first-person to third-person. Second, they do not highlight the main reason that God's monologue in chapter 41 discusses Leviathan. Wilcox rejects the textually superior reading in favor of emending third-person pronouns largely because he rejects what he thinks is a necessary implication of reading 41:2-3 with the first-person pronouns referring

---

4. Rowley, *Job*, 261; Gordis, *Book of Job*, 483. Cf. Driver and Gray, *Job*, 363-64; Ball, *Job*, 449; Dhorme, *Job*, 630-32; Pope, *Job*, 335-38; Wilde, *Hiob*, 388; Rowold, "מִי הוּא? לִי!הוּא," 104-9; Fohrer, *Hiob*, 527; Reyburn, *Job*, 755-56; Clines, "Job," 483.

5. Pope, *Job*, 337.

6. Gibson, *Job*, 252-53. Cf. idem, "New Look," 132.

7. Newsom, "Job," 622-23; idem, *Job*, 251.

8. See §3-4 in ch. 4 above. Cf. Terrien, "Job," 1189; Rowold, "Theology," 44-45, 154-56; Udd, "Evaluation," 111-20; Habel, *Job* (1985), 555; Hartley, *Job*, 527, 531-32; Caquot, "Le Léviathan," 54-56; Alden, *Job*, 402; Perdue, *Wisdom and Creation*, 178-79; Clifford, *Wisdom*, 93; Fyall, *Now*, 160-62.

to God: "The general idea that might makes right, or that a powerful being may rightly do as he pleases with the weak, is incompatible with the conception of morality worked out so elaborately in the central dialogues."[9] What Wilcox assumes is a necessary implication is a *non sequitur*.[10]

1.3. Textual Issues in Rom 11:34–35

There are no textual variants in Rom 11:34–35. The only textual issues involve its relation to the MT and LXX (see §2 below).

2. A COMPARISON OF THE MT, LXX, AND GREEK NT

Archer and Chirichigno classify OT quotations in the NT in six major categories (labeled A–F), several of which may be further subdivided.[11] (A) The NT quotes the LXX, which accurately renders the MT (268 total; e.g., Gen 2:2 in Heb 4:4). (B) The NT "quite closely adheres to the wording of the LXX," which "deviates somewhat" from the MT without distorting the MT's "real meaning" (50 total; e.g., Joel 2:32 in Rom 10:13). (C) The NT follows the MT "more closely" than the LXX, either because the author consulted the MT directly or possibly "the Proto-Theodotion Greek translation" (33 total; e.g., 1 Kgs 19:10 in Rom 11:3). (D) The NT "adheres quite closely to the LXX," which "deviates somewhat from the MT" (22 total; e.g., Isa 29:16 in Rom 9:20). (E) The NT quotations "give the impression that unwarranted liberties were taken with the Old Testament text in the light of its context" (13 total; e.g., Hos 11:1 in Matt 2:15). (F) The NT's "application" has a "close resemblance or complete identity" with the OT (32 total though many more could be added; e.g., 1 Sam 12:22 in Rom 11:2). Archer and Chirichigno label the use of Isa 40:13 in Rom 11:34 as category B and Job 41:3a in Rom 11:35 as category C.[12]

Table 6 highlights significant differences between Isa 40:13 and Job 41:3 (MT and LXX) and Rom 11:34–35.

---

9. Wilcox, *Job*, 200.

10. Again, see §3–4 in ch. 4 above.

11. Archer and Chirichigno, *OT Quotations*, xxv–xxxii.

12. Ibid., 57, 113. They label Paul's use of Isa 40:13 in 1 Cor 2:16 as category C (113). For Paul's use of Isa 40:13 in 1 Cor 2:16, see §1.5 in ch. 6 below.

TABLE 6. Significant Differences between
Isa 40:13, Job 41:3, and Rom 11:34–35

vv.	BHS	LXX (NETS)	NA²⁷
Isa 40:13 & Rom 11:34	מִי־תִכֵּן אֶת־רוּחַ יְהוָה וְאִישׁ עֲצָתוֹ יוֹדִיעֶנּוּ	τίς ἔγνω νοῦν κυρίου καὶ τίς αὐτοῦ σύμβουλος ἐγένετο ὃς συμβιβᾷ αὐτόν	τίς γὰρ ἔγνω νοῦν κυρίου; ἢ τίς σύμβουλος αὐτοῦ ἐγένετο;
	Who has measured the Spirit of the LORD, or what man shows him his counsel?	Who has known the mind of the Lord, and who has been his counselor to instruct him?	"For who has known the mind of the Lord, or who has been his counselor?"
Job 41:3 & Rom 11:35	מִי הִקְדִּימַנִי וַאֲשַׁלֵּם תַּחַת כָּל־הַשָּׁמַיִם לִי־הוּא	ἢ τίς ἀντιστήσεταί μοι καὶ ὑπομενεῖ εἰ πᾶσα ἡ ὑπ'οὐρανὸν ἐμή ἐστιν	ἢ τίς προέδωκεν αὐτῷ, καὶ ἀνταποδοθήσεται αὐτῷ;
	Who has first given to me, that I should repay him? Whatever is under the whole heaven is mine.	Or who will withstand me and survive, if the entire earth beneath the sky is mine?	"Or who has given a gift to him that he might be repaid?"

2.1. A Comparison of Isa 40:13 with Rom 11:34

Shum questions whether Paul actually quotes Isa 40:13:

> Due to the lack of any citation formula and to the syntactical smoothness between v. 34 and its context, it does not seem farfetched to claim that Paul here did not actually intend an explicit quotation from Isa 40.13 but rather a mere linguistic borrowing from the Isaianic passage.[13]

But it is likely that Paul is quoting Isaiah here because he is using nearly the exact language of Isa 40:13 LXX and because Paul has deliberately quoted from Isaiah multiple times throughout Rom 9–11. Further, if Rom 11:33–36 is a hymn of praise, then its genre explains the omission of a citation formula.

---

13. Shum, *Paul's Use*, 245.

Romans 11:34 closely follows Isa 40:13 LXX, which essentially follows Isa 40:13 MT with four—possibly five—qualifications.[14] First, ἔγνω in Isa 40:13 LXX and Rom 11:34 ("has known") is a more general rendering of תִכֵּן in Isa 40:13 ("has measured"). The former refers to knowing or comprehending, and the latter refers either to measuring, marking off, or determining as a metaphor for comprehending, fathoming, or plumbing, which carries the sense of directing or advising. In other words, Isa 40:13 is asking who can comprehend (metaphorically expressed by measuring) Yahweh's mind with the result that he can advise him.[15]

Second, the questions καὶ τίς αὐτοῦ σύμβουλος ἐγένετο ὃς συμβιβᾷ αὐτόν in Isa 40:13 LXX and ἢ τίς αὐτοῦ σύμβουλος ἐγένετο; in Rom 11:34 ("or who has been his counselor?") differ from וְאִישׁ עֲצָתוֹ יוֹדִיעֶנּוּ in Isa 40:13 ("[who] gives him instruction as his counselor?" [NET]). In both cases, the LXX and NT are less precise renderings of the MT, but they are consistent with the meaning of Isa 40:13.

Third, Rom 11:34 adds the word γάρ. Paul adds this word to indicate that strophe 2 (11:34–35) supports strophe 1 (11:33) by exulting in three specific reasons that God's riches, wisdom, and knowledge are deep.[16]

Fourth, Rom 11:34 omits ὃς συμβιβᾷ αὐτόν. Paul most likely omits these three words for aesthetic reasons. Strong evidence that Paul adapts the verse here is that Paul knew the entire verse of Isa 40:13 LXX, the rest of which he quotes in 1 Cor 2:16.[17]

Some may cite a fifth exception: νοῦν ("mind") appears to differ from רוּחַ. (Spirit, spirit, wind, breath, mind). Some insist that this רוּחַ is the same as the One involved in creation in Gen 1:2, namely, the Holy

---

14. Cf. Meyer, *Romans*, 2:245; Murray, *Romans*, 2:107; Bornkamm, "Praise," 106–7; Zutphen, "Studies," 34; Cranfield, *Romans*, 2:590; Käsemann, *Romans*, 318; Dunn, *Romans 9–16*, 700; Johnson, *Function*, 167; Black, *Romans*, 164; Oss, "Paul's Use," 45; Fitzmyer, *Romans*, 634; Witherington, *Romans*, 277; Schreiner, *Romans*, 635; Jewett, *Romans*, 718–19; Seifrid, "Romans," 678–79; Harrison and Hagner, "Romans," 180. Wagner's conclusion is well-reasoned: "Once again, *contra* Lim, there is no reason to suppose that Paul's citations have been influenced by a Hebrew *Vorlage*. The hypothesis that Paul modifies LXX Isaiah here explains the data more fully and more economically" (*Heralds*, 304n250).

15. Cf. Pinto, "Contribution," 175–78.

16. See §3.2 in ch. 2 above.

17. Cf. Oss, "Paul's Use," 61.

Spirit.[18] The variation in Rom 11:34, however, is not significant since רוּחַ may mean mind and likely does in this context.[19]

2.2. A Comparison of Job 41:3a with Rom 11:35

Smick questions whether Paul actually quotes Job 40:3a: "If Paul has this verse in mind in Rom 11:35, he is at best paraphrasing; for he follows neither the Hebrew nor the LXX fully."[20] Other commentators are open but cautious to identify Job 41:3a as a direct citation in Rom 11:35.[21] It is true that Paul follows neither the MT nor LXX "fully," but it seems unwarranted to claim that he follows neither at all.

The evidence suggests that Rom 11:35 follows the MT with three qualifications.[22] The first two regard the words προέδωκεν αὐτῷ in Rom 11:35 ("has first given to him" [NASB]) as opposed to הִקְדִּימַנִי in Job 40:3a ("has confronted me" [NET]). Αὐτῷ, a third-person pronoun, varies from ־נִי, a first-person pronominal suffix. Paul's pronominal shift, which differs from both the MT and LXX, is more appropriate for the context of Rom 11:33–36, which uses only third-person pronouns.

Second, the LXX mistranslates הִקְדִּים as ἀντιστήσεται ("will withstand") [NETS]), but the NT captures the idea precisely, which may to some degree explain some translations of הִקְדִּים (NASB, RSV: "has given"; ESV: "has first given"; cf. NIV: "has a claim against").

Third, ἀνταποδοθήσεται αὐτῷ in Rom 11:35 ("it might be paid back to him again" [NASB]) is not equivalent to וַאֲשַׁלֵּם in Job 40:3a ("that I should repay him"). But the NT accurately renders the MT here,[23] the only difference being its switch from the first-person to third-person.

---

18. E.g., Grogan, "Isaiah," 726.

19. See §4.2 in ch. 3 above.

20. Smick, "Job," 1054. Cf. Kroeze, Job, 454–55; Lindars, NT Apologetic, 246; Hall, "Paul," 209 (cf. 163); Moyise, "Quotations," 15–16.

21. Fitzmyer, Romans, 635; Moo, Epistle, 742.

22. Cf. Tholuck, Romans, 395; Shedd, Romans, 354; Meyer, Romans, 2:246; Liddon, Romans, 225; Sanday and Headlam, Romans, 340; Lagrange, Romains, 290; Denney, "Romans," 686; Viard, Romains, 254; Käsemann, Romans, 318; Cranfield, Romans, 2:591; Smith, "Pauline," 269, 272 ("Rom. 11:34" on p. 272 should say "Rom. 11:35"); Murray, Romans, 2:107; Dunn, Romans 9–16, 701; Morris, Romans, 428n147; Schreiner, Romans, 636. Lloyd-Jones argues that Paul translates the MT because "he knew that it [i.e., Job 41:3 LXX] was not a good translation" (Romans, 280).

23. Esp. as opposed to the LXX, which NETS translates "Or who will withstand me and survive" (Pietersma and Wright, "Iob," 695, emphasis added).

Thus, the most plausible explanation of Rom 11:35 is that Paul translates the MT and adapts it to his context, namely, by changing the first-person pronoun to third-person. Two less likely possibilities are that Paul translates from a targum[24] or quotes a non-LXX Greek version.[25] D. A. Carson's observation about the Gospel of Matthew applies here as well: "Doubtless both Hebrew and Greek OT textual traditions were somewhat fluid during the first century (as the Dead Sea Scrolls attest); and so it is not always possible to tell where the evangelist is using a text form known in his day and where he is providing his own rendering."[26]

3. CONCLUSION

The integrity of Isa 40:13, Job 41:3, and Rom 11:34–35 is unassailable. Although some question whether Paul directly cites Isa 40:13 and Job 41:3a in Rom 11:34–35, the external and internal evidence strongly favors direct, slightly adapted citations.

---

24. Wilckens, *Römer*, 2:271; Hanson, *NT Interpretation*, 84–89.

25. Munck, *Christ*, 142; Zutphen, "Studies," 31–37; Michel, *Römer*, 361; Schaller, "Hiobzitate," 21–26; Zeller, *Römer*, 201. Jewett's conclusion is more feasible: "It appears certain that Paul's ironic version [of Job 41:3] returns in one way or another to the spirit, if not the precise wording, of the original Hebrew text . . . No evidence has yet appeared of this [i.e., Schaller's] hypothetical pre-Christian correction of the Job text, and it is more plausible to conclude that Paul himself is responsible for the corrected translation" (*Romans*, 720).

26. "Matthew," 52.

6

Relevant Uses of Isaiah 40:13 and Job 41:3a in Jewish Literature

WHEN THE NT QUOTES a passage from the OT, it is helpful to study how that OT passage is used in other Jewish literature, especially the literature of Second Temple Judaism. Beale and Carson list five reasons to study such Jewish literature:

> (1) They may show us how the OT texts were understood by sources roughly contemporaneous with the NT . . . (2) They sometimes show that Jewish authorities were themselves divided as to how certain OT passages should be interpreted . . . (3) In some instances, the readings of early Judaism provide a foil for early Christian readings. The differences then demand hermeneutical and exegetical explanations . . . (4) Even where there is no direct literary dependence, sometimes the language of early Judaism provides close parallels to the language of the NT writers simply because of the chronological and cultural proximity. (5) In a handful of cases, NT writers apparently display direct dependence on sources belonging to early Judaism and their handling of the OT.[1]

Other resources further demonstrate the rationale for this chapter by explaining the nature and significance of Jewish extracanonical literature.[2] Six Jewish bodies of literature are most significant: the OT Apocrypha,

---

1. Beale and Carson, "Introduction," xxiv.
2. E.g., Fitzmyer, *Essays*; Drane, "Religious," 116–24; Bauckham, "Relevance," 90–108; Hatina, "Jewish," 46–76; Trebilco, "Jewish Backgrounds," 359–88; Evans and Porter, *Dictionary*; Scott, *Jewish*; Helyer, *Exploring*; Ferguson, *Backgrounds*; Evans, *Ancient*; Nickelsburg, *Jewish*; Harlow, "Jewish," 373–80; Fantin, "Background," 167–96.

OT Pseudepigrapha, Dead Sea Scrolls, Philo, Josephus, and Rabbinic literature (i.e., Targums, Talmuds, and midrash).³ This chapter investigates if and how Isa 40:13 and Job 41:3a are used in these Jewish bodies of literature and also examines the use of Isa 40:13 in 1 Cor 2:16.⁴

Before proceeding, a word of caution from Samuel Sandmel is in order.⁵ At this step of studying the use of the OT in a NT passage, some err by assuming and exaggerating. They make three assumptions: (1) they have correctly identified literary parallels; (2) there is "a direct organic literary connection" between the alleged parallels and the NT passage; and (3) the flow of source and derivation is from the parallels to the NT passage. Sandmel labels this "parallelomania," which he defines as "that extravagance among scholars which first overdoes the supposed similarity in passages and then proceeds to describe source and derivation as if implying literary connection flowing in an inevitable or predetermined direction."⁶ What follows identifies probable parallels while attempting to avoid parallelomania.⁷

1. ISA 40:13 IN JEWISH LITERATURE

Isaiah 40:13 is used in four of the six most significant Jewish bodies of literature: the OT Apocrypha, OT Pseudepigrapha, Dead Sea Scrolls, and Rabbinic literature. Nowhere in this literature is the verbal correspondence to Isa 40:13 as explicit as Paul's use of it in 1 Cor 2:16 and Rom 11:34, but repeatedly the literature reflects the message of Isa 40:13, namely, that humans cannot understand God and his ways. The literature also uses the same rhetorical-question form as Isa 40:13. "The rhe-

---

3. Dating Rabbinic literature is particularly challenging. The literature may be categorized as Tannaic (c. 50 B.C.–A.D. 200), Amoraic (c. 220–500), saboraic (c. 500–650), and geonic (650–1050) (cf. Evans, *Ancient*, 217). On criteria for dating and analyzing Rabbinic literature, see esp. Instone-Brewer, *Techniques*.

4. Less significant are possible parallels in non-Jewish sources. For example, in *Strom.* 5.14, Clement of Alexandria quotes Isa 40:13 and then cites Hesiod and Solon as agreeing with it. Clement of Alexandria quotes Hesiod as writing, "No prophet, sprung of men that dwell on earth, can know the mind of Aegis-bearing Zeus," and Solon, "The immortal's mind to men is quite unknown" (Roberts, Donaldson, and Coxe, *Ante-Nicene Fathers*, 2:473).

5. Sandmel, "Parallelomania," 1–13.

6. Ibid., 1.

7. Cf. some further cautions—presented as five "basic assumptions"—in Hays and Green, "Use," 229–31.

torical question in this form is characteristic, particularly in post-exilic Judaism (Ps 106:2; Jer 10:7; Sir 16:20; Wisd Sol 9:16–17; 11:21; Pss Sol 5:3, 12; 15:2; *1 Enoch* 93.11–14; *2 Apoc. Bar.* 14.8–9 . . .)."[8]

1.1. Isa 40:13 in the OT Apocrypha

The message of Isa 40:12–13 occurs in several places in the OT Apocrypha, but what follows examines passages that are most similar lexically, syntactically, and thematically. Other passages that are similar thematically include Sir 1:1–10; 16:20; 18:1–7; 24:28–29; and 42:21.

1.1.1. Isa 40:13 in Wis 9:13, 17

In the anonymous Wisdom of Solomon, Solomon prays for wisdom (9:4, 10).[9] His prayer offers several reasons that God should grant his request: Solomon is limited in his strength and understanding (9:5); he will be regarded as nothing without God's wisdom (9:6); God chose him to be king (9:7–8); wisdom belongs to God alone (9:9); God's wisdom will help Solomon please God (9:10–12); and in order to have God's wisdom, God must give it because no one can discern it (9:13–18). It is this final reason—particularly verses 13, 16, and 17—that uses the language of Isa 40:12–13:

> [13] For who can learn the counsel [βουλήν] of God?
>   Or who can discern what the Lord wills?
> [14] For the reasoning of mortals is worthless,
>   and our designs are likely to fail;
> [15] for a perishable body weighs down the soul,
>   and this earthy tent burdens the thoughtful mind.
> [16] We can hardly guess at what is on earth,
>   and what is at hand we find with labor;
>   but who has traced out what is in the heavens?
> [17] Who has learned your counsel [βουλήν],
>   unless you have given wisdom
>   and sent your holy spirit from on high?
> [18] And thus the paths of those on earth were set right,
>   and people were taught what pleases you,
>   and were saved by wisdom. (Wis 9:13–18, NRSV)

---

8. Dunn, *Romans 9–16*, 700.

9. On Isa 40:13 in Wis 9:13–18, cf. Goodrick, *Wisdom*, 221; Scroggs, "Paul," 50; Clarke, *Wisdom*, 65; Winston, *Wisdom*, 206; Hanson, *NT Interpretation*, 82–83; Hübner, *Weisheit*, 129; Williams, *Wisdom*, 218–19; Wagner, *Heralds*, 303n247; Ciampa and Rosner, "1 Corinthians," 702.

Winston translates βουλήν in 9:13 and 17 as "plan" and "design" instead of "counsel":

> [13] For what man can comprehend the plan [βουλήν] of God,
>   or who can grasp what the Lord wills? . . .
> [17] Who was privy to your design [βουλήν],
>   unless you gave him Wisdom,
>   and sent your holy spirit from on high?[10]

Not only the words but the form and content suggest that this passage is related to Isa 40:13. It uses the form of rhetorical questions, and it emphasizes that humans cannot understand God and his ways.

Paul likely was familiar with this passage because his writings evidence a noteworthy familiarity with the Wisdom of Solomon.[11] In fact, "The influence of the [Wisdom of Solomon] on the early Christian church appears to have been remarkable, and far surpasses all other OT apocryphal books in importance."[12] In Wis 9:13-18, the author repeats themes common to Isa 40 such as God's supreme power and wisdom as creator and king. He moves a step beyond Isa 40:12-14 by explicitly exalting wisdom and by asserting that no one can comprehend God's plan unless God himself reveals it. God's plan in Wis 9:13-18 includes his salvation-historical plan.[13]

1.1.2. Isa 40:13 in Jdt 8:14

This passage from the book of Judith does not quote Isa 40:13, but it is probably an allusion because Jdt 8:14 repeats the same theme of Isa 40:13.[14] Judith, the book's protagonist, here confronts the leaders of Israel for capitulating to the demands of the army of Nebuchadnezzar, king of Assyria:

> [12] Who are you to put God to the test today, and to set yourselves up in the place of God in human affairs? [13] You are putting the Lord Almighty to the test, but you will never learn anything! [14] You cannot plumb the depths of the human heart or understand the workings of the human mind; how do you expect to search out God, who made all these things, and find out his mind or

---

10. Winston, *Wisdom*, 206.
11. deSilva, *Apocrypha*, 149-52.
12. Hagner, "Wisdom," 1101.
13. Williams, *Wisdom*, 218-19, 225.
14. On Isa 40:13 in Jdt 8:14, cf. Hunt, *Inspired*, 56-57; Williams, *Wisdom*, 224.

comprehend his thought? No, my brothers, do not anger the Lord our God. ¹⁵ For if he does not choose to help us within these five days, he has power to protect us within any time he pleases, or even to destroy us in the presence of our enemies. ¹⁶ Do not try to bind the purposes of the Lord our God; for God is not like a human being, to be threatened, or like a mere mortal, to be won over by pleading. ¹⁷ Therefore, while we wait for his deliverance, let us call upon him to help us, and he will hear our voice, if it pleases him. (Jdt 8:12–17, NRSV)

Compare Moore's slightly different rendering of 8:14a: "If you cannot plumb the depths of a person's heart or understand the thoughts of his mind, then how can you fathom God, who made all these things, or read his mind or understand his reasoning?"[15] In the rest of the book, Judith proceeds to deliver Israel singlehandedly from their enemy by alluring and beheading Holofernes, the head of Assyria's army. Here she persuades Uzziah, the king of Israel, that his decision to surrender is wrong partly by underscoring that humans cannot fully understand God and his ways (Jdt 8:14, 28–29).

1.2. Isa 40:13 in the OT Pseudepigrapha

Four books of the OT Pseudepigrapha are noteworthy here: *1 Enoch*, *2 Enoch*, *4 Ezra*, and *2 Baruch*.

1.2.1. Isa 40:13 in 1 En. 93:11–14

First Enoch asks a series of rhetorical questions to underscore that humans cannot fully understand God's thoughts and ways, let alone the dimensions of the vast universe God created.[16]

> ¹¹ For what kind of a human being is there that is able to hear the voice of the Holy One without being shaken? Who is there that is able to ponder his (deep) thoughts? Who is there that can look directly at all the good deeds? ¹² What kind of a person is he that can (fully) understand the activities of heaven, so that he can see a soul, or even perhaps a spirit—or, even if he ascended (into the heavens) and saw all (these heavenly beings and) their wings and contemplated them; or, even if he can do (what the heavenly beings) do?—and is able to live? ¹³ What kind of a person is anyone

---

15. Moore, *Judith*, 177.

16. On Isa 40:13 in *1 En.* 93:11–14, cf. Winston, *Wisdom*, 206; Black, *Enoch*, 286–87; Johnson, *Function*, 169; Williams, *Wisdom*, 221–22; Wagner, *Heralds*, 303n247.

that is able to understand the nature of the breadth and length of the earth? To whom has the extent of all these been shown? [14] Is there perchance any human being that is able to understand the length of heaven, the extent of its altitude, upon what it is founded, the number of the stars, and (the place) where all the luminaries rest? (1 Enoch 93:11–14, OTP)

Although most commentators regard this passage as an interpolation "drawn from another context in the book (perhaps the Book of Luminaries) and appended here as a gloss on 93:10," Nickelsburg concludes, "The discovery of the Aramaic fragments requires us to revise this hypothesis" with the result that the passage may not be "an erratic block dropped into the present context."[17] Whether or not 1 En. 93:11–14 is an interpolation, it is probably an allusion to Isa 40:12–14 because it uses both the form of rhetorical questions and the theme that God is incomparably powerful, wise, and immense. The only humans who can acquire a degree of God's wisdom are those to whom God reveals himself.

1.2.2. Isa 40:13 in 2 En. 33:4

This passage from 2 Enoch does not quote Isa 40:13 and may not even be an allusion, but it at least repeats the same theme.[18]

> [3] And now, Enoch, whatever I have told you, and whatever you have understood, and whatever you have seen in the heavens, and whatever you have seen on the earth, and whatever I have written in the books—by my supreme wisdom all these things I planned to accomplish. And I created them from the highest foundation to the lowest, and to the end.
>
> [4] And there is no adviser and no successor to my creation. I am self-eternal and not made by hands. My thought is without change: My wisdom is my adviser and my deed is my word. And my eyes look at all things. (If I look at all things), then they stand still and shake with terror; but, If I should turn my face away, then all things would perish. (2 Enoch 33:3–4, OTP)

Like Isa 40:13, this affirms that God has no counselors. As in 1 En. 93:11–14, the only humans who can acquire a degree of God's wisdom are those to whom God reveals himself.

---

17. Nickelsburg, 1 Enoch, 451–53.

18. On Isa 40:13 in 2 En. 33:4, cf. Williams, *Wisdom*, 224; Wagner, *Heralds*, 303n247.

1.2.3. Isa 40:13 in 4 Ezra 4:1–12 and 5:33–40

Like the book of Habakkuk, *4 Ezra* (= *2 Esd* 3–14) wrestles with how God can punish Israel with a godless nation (cf. *4 Ezra* 6:55–59).[19] For Habakkuk, that nation is Babylon, and for *4 Ezra* it is Rome. Part of the answer to that question about God's justice in *4 Ezra* is that humans cannot fully understand God and his ways:

> [1] Then the angel that had been sent to me, whose name was Uriel, answered [2] and said to me, "Your understanding has utterly failed regarding this world, do you think you can comprehend the way of the Most High? [3] Then I said, "Yes, my lord." And he replied to me, "I have been sent to show you three problems. [4] If you can solve one of them for me, I also will show you the way you desire to see, and will teach you why the heart is evil."
>
> [5] I said, "Speak on, my lord."
>
> And he said to me, "Go, weigh for me the weight of fire, or measure for me a measure of wind, or call back for me the day that is past."
>
> [6] I answered and said, "Who of those that have been born can do this, that you ask me concerning these things?"
>
> [7] And he said to me, "If I had asked you, 'How many dwellings are in the heart of the sea, or how many streams are at the source of the deep, or how many streams are above the firmament, or which are the exits of hell, or which are the entrances of Paradise?" [8] perhaps you would have said to me, 'I never went down into the deep, nor as yet into hell, neither did I ever ascend into heaven.' [9] But now I have asked you only about fire and wind and the day, things through which you have passed and without which you cannot exist, and you have given me no answer about them!" [10] And he said to me, "You cannot understand the things with which you have grown up; [11] how then can your mind comprehend the way of the Most High? And how can one who is already worn out by the corrupt world understand incorruption? When I heard this, I fell on my face [12] and said to him, "It would be better for us not to be here than to come here and live in ungodliness: and to suffer and not understand why." (*4 Ezra* 4:1–12, *OTP*)

---

19. On Isa 40:13 in *4 Ezra*, cf. Winston, *Wisdom*, 206; Williams, *Wisdom*, 222–24; Wagner, *Heralds*, 303n247.

> [33] "Speak on, my lord," I said. And he said to me, "Are you greatly disturbed in mind over Israel? Or do you love him more than his Maker does?"
> [34] "No, my lord," I said, "but because of my grief I have spoken; for every hour I suffer agonies of heart, while I strive to understand the way of the Most High and to search out part of his judgment."
> [35] He said to me, "You cannot." And I said, "Why not, my lord? Why then was I born? Or why did not my mother's womb become my grave, that I might not see the travail of Jacob and the exhaustion of the people of Israel?"
> [36] He said to me, "Count up for me those who have not yet come, and gather for me the scattered raindrops, and make the withered flowers bloom again for me; [37] open for me the closed chambers, and bring forth for me the winds shut up in them, or show me the picture of a voice; and then I will explain to you the travail that you ask to understand."
> [38] "O sovereign Lord," I said, "who is able to know these things except he whose dwelling is not with men? [39] As for me, I am without wisdom, and how can I speak concerning the things which you have asked me?"
> [40] He said to me, "Just as you cannot do one of the things that were mentioned, so you cannot discover my judgment, or the goal of the love that I have promised my people." (4 Ezra 5:33–40, OTP)

Both passages (esp. *4 Ezra* 4:5–9; 5:36–37) also have overtones of Job 38–41 (esp. Job 38:16–17),[20] implying that (1) those who are protesting the way God is judging Israel are too large in their own eyes; (2) God is too small in their eyes; (3) God is not obligated to answer their questions; and (4) only God is all-wise. Further, as in *1 En.* 93:11–14 and *2 En.* 33:3–4, the only humans who can acquire a degree of God's wisdom are those to whom God reveals himself.

1.2.4. Isa 40:13 in 2 Bar. 14:8–11; 54:11–12; and 75:1b–5

Second Baruch wrestles with how God can punish Israel, his chosen people.[21] Chapter 14 contains what Johnson calls "the closest parallel" to "the three rhetorical questions about God's wisdom" in Rom 11:34–35.[22]

---

20. Cf. Myers, *Esdras*, 172–73, 181; Stone, *Fourth Ezra*, 84–85.

21. On Isa 40:13 in 2 *Baruch*, cf. Winston, *Wisdom*, 206; Klijn, "2 Baruch," 646; Johnson, *Romans 9–11*, 168–69; Williams, *Wisdom*, 220–21; Wagner, *Heralds*, 303n247.

22. Johnson, *Romans 9–11*, 168.

> [8] O Lord, my Lord, who can understand your judgment? Or who can explore the depth of your way? [9] Or who can discern the majesty of your path? Or who can discern your incomprehensible counsel? Or who of those who are born has ever discovered the beginning and the end of your wisdom? [10] For we all have been made like breath. [11] For as breath ascends without human control and vanishes, so it is with the nature of men, who do not go away according to their own will, and who do not know what will happen to them in the end. (*2 Bar.* 14:8–11, *OTP*)

This contrasts, however, with Paul's use of Isa 40:13 in Rom 11:34. The rhetorical questions in *2 Bar.* 14:8–9 express that no one can understand the Lord's deep, majestic, wise ways. But the primary function of the rhetorical questions in Rom 11:34 is to praise God for revealing—to some degree—his deep, wise ways.[23]

The tone of *2 Bar.* 14:8–11 is despairing, but twice the book later asks rhetorical questions that triumphantly praise God for his deep, incomprehensible ways.

> [11] For I shall not be silent in honoring the Mighty One but with the voice of glory I shall narrate his marvelous works. [12] For who is able to imitate your miracles, O God, or who understands your deep thoughts of life? (*2 Bar.* 54:11–12, *OTP*)

> [1] Who can equal your goodness, O Lord?
>   for it is incomprehensible.
> [2] Or who can fathom your grace
>   which is without end?
> [3] Or who can understand your intelligence?
> [4] Or who can narrate the thoughts of your spirit?
> [5] Or who of those born can hope to arrive at these things,
>   apart from those to whom you are merciful and gracious?
> (*2 Bar.* 75:1b–5, *OTP*)

Those two passages function similarly to Rom 11:34 by exulting in God's deep incomprehensibility.

All three of the above passages, like Isa 40:13, use rhetorical questions to convey that humans cannot fully understand God and his ways. They also "occur immediately before or after divine revelation," which suggests "that these parallels to Isa. 40:13 are associated with the revelation of God's plan of salvation."[24]

---

23. Cf. Käsemann, *Romans*, 319; Johnson, *Romans 9–11*, 168.
24. Williams, *Wisdom*, 221.

1.3. Isa 40:13 in the Dead Sea Scrolls

Isaiah 40:13 in the Dead Sea Scrolls occurs only in the Qumran documents, both biblical and non-biblical.[25]

TABLE 7. Isa 40:12–14 in the MT and 1QIsa[a]

MT	1QIsa[a]
¹²מִי־מָדַד בְּשָׁעֳלוֹ מַיִם וְשָׁמַיִם בַּזֶּרֶת תִּכֵּן וְכָל בַּשָּׁלִשׁ עֲפַר הָאָרֶץ וְשָׁקַל בַּפֶּלֶס הָרִים וּגְבָעוֹת בְּמֹאזְנָיִם: ¹³מִי־תִכֵּן אֶת־רוּחַ יְהוָה וְאִישׁ עֲצָתוֹ יוֹדִיעֶנּוּ: ¹⁴אֶת־מִי נוֹעָץ וַיְבִינֵהוּ וַיְלַמְּדֵהוּ בְּאֹרַח מִשְׁפָּט וַיְלַמְּדֵהוּ דַעַת וְדֶרֶךְ תְּבוּנוֹת יוֹדִיעֶנּוּ:	¹²מיא מדד בשועלו מי ים ושמים בזרתן תכן וכל בשליש עפר הארץ ושקל בפלס הרים וגבעות במוזנים ¹³מיא תכן את רוח יהוה אי[ש][a] ועצתו יודיענה ¹⁴את מי נועץ ויבינהו וילמדהו באורח משפט וילמדהו דעת ודרך תבונות יודיענו

[a]The ו is marked, either in order to delete it or to indicate that it should be followed by the interlinear word.[26] |
| ¹² Who has measured the waters in the hollow of his hand and marked off the heavens with a span, enclosed the dust of the earth in a measure and weighed the mountains in scales and the hills in a balance? ¹³ Who has measured the Spirit of the LORD, or what man shows him his counsel? ¹⁴ Whom did he consult, and who made him understand? Who taught him the path of justice, and taught him knowledge, and showed him the way of understanding? | ¹² Who has measured *the waters of the sea* in his palm? marked out the heavens with *his* compass and measured out the dust of the earth in a measuring bowl? weighed the mountains in scales and the hills in a balance? ¹³ Who has directed the spirit of the Lord, or as his counselor has taught *him*? ¹⁴ With whom did he consult, to instruct him and guide him in the ways of justice? *or taught him knowledge or showed him the ways of wisdom?*[27] |

---

25. Cf. Käsemann, *Romans*, 320; Lim, *Holy Scripture*, 159-60; Johnson, *Romans 9–11*, 169-71; Williams, *Wisdom*, 219-20 (Williams references 1QHa 15.31b-32 as 1QH 7.32-33 and 1QHa 18.1-4 as 1QH 10.1-4); Wagner, *Heralds*, 70n87, 303n247; Ciampa and Rosner, "1 Corinthians," 702.

26. Parry and Qimron, *Isaiah Scroll*, 66-67.

27. Abegg, Flint, and Ulrich, *DSS*, 333 (emphasis in original).

1.3.1. Isa 40:13 in 1QIsa^a

The *Great Isaiah Scroll* (1QIsa^a) is probably the single most famous Qumran document because it is the only one that preserves an entire biblical scroll. It preserves nearly the entire book of Isaiah and for the most part differs only incidentally from the MT. Table 7 demonstrates how similar Isa 40:12–14 is in the MT and 1QIsa^a. The rendering of Isa 40:13 in 1QIsa^a is consistent with our understanding of the passage in its context.[28]

1.3.2. Isa 40:13 in Non-Biblical Qumran Texts

At least four passages in non-biblical Qumran texts appear to allude to Isa 40:13 by emphasizing that humans cannot fully understand God and his ways. These passages occur in three documents.

1. The *Rule of the Community* (1QS), also called the *Discipline Scroll* and *Manual of Discipline*, regulates community life. The following passage contrasts lowly humans with the powerful, all-wise God:

> [20] Who can endure your glory? What, indeed, is the son of man, among all your marvellous deeds?
> [21] As what shall one born of woman be considered in your presence? Shaped from dust has he been, maggots' food shall be his dwelling; he is spat saliva,
> [22] moulded clay, and for dust is his longing. What will the clay reply and the one shaped by hand? And what advice will he be able to understand? (1QS 11.20–22)[29]

The final question ("what advice will he [i.e., a human] be able to understand?") reverses the question in Isa 40:13b ("what man shows him [i.e., God] his counsel?"). Not only do humans have no advice to offer God, humans are not even able to understand God's ways. Rather than praising God for revealing his ways as in Rom 11:34, this passage emphasizes God's transcendence and incomprehensibility.

2. 1QH^a, the largest scroll of the *Thanksgiving Hymns*, includes two significant passages. Both emphasize that humans are lowly compared to God and that they cannot fully understand God and his ways.

---

28. See §4 in chap. 3 above.
29. Martínez and Tigchelaar, *DSS*, 1:99.

> ³¹ ... For you are an eternal God and all your paths remain from eternity
> ³² [to e]ter[nity.] And there is no-one apart from you. What is the man of emptiness, or the owner of futility, to understand your wonderful [great] deeds? (1QHª 15.31b–32 [previously numbered as 7.32–33])³⁰

The second passage praises God for revealing his wise ways to his servants.

> ¹ [...] has become [...] the plan of your heart [...]
> ² [...] And without your will it shall not be. And no-one understands [your] wis[dom,]
> ³ your [...], no-one contemplates them. What, then, is man? He is nothing but earth. *Blank* [From clay]
> ⁴ he is fashioned and to dust he will return. But you teach him about wonders
> like these and the foundations of [your] tru[th]
> ⁵ you show to him. (1QHª 18.1–5a [previously numbered as 10.1–4])³¹

3. A passage in the *Songs of the Sage* (4Q510–511) comes closest to quoting Isa 40:13 (4Q511 30.6). This is fragment 30 from 4Q511 in its entirety:

> ¹ you have sealed [... ea]rth ... [...]
> ² and deep are [... the] heavens and the abysses and [...]
> ³ You, my God have sealed them all up, and nobody opens them. And to whom [...]
> ⁴ Can perhaps the waters of the deep be gauged in the hollow of a man's hand? And [the span of the heavens] be calculated in palms? [Who, in a bushel]
> ⁵ can hold the dust of the earth, weigh the mountains with scales, or the hills on a balanc[e? *Blank?*]
> ⁶ Man does not do these things. [How, then,] can man measure the spirit [of God?] (4Q511 30.1–6)³²

---

30. Ibid., 1:180.
31. Ibid., 1:187.
32. Ibid., 2:1034.

1.4. Isa 40:13 in Rabbinic Literature

The paraphrase of Isa 40:12–14 in the Targum of Isaiah significantly alters the meaning of 40:13:[33]

> [12] Who *says these things? One who lives, speaks and acts, before whom all the waters of the world are reckoned as the drop* in the hollow of *a* hand and *the length of* the heavens *as if* with *the* span *established*, the dust of the earth *as if measured* in a measure and *the* mountains *as if indeed* weigh*ed* and *the* hills, *behold, just as* in *the* balance. [13] Who *established* the *holy* spirit *in the mouth of all the prophets, is it not* the LORD? And *to the righteous who perform his Memra* [i.e., command] he makes known *the words of his pleasure*. [14] *Those who besought before him* he *caused to apprehend wisdom* and taught *them* the path of judgment and *gave their sons the law* and showed the way of understanding *to their sons' sons*.[34]

Instead of asking who has known the mind of the Lord or been his counselor, the Targum asks who has directed the Holy Spirit's disclosure of revelation through the prophets. Instead of the answer to the rhetorical question being no one, the answer to the Targum's question is the Lord. Further, the Targum adds that the Lord reveals things to the righteous.

1.5. Isa 40:13 in 1 Cor 2:16

> [14] The natural person does not accept the things of the Spirit of God, for they are folly to him, and he is not able to understand them because they are spiritually discerned. [15] The spiritual person judges all things, but is himself to be judged by no one. [16] "For who has understood the mind of the Lord so as to instruct him?" But we have the mind of Christ. (1 Cor 2:14–16)

The use of Isa 40:13 in 1 Cor 2:16 is especially significant for understanding its use in Rom 11:34 because 1 Corinthians and Romans share so many characteristics: (1) Paul authored both of them; (2) both are canonical Scripture; (3) both are the same epistolary genre; and (4) Paul probably wrote them within a few years of each other, likely penning 1 Corinthians before Romans.[35]

---

33. On Isa 40:13 in Rabbinic literature, cf. Stenning, *Targum*, 132–33; Hanson, *NT Interpretation*, 82; Chilton, *Targum*, 78.

34. Chilton, *Targum*, 78 (emphasis in original).

35. Carson and Moo (*Introduction*, 393–94, 447–48) argue that Paul wrote 1 Corinthians early in A.D. 55 and Romans in A.D. 57. Cf. Guthrie, *NT Introduction*, 406–8, 457–59.

Paul quotes Isa 40:13 in 1 Cor 2:16 in a way that may seem inconsistent with his use of it in Rom 11:34. There are at least three differences between how Paul uses Isa 40:13 in 1 Cor 2:16 and Rom 11:34.

1. Paul focuses on Jesus in 1 Cor 2:16, and he focuses on God the Father in Rom 11:34.[36] The "Lord" in Rom 11:34 refers to God the Father, but Paul explicitly identifies the "Lord" in 1 Cor 2:16 as Christ.[37]

2. First Corinthians 2:16 quotes the first and third clauses of Isa 40:13, and Rom 11:34 quotes the first two clauses of Isa 40:13. Lim concludes, "Clearly, Paul is tolerant of two slightly different versions of Isaiah 40:13."[38] But contra Lim, "it would be more accurate to say that Paul knew one form (quite close to the LXX) and quoted it in two different ways."[39]

3. Paul's answer to the rhetorical question of Isa 40:13 is slightly different in 1 Cor 2:16 than his implied answer in Rom 11:34. The implied answer to Rom 11:34 is the same as Isa 40:13: *no one* has known the mind of the Lord. But after quoting Isa 40:13 in 1 Cor 2:16, Paul answers the rhetorical question differently than implied in the context of Isa 40. While its implied answer is still "no one," on the other hand Paul continues that we *can* know the mind of the Lord: "But we have the mind of Christ" (1 Cor 2:16b).[40] So by application, those who now have the Holy Spirit have "God's profound wisdom regarding salvation through a crucified Messiah, which was hidden but now revealed by the Holy Spirit."[41]

4. Some argue for a fourth difference, namely, that 1 Cor 2:16 emphasizes that God reveals previously hidden truths to his people while Rom 11:34 emphasizes that God's ways are unknowable.[42] But this dichotomy does not hold since Rom 11:33–36 exults in the ways of God that Paul just explained in Rom 9–11.[43] The context of both 1 Cor 2:16 and Rom

---

36. Dunn, *Romans 9–16*, 700.
37. Cf. Thiselton, *Corinthians*, 275.
38. Lim, *Holy Scripture*, 159.
39. Wagner, *Heralds*, 304. See also Figure 4.8 (p. 303) and 304n250.
40. Cf. Hays, *First Corinthians*, 47.
41. Ciampa and Rosner, "1 Corinthians," 702. Williams argues that the "mind" of 1 Cor 2:16 is God's salvation-historical plan (*Wisdom*, 225–35).
42. Cf. Youngblood, *Isaiah*, 115.
43. See §3.1 in ch. 2 above.

11:34 includes God's disclosure of revelation, and both passages teach that God is incomprehensible and that he graciously reveals some things to his people. Paul uses Isa 40:13 in 1 Cor 2:16 to support 2:15, namely, "that the mind of Christ is alien to the unbeliever, and insofar as we have the mind of Christ we will be alien to the unbeliever as well."[44] Schreiner rightly concludes that Rom 11:34 is "remarkably similar in theme to 1 Cor. 2:16: human beings cannot know God's wisdom unaided, but they can access it as the Holy Spirit reveals it."[45] "The point," explains Osborne as he agrees with Schreiner, "is that God's knowledge of salvation history is absolute while ours is finite, so none of us can be his *counselor*."[46]

2. JOB 41:3A IN JEWISH LITERATURE

The use of Job 41:3a in Jewish literature is much thinner than the use of Isa 40:13. Besides the use of Leviathan in Jewish literature, the use of Job 41:3a is sparse; it does not occur in the OT Apocrypha, OT Pseudepigrapha, Dead Sea Scrolls, Philo,[47] or Josephus.

2.1. Job 41:3a in Rabbinic Literature

Beyond the Aramaic translations of the book of Job (4Q157 and 11Q10), only four manuscripts of Job were discovered at Qumran. These remnants contain only small portions of chapters 8–9, 13–14, 31–33, and 35–37, and an English translation of them fills only two and a half pages of a normal-size book.[48] The Aramaic Targum of Job (11Q10)[49] trans-

---

44. Cf. Carson, *Cross*, 61.

45. Schreiner, *Romans*, 636. Cf. Fitzmyer, *First Corinthians*, 185; Käsemann, *Romans*, 320; Fee, *Corinthians*, 119–20. Contra Mortenson, "Text," 75; Jewett, *Romans*, 719.

46. Osborne, *Romans*, 315–16.

47. But see Gundry, "Rom 11,35," 25–53. Gundry, who does not address the use of Job 41:3a in Rom 11:35, draws "some parallels between the two views of the divine Benefactor in Paul's interaction with the Roman Gentiles, on the one hand, and Philo's two chief divine powers, on the other hand. [1] Philo's beneficent creative power bestows gifts upon all without ceasing in expression of the eternal divine nature, [2] whereas the ruling power metes out both reward and punishment, as appropriate to the human disposition dependent on such activity. Philo esteems the beneficent creative power higher than the ruling power" (30–31).

48. Abegg, Flint, and Ulrich, *DSS*, 591–93.

49. Martínez and Tigchelaar, *DSS*, 2:1185–1201; Wise, Abegg, and Cook, *DSS*, 577–88.

lates Job 17:14—42:12 but skips 41:1–6.[50] Strack-Billerbeck suggests that Paul's wording in Rom 11:35 derives from an early form of the Targum of Job on Job 41:3,[51] but Jewett rightly counters, "the formulation is not close enough to be very plausible: 'Who comes before me in the works of creation, that I must repay him?'"[52]

Hanson traces the use of Job 41:3a in early Rabbinic exegesis.[53] Two sources are significant. First, *Pesikta Rabbati* uses Job 41:3

> to remind those in Israel who are under obligation to tithe that "all things come of God,"[54] i.e., they do not possess anything which God has not already given them. The verse is understood as meaning "Who has given me anything beforehand, that I should repay him?," precisely the sense in which Paul takes it. Then follows a series of questions, all emphasizing that God does not ask anything of a man until he has first given the man something, e.g. no one is required to circumcise his son till God has given him one. God is represented as saying: "I have not asked for a portion of that which is yours: I have asked for a portion of that which is mine." This agrees well enough in general with Paul's thought in Romans: we have no ground on which we can of ourselves establish a claim against God.[55]

Second, R. Tanhuma explains Job 41:3 in *Pesikta de Rab Kahana*.

> Whoever, without being required to, bestirs himself [to help provide instruction in the Torah which] under the whole heaven was [first] mine, I will repay him [by not turning a deaf ear to his prayer for male children].[56]

R. Tanhuma continues in the name of R. Jeremiah ben Eleazar:

> Whosoever without being required to bestirs himself [to provide instruction in the Torah which] under the whole heaven

---

50. Martínez and Tigchelaar, *DSS*, 2:1200; Wise, Abegg, and Cook, *DSS*, 587.

51. Str-B 3:295.

52. Jewett, *Romans*, 720.

53. Hanson, *NT Interpretation*, 86–89.

54. Hanson is citing *Piska* 25.2 from William G. Braude, *Pesikta Rabbati: Discourses for Feasts, Fasts, and Special Sabbaths* (Yale Judaica 18; New Haven: Yale University Press, 1968), 514.

55. Hanson, *NT Interpretation*, 86–87.

56. Hanson (ibid., 87) is citing *Piska* 9.2 from William G. Braude and Israel J. Kapstein, *Pesikta de Rab Kahana: R. Kahana's Compilation of Discourses for Sabbaths and Festal Days* (London: Routledge & Paul, 1975), 173.

was [first] mine, I will repay him [by having a Voice proclaim] under the entire heaven [that such a man has wrought as I have wrought].⁵⁷

These two quotations from *Pesikta de Rab Kahana* are not consistent with the context of either Job 41:3a or Rom 11:35. Instead, they reverse the meaning of those passages by speaking of meriting God's favor and thus making God their creditor—the very thing that Job 41:3a and Rom 11:35 deny.

2.2. Leviathan in Jewish Literature

Leviathan, the fearsome creature God describes in Job 40:25—41:26 (Eng. 41:1-34), is mentioned three times in the OT Pseudepigrapha (*1 En.* 60:7-9; *4 Ezra* 6:49-54; *2 Bar.* 29:4)⁵⁸ and several times in Rabbinic literature.⁵⁹ The most up-to-date and thorough treatment of this is Whitney's published dissertation on the subject.⁶⁰ The Leviathan-passages in Second Temple and Rabbinic Judaism are for the most part consistent with the view that Leviathan is a real creature that symbolizes larger cosmic realities, but their focus is on those larger cosmic realities.⁶¹

3. CONCLUSION

The few uses of Job 41:3a in the Jewish literature cited above are not significant for understanding the use of the OT in Rom 11:35. The use of Leviathan in Jewish literature, however, is at least partially consistent with the larger cosmic realities present in Job 40-41.

The apparent quotations of and allusions to Isa 40:13 in the Jewish literature cited above share at least two themes. First, humans cannot fully understand God's thoughts and ways. This includes God's thoughts and ways in salvation history: "The link to God's plan of salvation is clear in various texts from Qumran that emphasize human inability to grasp

---

57. Cited in Hanson, *NT Interpretation*, 87.

58. Cf. Myers, *Esdras*, 128-29, 229n49; Caquot, "Léviathan," 111-22; Stone, *Fourth Ezra*, 182-83, 186-88.

59. See Jacobs, "Elements," 4-7. Cf. Ginzberg, *Legends*, 5:26n73, 43-46n127; Pfeiffer, "Lotan," 209-11; Uehlinger, "Leviathan," 514-15.

60. Whitney, *Two Strange Beasts*.

61. Cf. Day, *God's Conflict*, 82-83n59; idem, "Leviathan," 296; Hartley, *Job*, 522n3.

God's spirit, mind, and ways."[62] Second, the only humans who can acquire a degree of God's wisdom are those to whom God reveals himself. These themes are also present in both Isa 40:13 and Rom 11:34.

There is both continuity and discontinuity between the uses of Isa 40:13 in Jewish literature and in Rom 11:34. (1) The continuity is that Paul writes within a rich Jewish heritage that understands all these texts. Sometimes when Paul quotes the OT, he takes a stance that non-Christian OT theologians would not take. When he reads the OT salvation-historically and sequentially, for example, he is outside the camp. But in Rom 11:34, he is not outside the camp. There is a whole corpus of literature that extols God's thoughts, and Paul writes in continuity with it. (2) The discontinuity is what triggers Paul's praise. What is innovative in Rom 11:34 is Paul's salvation-historical reflection on God's sovereign ways specifically with reference to the salvation of Jews and Gentiles.

---

62. Ciampa and Rosner, "1 Corinthians," 702.

7

Paul's Hermeneutical Warrant for Using Isaiah 40:13 and Job 41:3a in Romans 11:34–35

STEPS 1–4 LAY THE groundwork for steps 5–6:

1. the NT context of Rom 11:34–35 (ch. 2)
2. the OT context of Isa 40:13 and Job 41:3a (chs. 3–4)
3. textual issues in Isa 40:13, Job 41:3, and Rom 11:34–35 (ch. 5)
4. relevant uses of Isa 40:13 and Job 41:3a in Jewish literature (ch. 6)
5. Paul's hermeneutical warrant for using Isa 40:13 and Job 41:3a in Rom 11:34–35 (ch. 7)
6. Paul's theological use of Isa 40:13 and Job 41:3a in Rom 11:34–35 (ch. 8)

"Once this groundwork has been laid," explain Beale and Carson, "it becomes important to try to understand how the NT is using or appealing to the OT. What is the nature of the connection as the NT writer sees it?"[1] By "warrant," I mean what the *Oxford English Dictionary* lists as definition 8a: "Justifying reason or ground for an action, belief, or feeling." By "hermeneutical warrant," I mean "how the NT is using or appealing to the OT" and "the nature of the connection as the NT writer sees it." So a NT author's hermeneutical warrant explains why and how he uses the OT. This chapter surveys various hermeneutical warrants, focuses on Paul's hermeneutical warrant in Rom 11:34–35, and then

---

1. Beale and Carson, "Introduction," xxiv.

briefly compares that with Paul's use of the OT in Rom 9–11 and the use of the OT in other NT doxologies.

1. A SURVEY OF THE NT AUTHORS' HERMENEUTICAL WARRANTS FOR USING THE OT

This section surveys some hermeneutical warrants for the way NT authors use the OT. Three qualifications are noteworthy: (1) Parts of this section paraphrase a forthcoming essay that updates a 1986 essay by Moo.[2] (2) This list could give the impression that these different warrants are completely separate, but they may overlap. Sometimes a NT author's warrant is multifaceted and combines more than one of these warrants. (3) This survey gives disproportionate space to the final two hermeneutical warrants (canonical approach and typology) because they are the most significant for our conclusions about the use of the OT in Rom 11:34–35.

1.1. Borrowed Language

NT authors may borrow the language of the OT to express something unrelated to the OT's original context.[3] The nature of the connection between such an OT quotation and a NT author's use of it is merely linguistic because NT authors were so steeped in the OT that it shaped they way they thought and talked. The speech of a person immersed in popular culture's movies, TV shows, and songs, for example, is understandably sprinkled with terms and idioms drawn from those forms of entertainment. Similarly, the NT writers sometimes use OT language as a vehicle of expression without intending to provide a "correct" interpretation of the OT text they are quoting. Examples of this warrant may include the use of Psalms 42–43 in Matt 2:38 and Mark 14:34.[4]

1.2. Alternative Points of View

NT authors may quote the OT merely to represent the opinion of their listeners or opponents. This phenomenon of quoting alternative points of view may occur when Paul quotes what appears to be slogans of the Corinthians rather than giving his own teaching (e.g., 1 Cor 6:12; 7:1;

---

2. Moo and Naselli, "Problem," updates Moo, "Problem."
3. Beale and Carson, "Introduction," xxiv–xxv.
4. Moo, *Old Testament*, 240–42.

8:1; 10:23). Examples of this warrant may include the use of Lev 19:18 in Matt 5:43[5] and Lev 18:5 in Gal 3:12 and Rom 10:5.[6] The context of Matthew 5 suggests this warrant because the quotation in Matt 5:43 is antithetical to Jesus' teaching. But when contextual indicators are not present, we must be especially cautious before hypothesizing this warrant because attributing an author's words to his opponents requires compelling evidence.

1.3. Jewish Exegetical Methods

NT authors may apply the OT to their own situations by using the same midrashic or pesher approaches as their non-Christian Jewish contemporaries.[7] Both the NT and Qumran documents, for example, share the conviction that the OT prophesies about their own times and experience. Further, both the NT and first-century Jewish sources utilize similar citation techniques. Examples include *gezerah shawah* (i.e., combining verses on the basis of verbal resemblance; cf. Pss 110:1 and 16:8–11 in Acts 2:25–34) and *qal wahomer* (i.e., arguing from the lesser to the greater; cf. John 7:23).

The value of this hermeneutical warrant is limited because it lacks explanatory power at the most significant levels. Granted, studying Jewish exegetical procedures may help (1) explain what the NT authors sometimes do with Scripture, (2) explain why they do it, and (3) show that the NT authors often use methods that many of their contemporaries knew and accepted. But the presence of first-century exegetical techniques does not answer whether the meaning that these techniques discover is really in the OT. It does not explain how Jewish Christians and non-Christians can arrive at contradictory conclusions by using the same exegetical methods. At the level of appropriation technique (i.e., "on the surface" methods that authors use to "appropriate" a text for a new situation), the NT can closely resemble contemporary Jewish methods, but below the surface, hermeneutical axioms (i.e., a community's

---

5. Cf. Carson, "Matthew," 191.

6. Silva, "NT Use," 159; idem, "OT in Paul," *DPL* 638.

7. Ellis, *Paul's Use*; idem, *Prophecy*; idem, "How the NT," 201–8; Barrett, "Interpretation," 379–403; McCartney, "NT Use," 101–16; Silva, "OT in Paul," 635–38; Longenecker, *Biblical Exegesis*; Evans, "OT in the New," 130–45; idem, "Jewish Exegesis," 380–84; Enns, *Inspiration*, 113–65; idem, "Fuller Meaning," 167–217; Gignilliat, *Paul*, 8–13; Lunde, "Introduction, 25–32.

basic convictions about Scripture, its own identity, and God's movement in history, which result in basic theological connections between the Testaments) provide the validating matrix for what may seem to be an arbitrary exegesis.[8]

1.4. Sensus Plenior

NT authors may appeal to an OT text's *sensus plenior*, namely, to a "fuller sense" than what its human author consciously intended but what God, Scripture's ultimate author, did intend.[9] This hermeneutical warrant affirms that God can intend a sense related to but more than what the OT author intends.[10] While typology involves the deeper meaning of things, *sensus plenior* involves the extended meaning of words.[11] The usual objections against the idea of a *sensus plenior* are not cogent, so there does not appear to be any compelling reason for rejecting the hypothesis.[12] But we should consider other hermeneutical warrants before this one because it has two difficulties: (1) The NT sometimes appeals to the human author of an OT text for what appears to be a questionable application (e.g., Acts 2:25-28). (2) The NT authors generally give the impression that others can also see the meaning they find in the OT, granted certain basic presuppositions (e.g., Mark 12:26; John 3:10), but if the NT authors appeal to a "hidden" sense of the text that the Spirit revealed only to them, then their argument will probably not seem compelling to others who have not received that revelation.

---

8. Moo, *Old Testament*, 75-78.

9. Brown, *Sensus Plenior*, 1955; Hagner, "OT in the NT," 92-104; Lunde, "Introduction," 13-18. Cf. Poythress, "Divine," 241-79.

10. One of the most outspoken evangelical opponents of *sensus plenior* in the last four decades has been Walter C. Kaiser Jr. See, for example, his "Single Intent," 123-41; *Uses*, 27-28, 63-70; "Single Meaning," 47-60, 223-24. Kaiser is not, however, staunchly opposed to the type of *sensus plenior* represented above because it is related to and consistent with the OT text's original meaning ("Single Meaning," 154). Thomas is a more insistent opponent of *sensus plenior* (which, for Thomas, includes the canonical approach and typology as advocated below); see, e.g., "Principle," 33-47; "NT Use," 79-98. Cf. how one of Thomas's students applies his approach to Romans 9:25-26, 10:20-21, and 11:25-27; Brackett, "Paul's Use."

11. Brown, *Sensus Plenior*, 92.

12. See Moo and Naselli, "Problem," forthcoming; cf. Moo, "Problem," 202-4.

1.5. Generic OT Expression

NT authors may use an OT expression to refer generically to a richly theological OT theme without having only one specific OT text in mind.[13] Beale and Carson explain that there may be times

> when a NT writer uses an expression that crops up in many OT passages (such as, say, "day of the Lord," especially common in the prophets), not thinking of any one OT text but nevertheless using the expression to reflect the rich mix of promised blessing and promised judgment that characterizes the particular instantiations of the OT occurrences . . . In this case, the NT writer may be very faithful to OT usage at the generic level, even while not thinking of any particular passage, that is, individual OT occurrences may envisage particular visitations by God, while the generic pattern combines judgment and blessing, and the NT use may pick up on the generic pattern while applying it to yet another visitation by God.[14]

1.6. Fulfillment of a Specific Prediction

NT authors may quote the OT to claim that a NT person or event specifically fulfills what an OT author predicted.[15] This one-to-one prediction and fulfillment is what most people think of when they think of prophecy. Examples of this warrant include the use of Zech 9:9 in Matt 21:4–5 and Isa 61:1–2a in Luke 4:18–20.

1.7. The Larger OT Context

NT authors may implicitly include the larger OT context when they quote just a small part of it. Scholars have generally accepted this hermeneutical warrant since the work of C. H. Dodd.[16] Dodd draws four interlocking conclusions, and the second of these explicitly explains this hermeneutical warrant that we are calling "the larger OT context":

> 1. The quotation of passages from the Old Testament (whether or not under a formula of quotation) is not to be accounted for

---

13. Waltke, *OT Theology*, 129–30.
14. Beale and Carson, "Introduction," xxv.
15. Ibid.
16. Dodd, *According*. Cf. Silva, "NT Use," 159–61; Marshall, "Assessment," 1–21, esp. 2–8; Lunde, "Introduction," 22–24.

by the postulate of a primitive anthology of isolated proof-texts. The composition of "testimony-books" was the result, not the presupposition, of the work of early Christian biblical scholars. The evidence suggests that at a very early date a certain *method* of biblical study was established and became part of the equipment of Christian evangelists and teachers....

2. The method included, first, the *selection* of certain large sections of the Old Testament scriptures, especially from Isaiah, Jeremiah and certain minor prophets, and from the Psalms. These sections were understood as *wholes*, and particular verses or sentences were quoted from them rather as pointers to the whole context than as constituting testimonies in and for themselves. At the same time, detached sentences from other parts of the Old Testament could be adduced to illustrate or elucidate the meaning of the main section under consideration. But in the fundamental passages it is *total context* that is in view, and is the basis of the argument.

3. The relevant scriptures were understood and interpreted upon intelligible and consistent principles, as setting forth "the determinate counsel of God" which was fulfilled in the gospel facts, and consequently as fixing the meaning of those facts.

4. This whole body of material—the passages of Old Testament scripture with their application to the gospel facts—is common to all the main portions of the New Testament, and in particular it provided the starting point for the theological constructions of Paul, the author to the Hebrews, and the Fourth Evangelist. It is the substructure of all Christian theology and contains already its chief regulative ideas.[17]

Examples of this warrant include the use of Isa 53:4 in Matt 8:17; and Isa 40:1–11 in 1 Pet 1:24–25.[18]

1.8. Application

NT authors may apply an OT principle or law to a new situation that the OT authors did not specifically, consciously intend, but the general meaning that the OT authors intended legitimately includes the NT

---

17. Dodd, *According*, 126–27 (emphasis in original).

18. Cf. Carson ("1 Peter," 1021) on Peter's use of Isa 40:1–11 in 1 Pet 1:24–25: "Almost certainly he expects them to pick up on all of Isa. 40, not just the two verses that he actually cites, and to direct the parallels in their own situation."

authors' application.[19] Examples of this warrant may include the use of Deut 25:4 in 1 Cor 9:9.[20]

1.9. Canonical Approach

NT authors may approach the OT by focusing on the ultimate canonical context of any single OT text as the basis on which to find a "fuller" sense in that text beyond what its human author consciously intends.[21] This hermeneutical warrant affirms that one can legitimately interpret any specific biblical text in light of its ultimate literary context—the whole canon—which receives its unity from its single divine author. The human authors may have had inklings that their words were pregnant with meanings that they did not yet understand, but they would not have been in a position to see the entire context of their words. Some biblical books written before them may not have been available to them, and they were unaware of subsequent revelation. Although Bock does not explicitly describe a salvation-historical reading that uses a biblical-theological method to trace themes throughout the Bible's storyline, he helpfully explains,

> Two ways to read a biblical text are the "historical-exegetical" reading and the "theological-canonical" reading. These terms are not altogether adequate, however. Exegesis is theological, and theology should be exegetical. Still, the terms are chosen because of what each reading emphasizes. An historical-exegetical reading is primarily concerned with discerning the original author's message to his immediate audience in its specific, historical situation. A theological-canonical reading views the text in light of subsequent revelation.
>
> In a theological-canonical reading, the progress of revelation may "refract" on an earlier passage so that the force of the earlier passage is clarified or developed beyond what the original author could have grasped. How this is done is debated among evangelicals and divides into three broad views. (1) Some argue that the later NT meaning tells us what the original OT author meant (even though in the original OT context that meaning was

---

19. Hirsch (*Validity*, 121–26) labels this phenomenon a "willed type." Cf. Beale and Carson, "Introduction," xxv.

20. Kaiser, "Current Crisis," 3–18.

21. Cf. Waltke, "Canonical," 3–18; Poythress, "Divine"; Bock, "Single Meaning," 105–51.

not very transparent). (2) Others argue that the OT revelation determines the meaning and defines the limits of the concept and thereby fixes that meaning. (3) Others argue that the NT meaning can develop or complement what the OT meant, but not in a way that ends up denying what the OT originally affirmed.[22]

Examples of the canonical approach include Ps 8:6 in 1 Cor 15:27; and Hab 2:4b in Rom 1:17 and Gal 3:11.

The canonical approach has at least four strengths:

1. It builds on a salvation-historical framework: the OT as a whole points forward to, anticipates, and prefigures Christ and the church.[23] The NT views the OT as a collection of books that, in each of its parts and in its whole, was incomplete until Jesus fulfilled it by coming and inaugurating the era of salvation. Jesus fulfills Israel's law (Matt 5:17), history (Matt 2:15), and prophecy (Acts 3:18). He also fulfills the meaning of many specific OT texts.

2. It has precedents within the OT itself because it gives deeper meaning to antecedent OT texts.

3. It decreases and may eliminate the questionable division between the human and divine authors' intentions in a given text because it appeals to the meaning of the text itself that takes on deeper significance as God's plan unfolds.[24]

4. Its conclusions are verifiable to some degree. So can we reproduce the NT's exegesis? In other words, can we interpret the OT the same way that the NT authors do and with the same results? On the one hand, we do not have the same revelatory authority to reproduce the NT's specific applications. But on the other hand, we can usually see the theological structure and hermeneutical principles on which the NT's interpretation

---

22. Bock, "Single Meaning," 115–16. Bock prefers the third view, noting, "Historically, the three options often reflect the difference between a Reformed amillennial approach (view 1), a traditional dispensational approach (view 2), and a progressive dispensational approach, which some historic premillenarians might also share (view 3)" (116n11).

23. On salvation history, see §3 of ch. 1; Cullmann, *Salvation*; Ridderbos, *Paul*, 44–90; Ellis, "How the NT," 209–10; VanGemeren, *Progress*; Moo, "Law of Christ," 321–22; Yarbrough, *Salvation*; idem, "Paul," 297–342; Rosner, "Salvation," 714–17; Waltke, *OT Theology*, 53, 133; Baker, *Two Testament*, 139–65, 272–73.

24. Cf. Compton, "Shared," 23–33.

of the OT rests, and our interpretation can follow the NT by applying similar criteria.

The canonical approach, however, is easily abused by interpreters who hold that God is Scripture's ultimate author. Such interpreters rightly insist on Scripture's unity, but they may hastily and anachronistically skip from exegesis to systematic theology without anchoring a canonical approach to biblical theology.[25] The result is a flat reading of Scripture without sufficient methodological controls; some may read a full-blown doctrine into earlier Scripture (e.g., reading God's tri-unity into Gen 1:26) that may merely adumbrate themes that Scripture gradually unpacks over time. The canonical approach integrates typology (see §1.10 below) as much as possible and on as wide a sweep as possible and never in an atemporal way.

1.10. Typology

NT authors may use the OT typologically to show that NT persons, events, and institutions fulfill OT persons, events, and institutions by repeating the OT situations at a deeper, climactic level in salvation history.[26] Typology is a core component of the canonical approach, and it explains how a type exemplifies or models its subsequent antitype. Goppelt calls it the NT's "predominant" and "characteristic" approach to the OT,[27] and Osborne observes, "It has increasingly been recognized that typology expresses the basic hermeneutic, indeed the attitude or perspective, by which both OT and NT writers understood themselves and their predecessors."[28] Baker's "working definitions" are helpful:

---

25. Cf. Carson, "Unity," 65-95, 368-75; idem, "Role," 39-76; idem, "Current," 17-41; idem, "NT Theology," 796-814; idem, "ST and BT," 89-104.

26. Goppelt, *Typos*; idem, "τύπος," 246-59; Foulkes, *Acts*; Ellis, *Paul's Use*, 126-35; idem, "How the NT," 210-12; Achtemeier, "Typology," 926-27; Johnson, *OT in the New*, esp. 53-79; idem, "Response," 791-99; Osborne, "Type; Typology," 930-32; idem, "Type, Typology," 1222-23; Beale, "Did Jesus," 89-96; Alsup, "Typology," 682-85; Hugenberger, "Introductory," 331-41; Dempster, *Dominion*, 231-34; Carson, "Mystery," 404-12, 425-28; Yoshikawa, "Prototypical," 8-35; Evans, "Jewish Exegesis," 383-84; France, "Relationship," 669; Treier, "Typology," 823-27; Waltke, *OT Theology*, 136-39, 141-42; Beale and Carson, "Introduction," xxv; Elliott, "Typology," 692; Lunde, "Introduction," 18-22; Harris, "Eternal," 15-19; Baker, *Two Testaments*, 169-89, 273.

27. Goppelt, *Typos*, 198.

28. Osborne, "Type, Typology," 1223.

> A *type* is a biblical event, person or institution which serves as an example or pattern for other events, persons or institutions.
>
> - *Typology* is the study of types and the historical and theological correspondences between them.
> - The *basis* of typology is God's consistent activity in the history of his chosen people.[29]

Osborne's definition of typology includes several examples:

> A hermeneutical concept in which a biblical place (Jerusalem, Zion), person (Adam, Melchizedek), event (flood, brazen serpent), institution (feasts, covenant), office (prophet, priest, king), or object (tabernacle, altar, incense) becomes a pattern by which later persons or places are interpreted due to the unity of events within salvation-history.[30]

Four clarifications help unpack the nature of this hermeneutical warrant:

1. Typology explains connections between events in textually rooted salvation history. It is "a pattern established by a succession of similar events over time."[31] It differs from allegory since the real meaning of allegory depends on an extratextual hermeneutical grid. Typology, or typological fulfillment, is a specific form of the larger "promise-fulfillment" framework essential for understanding the relationship between the Testaments. This salvation-historical movement from OT to NT permeates the NT and ultimately validates its specific, extensive use of the OT. Both the OT and NT unfold God's character, purpose, and plan, but God's salvation through Christ "fulfills" OT history, law, and prophecy.[32]

2. The OT functions prophetically in the sense that the NT authors view the OT as pointing towards the future.[33] But this does not mean that the

---

29. Baker, *Two Testaments*, 180.
30. Osborne, "Type; Typology," 930.
31. Beale and Carson, "Introduction," xxv.

32. This is why some argue that typology must include heightening or escalation (e.g., Goppelt, *Typos*, 199, 202), although others reject this as a necessary characteristic of a type. Cf. Baker, *Two Testaments*, 183: "The essence of a type is that it is exemplary, and it is also possible for something more advanced to be typical of something less advanced. Moreover it is possible for one thing to be a type of its opposite."

33. Beale and Carson ("Introduction," xxv) ask an important question regarding typological fulfillment: "Are the NT writers coming to their conclusion that this fulfillment has taken place to fulfill antecedent events simply out of their confidence in the

OT intends the NT's typological correspondence in the sense that the OT authors or the participants in the OT situation were always aware of the typological significance. While the OT authors and participants in these typological situations may have dimly perceived anticipatory elements, God ordered typological situations to function prophetically. Typology has a prospective element, but sometimes people can recognize it only retrospectively.[34] The Israelites and OT authors certainly recognized the symbolic value of some of their history (e.g., the Exodus) and institutions (e.g., their cultus), but they did not recognize all of the OT types that God designed. Paul simultaneously recognizes both continuity and discontinuity, and he feels no tension between them "because they genuinely lock together":

> *First*, there is no evidence that Paul himself was aware of any tension between these two stances; and *second*, within the patterns of promise and fulfillment, regularly connected with continuity, various kinds of discontinuity emerged, while within the patterns of mystery and fulfillment, regularly connected with discontinuity, various kinds of continuity emerged in that the revelation of the mystery was on occasion tied to (revelatory) exegesis of Scripture. These two matters dovetail. The reason Paul does not sense any tension between the two stances is because they genuinely lock together. For instance, much of the Old Testament's promise is expressed (in Paul's understanding) in one kind or another of typology, and fulfilled in the antitype. Sometimes there is a considerable conceptual gap between the type and the antitype . . . Paul certainly does not insist that when the stipulations regarding the Passover lamb were first written down, both writer and readers understood that they were pointing to the ultimate "lamb," the Messiah himself. So it would be fair to say that such notions were still hidden—hidden in plain view, so to speak, because genuinely there in the text (once one perceives the trajectory of the typology), but not yet revealed. And that, perhaps, is why a "mystery" *must* be *revealed*, but also why it *may* be revealed *through the prophetic writings*. In other words, Paul feels no tension between these two stances because, as he understands them, there isn't any. And this is why the gospel itself, not

---

sovereign God's ordering of all things, such that he has established patterns that, rightly read, anticipate a recurrence of God's actions? Or are they claiming, in some instances, that the OT texts themselves point forward in some way to the future?" The answer is the latter. See Carson, "Mystery," 405–6.

34. Davidson, *Typology*. Contra Kaiser, "Single Meaning," 60–72; Baker, *Two Testaments*, 181, 183.

to say some of its chief elements, can be simultaneously seen as something that has been (typologically) predicted and now fulfilled, and as something that has been hidden and has now been revealed. What starts off as almost intolerable paradox emerges as a coherent and interlocking web.[35]

3. Types and antitypes have degrees of similarities and dissimilarities. "The types to which Paul appeals are of various kinds, measured by the degree of likeness or unlikeness that subsists between type and antitype."[36]

4. Although the NT need not specifically designate an OT situation as a type for it to be a type, (1) we would not know of some types if the NT did not reveal them to us, and (2) any types we may suggest lack Scripture's authority.[37] Examples of typology include the use of Psalm 22 in the Gospels;[38] Paul's historical reading of the Abrahamic promise and the Mosaic Law in Galatians 3 and Romans 4; the use of Psalm 95 in Heb 4:1–13; and Melchizedek in Hebrew 7.

2. ELIMINATING AND EVALUATING HERMENEUTICAL WARRANTS FOR PAUL'S USE OF THE OT IN ROM 11:34–35

Not all of the ten hermeneutical warrants listed above can feasibly explain how Paul uses the OT in Rom 11:34–35. Silva explains,

> We may have as many as fifteen or even twenty distinct approaches to the difficulties raised by the New Testament writers' use of the Old Testament, though only a couple of them may be applicable at any one time. It is clear, therefore, that we should avoid quick solutions and simplistic answers.[39]

---

35. Carson, "Mystery," 426–27.

36. Ibid., 407; see 407–10.

37. Note, however, Hebrews 9:5b: "Of these things we cannot now speak in detail." This presupposes that (1) the author of Hebrews could have explained the typological significance of the temple in much more detail and (2) Christians could and should be making such typological connections. So, although interpretations not explicitly grounded in Scripture have less warrant, there are other typological connections that readers should understand.

38. Goppelt, *Typos*, 103; Moo, *Old Testament*, 289–300.

39. Silva, "NT Use of the OT," 155.

2.1. Eliminating Six Nonviable Hermeneutical Warrants

We may quickly eliminate the first six of the ten hermeneutical warrants above as possible explanations for Paul's use of the OT in Rom 11:34–35.

1. *Borrowed Language.* Paul is not merely borrowing the language of Isa 40:13 and Job 41:3a to express something unrelated to their original contexts. He uses those OT verses in a way consistent with their original contexts.

2. *Alternative Points of View.* Paul is not quoting Isa 40:13 and Job 41:3a merely to represent the opinion of his listeners or opponents. He agrees with what he quotes.

3. *Jewish Exegetical Methods.* Paul is not applying Isa 40:13 and Job 41:3a to his own situation by using the same midrashic or pesher appropriation techniques as his non-Christian Jewish contemporaries in any noteworthy way.[40]

4. *Sensus Plenior.* Paul is not appealing to senses of Isa 40:13 and Job 41:3a that are fuller than what their human authors consciously intended but what God did intend when the OT authors wrote those passages.

5. *Generic OT Expression.* Paul is not using an OT expression to refer generically to a richly theological OT theme without having only one specific OT text in mind. He quotes specific texts.

6. *Fulfillment of a Specific Prediction.* Paul is not quoting Isa 40:13 and Job 41:3a to claim that a NT person or event specifically fulfills what their OT authors predicted. Neither Isa 40:13 nor Job 41:3a predict anything, and Paul is not claiming a one-to-one prediction and fulfillment.

2.2. Evaluating Four Viable Hermeneutical Warrants

Four hermeneutical warrants remain as viable possibilities: the larger OT context, application, the canonical approach, and typology. These are not mutually exclusive warrants, but the challenge is to articulate as precisely as possible the nature of the connection between the OT passages that Paul quotes and his use of them in Rom 11:34–35.

---

40. See §1.3 above for an explanation of the distinction between appropriation techniques and hermeneutical axioms.

2.2.1. The Larger Contexts of Isa 40:13 and Job 41:3a

Paul implicitly includes the larger OT contexts of Isa 40:13 and Job 41:3a when he quotes just those small portions. He applies both Isa 40:13 and Job 41:3a in accordance with their contexts, and those contexts include far more than just the words he cites. As the rest of §2 demonstrates, Paul evokes at least the immediate contexts of Isa 40:12-31 and Job 38:1—42:6.[41] Those larger contexts exalt the sheer grandeur of God, and Paul is doing the same in Rom 11:33-36. After three exclamations about the infinite nature of God's attributes and ways (Rom 11:33), Paul cites these two OT passages to support his exclamations as well as to use the OT to convey his thoughts in the context of Rom 11. He is not merely borrowing the language of those two OT passages.

2.2.2. Application

Paul applies Isa 40:13 and Job 41:3a to a new situation that the OT authors did not specifically, consciously intend, but the general meaning that the OT authors intended legitimately includes Paul's application. There is no question that Paul is applying the OT in this way in Rom 11:34-35 (see §2.2.3 below). The question is whether that is all Paul is doing. Does Rom 11:34-35 typologically fulfill Isa 40:13 and Job 41:3a in some way? If not, then Paul's hermeneutical warrant lies at the level of application, but if so, then Paul's hermeneutical warrant is more complex.

2.2.3. Canonical Approach

Paul may be approaching Isa 40:13 and Job 41:3a by focusing on the ultimate canonical context of those OT texts as the basis on which to find a "fuller" sense in those texts beyond what its human author consciously intend. This appeal, then, is not just to the larger OT context but to the ultimate literary context of those two OT texts: the whole canon.

If interpreters avoid the anachronistic error of insufficiently rooting systematic theology in biblical theology (see the last paragraph of §1.9 above), they may legitimately interpret any specific biblical text in light of the canon because the canon's single divine author guarantees its unity. Paul seems to be using a canonical approach in Rom 11:34-35 because his appeal not only makes perfect sense in a straightforward analogical sense; it also appears to have a deeper typological sense when one accounts for the larger OT contexts of Isa 40:13 and Job 41:3a. Since

---

41. Cf. Dunn, *Romans 9–16*, 700, 703.

typology is a core component of the canonical approach, we will unpack this under typology immediately below.

2.2.4. Typology

Paul's use of the OT in Rom 11:34–35 may appear to be relatively uncontroversial, especially in comparison with other passages in near proximity and elsewhere that require much more nuanced explanations, some of which involve typology to account for changed referents.[42] But is Paul's use of the OT in Rom 11:34–35 as straightforward as it may initially seem? We make the case below that Paul's hermeneutical warrant is typology.

Types and antitypes have degrees of similarities and dissimilarities. If the relationship between the OT and Rom 11:34–35 is typological, then those two OT passages lie on an extreme of that spectrum that is least prospective and primarily retrospective. In Rom 11:34–35, Paul appeals to the OT to highlight God's character as he has revealed himself in history. God's character as he revealed it in those OT passages is especially relevant to conclude Rom 9–11, and God's character as he revealed it in history to Job in Job 41:3a and to Israel in Isa 40:13 connects with his revelation to the Christians Paul addresses in Rom 9–11. The question is whether we should label those connections as typology. To answer that question, it would be prudent to begin by analyzing Isa 40:13 and Job 41:3a separately.

A Typological Connection between Isa 40:13 and Rom 11:34—Isaiah 40:13 is an ideal passage to quote in order to evoke God's unrivaled wisdom and incomparable greatness as a prelude to a grand doxology. But that does not go far enough because Paul imports more than that into Rom 11:34. Both passages exalt God's limitless knowledge in his dealings with Israel, and Paul's theological argument regarding God's activities in salvation history draws on Isaiah's theological argument regarding God's activities in salvation history.[43]

Paul uses Isaiah here consistent with his previous uses in Rom 9–11:

---

42. E.g., Deut 30:12–14 in Rom 10:6–8; Ps 19:4 in Rom 10:18; Isa 65:1–2 in Rom 10:20–21; the catena of OT passages in Rom 3:10–18; Hos 11:1 in Matt 2:15; Isa 53:4 in Matt 8:16–17. See Moo, *Epistle*, 650–57, 666–67, 669–70, 197–210; Carson, "Matthew," 118–20.

43. Cf. Viard, *Romains*, 254; Dunn, *Romans 9–16*, 703; Shum, *Paul's Use*, 246; Wright, "Romans," 696.

Paul's appropriation of Isaiah 40:13 is of a piece with his use of other Isaianic texts in Romans to speak about contemporary Israel, particularly Isaiah 29:16/45:9 (Rom 9:20), Isaiah 28:16/8:14 (Rom 9:33), and Isaiah 40:21/28 (Rom 10:18, 19). In each case, the wider context in Isaiah portrays Israel challenging God's wisdom and doubting God's power and faithfulness to save them. Paul appears to have found in these Isaianic oracles an analogue to the resistance his message now faces from his contemporaries, as they question how Paul's gospel could be the announcement of their long-awaited deliverance.[44]

Bock illustrates how typological patterns can have multiple referents by explaining Isaiah 40:

> When Isaiah spoke of a new Exodus in Isaiah 40, he referred to the redemption of the nation out of exile, and yet his language also applies to what ultimate redemption will be like.[45]

> But what happens when a text discusses a typological pattern as opposed to one event? The sense becomes key in the text, and the referents multiply as each context is addressed. In Isaiah 40:1–11, exile [and deliverance from exile] can refer both to the short-term situation (Israel's rescue through Cyrus) and to the long-term one (complete salvation) at one time. This is a simple example of the language-referent process. Salvation in the short-term setting merely refers to "deliverance from exile"; but in the long-term view of the NT the referent is "salvation in Christ" or "eternal life." Such a distinction reflects biblical typology and the progress of revelation, where the event escalates in its later fulfillment.
>
> This type of pattern fulfillment may mean that though the sense of a term is maintained at one level in all the fulfillments, the referent is heightened to a new level of realization in the later fulfillment because of the new context's escalation of scope.[46]

In Isa 40, God comforts Israel, anticipating their Babylonian captivity and future restoration, and in Rom 11, Paul's discussion of election provides a ground for comforting Israel by explaining their current condition and future restoration. In neither situation does anyone give God

---

44. Wagner, *Heralds*, 304. See also Wagner's summarizing analysis of Paul's "juxtaposition of texts" in Rom 9–11 and 15 (349–51).

45. Bock, "Scripture," 262.

46. Bock, "Single Meaning," 113–14.

advice,[47] and the sequence of Isa 40 and Rom 11 are parallel (with the exception that in Isa 40 Israel receives revelation from God about God's stripping them of blessing in the near future):

1. Israel has been experiencing God's blessing.
2. God strips them of that blessing to some degree in a way that seems unfair to them and makes restoration seem impossible.
3. They question God's righteousness and assert their own.
4. They receive revelation from God that is difficult to accept and does not provide all the answers they want. This revelation includes the prominent role of Gentiles with reference to Israelites. They are tempted to doubt God's wisdom.
5. They must repent of their flawed view of God and themselves, and they must trust God.
6. They will experience God's restored blessing to an even greater degree and in an unexpected way.
7. This God-designed plan in salvation history demonstrates God's wisdom, kindness, and sovereignty.

Compare Schreiner's explanation:

> The thematic connection to Rom. 9–11 should not be missed. Just as Yahweh promised to save Israel when such deliverance seemed impossible and they had virtually given up, so too he has planned history in such a way that he fulfills the covenantal promises made in Isaiah in an unexpected way. He has extended salvation to uncircumcised Gentiles and at the end of history will again fold in unbelieving Jews. Does the inclusion of Israel again seem incredible? It is no more incredible than the pledge to rescue Israel from the dominion of Babylon. God effects salvation for the weak so that the glory of his strength is impressed upon all. Captive Israel in Babylon did not perceive the mind of the Lord, that it was his plan to rescue them from their plight; similarly no human being could anticipate the wisdom of God's plan by which he has arranged history to bring about the salvation of both Jews and Gentiles in a most improbable way.[48]

---

47. Bultema, *Isaiah*, 381.
48. Schreiner, *Romans*, 635.

"Just as formerly the hope of the return from exile and the rebirth of the people remained, so Paul awaits the redemption of the nation."⁴⁹ The connection between Isa 40:13 and Rom 11:34 is likely typological because the events of Rom 11 fulfill the events of Isa 40 by repeating the OT situation at a deeper, climactic level in salvation history. This typology is primarily retrospective rather than prospective.⁵⁰

A Typological Connection between Job 41:3a and Rom 11:35—If the relationship between Job 41:3a and Rom 11: 35 is typological, then it is also primarily retrospective rather than prospective. At first glance it seems like Paul's hermeneutical warrant for using Job 41:3a in Rom 11:35 is a straightforward application.

The argument for application goes something like this: Paul uses Job 41:3a as part of his salvation-historical argument in Rom 9–11, but his use of Job 41:3a itself is not salvation-historical because there is not a sense in which what Paul explains in Rom 9–11 *fulfills* Job 41:3a. Rather, Paul's use of Job 41:3a is analogical. Paul applies the principle of Job 41:3a to a new situation that the author of Job did not specifically, consciously intend, but the general meaning that the OT author intended legitimately includes Paul's application.

But is this exclusively an instance of application? Is the connection deeper than that? Is there a sense in which Rom 11:35 and its context *fulfills* Job 41:3a and its context? We make the case below that the warrant for Job 41:3a in Rom 11:35 is typological and more than just an analogical application. Like Isa 40 and Rom 11, the sequences of Job and Rom 11 are parallel:

1. Both Job and Israel have been experiencing God's blessing.
2. God strips them of that blessing to some degree in a way that seems unfair to them and makes restoration seem impossible.
3. They question God's righteousness and assert their own.
4. They receive revelation from God that is difficult to accept and does not provide all the answers they want. They are tempted to doubt God's wisdom. Further, in Job 38–41, God rebukes Job for questioning his justice with reference to Job's suffering, and in

---

49. Seifrid, "Romans," 671.

50. Cf. §1.10 above: "Typology has a prospective element, but sometimes people can recognize it only retrospectively."

Rom 9:6–29, God similarly rebukes Israelites (and Gentiles) for questioning his justice with reference to election.

5. They must repent of their flawed view of God and themselves, and they must trust God.

6. Job experiences and Israel will experience God's restored blessing to an even greater degree and in an unexpected way.

7. This God-designed plan in salvation history demonstrates God's wisdom, kindness, and sovereignty. In both cases "the kindness and the severity of God" (Rom 11:22) are abundantly evident.

Job 41:3a exalts God's sovereign freedom as no human's debtor, and Paul exults in that truth in Rom 11:35. Again, compare Schreiner's explanation:

> Once again the larger OT context of the citation is significant. One of Job's major complaints during his suffering was that God was unjust. This led Job to doubt God's wisdom. In Job 38–41 God reveals himself to Job and rebukes him for questioning God's justice and mode of operation in the world. Job is too limited and finite to superintend the world and all that is in it. God reveals to Job through his speech that he indeed has the capacity to superintend the world he has established. Job responds to God's speech (Job 42:3) by admitting that he has transgressed beyond his sphere, that his knowledge is too limited, and that no one can thwart God's plan (42:2). Just as Job doubted God's wisdom and ability in his suffering, so too the Roman Christians might be inclined to question God's wisdom in terms of his saving plan for world history. Job's vision of God's greatness was too circumscribed. God accomplished his plan with respect to Job in wisdom and justice, and so too his plan to save some Jews and Gentiles is wise and just. He is debtor to no one's wisdom, strength, or goodness, and he has accomplished his purposes by his own initiative.[51]

The book of Job and Rom 9–11 are similar in genre: both are theodicies with the motif of praise. Wagner notes "a number of intriguing resemblances between Romans 9:19–20 and several passages in Job where the suffering protagonist questions God's justice."[52] Indeed,

---

51. Schreiner, *Romans*, 635. Cf. Parsons, "Job 38:1—42:6," 256; Herzer, "Jakobus," 346–49.

52. Wagner, *Heralds*, 56–57, 302n246.

"particularly prominent" in Rom 11:33–36, notes Dunn, "are the links with Job."[53] Hartley calls "the essential nature" of Job 38–41 "a hymn of praise,"[54] which aptly labels Rom 11:33–36. Job 38–41 is disputation in which the motif of praise dominates.[55] The connection between Job 41:3a and Rom 11:35 is typological because the events of Rom 11 fulfill the events of Job by repeating the OT situation at a deeper, climactic level in salvation history.

A Typological Connection between Isa 40:13, Job 41:3, and Rom 11:34–35—Paul quotes Isa 40:13 and Job 41:3a in Rom 11:34–35 as the second of three strophes designed to exalt God's inscrutable ways with reference to his salvation-historical plan. After a cursory look into the use of the OT in Rom 11:34–35, some may concede too much by concluding that these two OT texts in their contexts do not address that soteriological aspect of God's inscrutable ways. (At least that was my initial impression.) But that concession wrongly conceals the glory of how Paul uses two ideal passages to parallel his vindication of God in Rom 9–11.

Understanding the role of the OT in Rom 9–11 and Paul's driving purpose in Rom 9–11 is crucial for understanding the connection between any OT passage that Paul quotes in this section of his letter. "Paul's references to the OT in these chapters do not simply illustrate points established independently; the OT itself often sets the agenda, establishes the themes, and moves the argument along."[56] Paul's doxological conclusion to Rom 9–11 is unquestionably grounded in the OT:

> Referring to H. Hübner, Silva speaks of over 100 references to the Old Testament in Roman 9–11 alone.[57] There is no reason to suppose that Paul is unaware of the historical mediation of these writings since, as seen above, he often lists various authors' names and can distinguish between different epochs and incidents in the history of Israel. This suggests that his appropriation of Old Testament theological and ethical affirmations may be viewed as implicit acknowledgment of the unfolding of God's saving plan in history . . . Every one of Romans' five benedictions

---

53. Dunn, *Romans 9–16*, 698; see also 703.

54. Hartley, *Job*, 488.

55. Westermann, *Hiob*, 108–24 (see also 30, 40–51, 84–92); Perdue, *Wisdom in Revolt*, 76–80, 201–2, 218.

56. Moo, *Epistle*, 550n9.

57. Silva, "OT in Paul," 631.

> [Rom 1:25; 9:5; 11:36; 15:33; 16:27], ascriptions of praise and glory to God, hinge on Old Testament affirmations preceding the benedictions in the discourse . . . Absent the Scriptures and Paul's conviction that they convey some real semblance of what God has done and willed, there would be no ground for such doxological summations.[58]

Moo explains how salvation history is integrally related to the reason Paul writes Rom 9–11:

> The gospel is "the gospel of God" (1:1), and the God of whom Paul speaks is none other than the God who has spoken and acted in Israel's history. Paul must, then, demonstrate that the God who chose and made promises to Israel is the same God who has opened the doors of salvation "to all who believe." To do so, Paul must prove that God has done nothing in the gospel that is inconsistent with his word of promise to Israel; that the gospel he preaches is not the negation but the affirmation of God's plan revealed in the OT (see, e.g., 1:2; 3:21). It is for this reason that Paul quotes the OT so often in Rom. 9–11 (almost a third of all Paul's quotations are found in these chapters): he is seeking to demonstrate "the congruity between God's word in Scripture and God's word in Paul's gospel." At the same time, then, Paul is demonstrating that God is consistent, faithfully fulfilling all his promises—whether they are found in the OT or the NT (cf. 9:6a) . . .
>
> Tied though these chapters are to the immediate needs and problems of both Paul and the Roman Christians, we should not miss the larger and enduring theological issue that they address. Israel's unbelief of the gospel is a matter of significance not only to the Roman Christians, or to first-century Christians generally, but to all Christians. For it raises the question of the continuity of salvation history: Does the gospel presented in the NT genuinely "fulfill" the OT and stand, thus, as its natural completion? Or is the gospel a betrayal of the OT, with no claim therefore to come from the same God who elected and made promises to Israel? We need to hear Paul's careful and balanced answer to these questions. He teaches that the gospel is the natural continuation of OT salvation history—against an incipient "Marcionism" that would sever the gospel from the OT and Judaism. But at the same time, he teaches that the gospel is also the fulfillment of salvation

---

58. Yarbrough, "Paul," 332–33.

history—against the Judaizing tendency to view the gospel in terms of the torah.[59]

Given this role of the OT in Rom 9–11 and Paul's driving purpose in Rom 9–11,[60] it becomes even more likely that Paul's use of the OT in Rom 11:34–35 is typological. The contexts of Isa 40:13, Job 41:3a, and Rom 11:34–35 all share the following sequence:

1. Both Job and Israel have been experiencing God's blessing.

2. God strips them of that blessing to some degree in a way that seems unfair to them and makes restoration seem impossible.

3. They question God's righteousness and assert their own.

4. They receive revelation from God that is difficult to accept and does not provide all the answers they want. They are tempted to doubt God's wisdom.

5. They must repent of their flawed view of God and themselves, and they must trust God.

6. Job experiences and Israel will experience God's restored blessing to an even greater degree and in an unexpected way.

7. This God-designed plan in salvation history demonstrates God's wisdom, kindness, and sovereignty.

The stages that God has designed in salvation history are a "mystery" that evokes praise (cf. Rom 11:25–36).[61] All three texts exalt God's rich generosity[62] and his infinite greatness in contrast with human finitude.[63] Isaiah 40:12–31 and Job 38–41 are polemic and doxological,[64] making them a perfect fit for the polemic in Rom 9–11 that climaxes with doxology.

A further connection between all three passages is wisdom. Isaiah 40:13, Job 41:3a, and Rom 11:34–35 are wisdom literature in some

---

59. Moo, *Epistle*, 550–51, 553. Contra Aageson, who argues that typology plays only limited roles in Paul's letters in general and Rom 9–11 in particular ("Paul's Use," 151–56, 211–80; "Typology," 51–72).

60. Cf. Smith, "Pauline," 285–86; Silva, "OT in Paul," 638.

61. Cf. Cullmann, *Christ and Time*, 77–78, 138.

62. Bonnard, "Trésors," 17.

63. Schreiner, *Romans*, 635–37.

64. Brueggemann, *Isaiah*, 22–28.

sense.⁶⁵ Romans 11:34–35 fulfills the OT because Jesus, who is preeminent in God's salvation-historical plan, embodies wisdom.⁶⁶ He alone understands and rightly interprets God's mind:

> The questions in these verses are obviously rhetorical, expecting the answer "no one." The first two stress that no human being can understand what God is doing in the world. But, as the wisdom tradition from which these questions are drawn teaches, what no human being can understand, "wisdom" can. And since Paul sees Christ as the embodiment of wisdom, we are probably justified in adding to our expected answer "no one" a qualification: "no one, except Jesus Christ, who has revealed to us in his own person the plan of God for salvation history."⁶⁷

2.3. Comparing Isa 40:13 and Job 41:3a

Why does Paul quote Isa 40:13 and Job 41:3a *together*?⁶⁸ Paul quotes the verses back-to-back, suggesting that he is not choosing two random, unrelated texts to serve his purpose in Rom 11:33–36. Paul quotes the two verses because they are remarkably similar in genre and content: they both are wisdom literature that uses God-exalting, human-diminishing disputation. Isaiah's questions in 40:12–31 are not unlike God's questions to Job in Job 38–41. For example, Clifford notes,

> Isaiah 40:12–31, a series of questions about who has created and now maintains the world, has its nearest parallel in Job 38–41. In Job, the questions are designed to sweep Job from his self-confidence and make him bow before the divine freedom and power.

---

65. On wisdom literature, see §1.2 in ch. 3. See also the following works, some of which specifically address Job, Isaiah, and/or Rom 9–11: Whedbee, *Isaiah*; Emerton, "Wisdom," 214–37; Morgan, *Wisdom*, esp. 114–19; Kidner, *Wisdom*; Crenshaw, "Wisdom," 369–407; idem, *OT Wisdom*; Johnson, *Function*, 164–74; Murphy, *Tree*; Waltke, *Proverbs*, 50–55; Perdue, *Wisdom Literature*; Wilson, "Wisdom," 145–67.

66. Paul connects wisdom and salvation history elsewhere (e.g., 1 Cor 1:17–2:16; Col 2:2–3).

67. Moo, *Epistle*, 743. Cf. Wilckens, "σοφία," 518–22; Lupieri, *Il cielo*, 84–85; Hanson, *NT Interpretation*, 90–91; idem, *Living*, 48; Schnabel, *Law*, 249–51, 261; Pépin, "Conseiller," 59–64.

68. Paul may be quoting two passages in accord with the Mosaic dictum (and Rabbinic hermeneutical rule) that "every charge may be established by the evidence of two or three witnesses" (Matt 18:16; cf. Num 35:30; Deut 19:15; John 8:17; 2 Cor 13:1; 1 Tim. 5:19; Heb. 10:28). But the question raised above is why Paul quotes *these two passages* together.

Second Isaiah has a number of affinities with Job; 40:12–31 is especially Joban.[69]

TABLE 8: Comparing Job 38:4–7 and Isa 40:12–14

Job 38:4–7	Isa 40:12–14
[4] Where were you when I laid the foundation of the earth? Tell me, if you have understanding. [5] Who determined its measurements— surely you know! Or who stretched the line upon it? [6] On what were its bases sunk, or who laid its cornerstone, [7] when the morning stars sang together and all the sons of God shouted for joy?	[12] Who has measured the waters in the hollow of his hand and marked off the heavens with a span, enclosed the dust of the earth in a measure and weighed the mountains in scales and the hills in a balance? [13] Who has measured the Spirit of the LORD, or what man shows him his counsel? [14] Whom did he consult, and who made him understand? Who taught him the path of justice, and taught him knowledge, and showed him the way of understanding?

God's addresses in both Isa 40:12–31 and Job 38–41 are strikingly strong and prolonged. After reading Isa 40:12–31, some readers might think, "Isn't God's answer to Israel overkill in response to the simple question 'Is God able to deliver Israel from the Babylonians?'" After reading Job 38–41, some readers might think, "Isn't God's answer to Job overkill in response to Job's simple 'Why?' questions?" Both of these passages are bold, dramatic climaxes that exalt God and diminish humans in the face of seemingly inexplicable circumstances. Table 8 shows one example of how similar the passages are by juxtaposing Job 38:4–7 and Isa 40:12–14; in both passages God highlights his sovereignty and familiarity with his universe in a way that makes humans feel very small and insignificant.

---

69. Clifford, "Isaiah," 497. Cf. idem, *Fair Spoken*, 79–80; McKenzie, *Second Isaiah*, 23; Whybray, *Heavenly Counsellor*, 20–21; Blenkinsopp, *Isaiah*, 190–91; Harrisville, *Romans*, 187–88; Hartley, *Job*, 12–15, 42; Oswalt, *Isaiah*, 59; Conrad, *Isaiah*, 65; Youngblood, *Isaiah*, 114; Kidner, "Isaiah," 656; Hanson, *Isaiah*, 27; Koole, *Isaiah*, 82, 87, 88, 91, 93; Brueggemann, *Isaiah*, 23–24; Briley, *Isaiah*, 2:119–20; Grogan, "Isaiah," 725; Friesen, *Isaiah*, 237; Smith, *Isaiah 40–66*, 106, 111n95.

2.4. Conclusion

The connection of Rom 11:34-35 to Isa 40:13 and Job 41:3a is typological. In Rom 11:34-35, Paul uses Isa 40:13 and Job 41:3a typologically to show that the NT event he describes in Rom 9-11 "fulfills" the events in Isa 40:13 and Job 41:3a by repeating the OT situations at a deeper, climactic level in salvation history. Further, Paul's use of the OT in Rom 11:34-35 illustrates a methodology that believers should use today, namely, quoting Scripture to confirm what God is doing and will do as expressed in its unfolding of his salvation-historical plan.[70]

3. COMPARING PAUL'S USE OF THE OT IN ROM 11:34-35 WITH ROM 9-11 AND OTHER NT DOXOLOGIES

How does Paul's use of the OT in Romans compare to his use of the OT in Rom 9-11 and the use of the OT in other NT doxologies?

3.1. Paul's Use of the OT in Rom 9-11

Paul uses the OT in Rom 11:34-35 consistently with the rest of chapters 9-11. He quotes the OT using multiple hermeneutical warrants including typology to make, prove, or support his point. Romans 9-11 vindicates God's righteousness by demonstrating the continuity and complexity of his salvation-historical plan, starting with God's promises in the OT and culminating with a heightened eschatological fulfillment in the NT. The NT does not abrogate God's OT promises, and Paul demonstrates this by repeatedly quoting the OT. Table 9 summarizes this by organizing all of Paul's OT quotations in Rom 9-11;[71] the table's third column, which provides succinct statements at the risk of oversimplification, is consistent with Moo's exegesis.[72]

---

70. Cf. how the early church used Neh 9:6 and Ps 146:6 (cf. Exod 20:11; 2 Chr 2:12; Pss 102:25; 124:8; 134:3) in their prayer in Acts 4:24.

71. It does not address allusions or what Richard B. Hays calls echoes. E.g., see Hays (*Echoes*, 68-70) on echoes in Rom 11:1-2.

72. Moo, *Epistle*, 574-744; idem, "Israel," 196-205.

TABLE 9: OT Quotations in Rom 9–11

Rom	OT quoted	Paul's Point
9:7	Gen 21:12	Ethnic and spiritual Israel are distinct.
9:9	Gen 18:10, 14	God caused Isaac's birth to fulfill his promise to Abraham.
9:12	Gen 25:23	God chose Jacob over Esau after their conception but before their birth.
9:13	Mal 1:2–3	God chose Jacob and rejected Esau.
9:15	Exod 33:19	God can have mercy on whomever he wants.
9:17	Exod 9:16	God can harden whomever he wants to accomplish his purposes.
9:25	Hos 2:23	God will include Gentiles as his beloved people.
9:26	Hos 1:10	God will include Gentiles as his children.
9:27–28	Isa 10:22–23	God will judge ethnic Israel and save only a remnant.
9:29	Isa 1:9	God will preserve ethnic Israel's remnant by leaving "a seed" (σπέρμα).
9:33	Isa 28:16; 8:14	Ethnic Israel will stumble over the Messiah, failing to believe in him.
10:5	Lev 18:5	Righteousness by practicing the law is impossible.
10:6–8	Deut 30:12–14	Righteousness by faith is accessible.
10:11	Isa 28:16	Faith is necessary for deliverance from judgment (i.e., salvation). Righteousness by faith is universally accessible for "whoever believes in" Jesus—whether ethnic Israel or Gentiles.
10:13	Joel 2:32	Righteousness by faith is universally accessible for "whoever will call on the name of the Lord"—whether ethnic Israel or Gentiles.
10:15	Isa 52:7	Ethnic Israel's rejection of Jesus is inexcusable because God fulfilled the first and second conditions for calling on Jesus: God sent preachers, and the preachers preached.

Rom	OT quoted	Paul's Point
10:16	Isa 53:1	Ethnic Israel's rejection of Jesus is inexcusable because they are responsible for not fulfilling the fourth condition for calling on Jesus: they must believe in Christ.
10:18	Ps 19:4	Ethnic Israel's rejection of Jesus is inexcusable because God fulfilled the third condition for calling on Jesus: they have heard the preaching.
10:19	Deut 32:21	Ethnic Israel not only heard—they should have understood that God would (1) use the Gentiles to provoke them to jealousy and (2) include the Gentiles after reaching out to Israel despite their disobedience.
10:20–21	Isa 65:1–2	
11:2	1 Sam 12:22; Ps 94:14	God has not rejected ethnic Israel (whom he foreknew).
11:3–4	1 Kgs 19:10, 14, 18	Though ethnic Israel's condition may seem hopeless, the faithful God is preserving and will preserve a remnant.
11:8–10	Deut 29:4; Isa 29:10; Ps 69:22–23	Ethnic Israel's rejection is partial—not total—because there is a remnant, the elect. God hardened the rest.
11:26–27	Isa 59:20–21; 27:9	πᾶς Ἰσραὴλ σωθήσεται: In the end times, God will save a large number of ethnic Israelites alive at that time, consummating his covenant with them.
11:34	Isa 40:13	God is incomprehensible and without counselors, so finite humans cannot understand his infinite ways or counsel him.
11:35	Job 41:3a (Eng 41:11a)	God is without creditors, so finite humans cannot place God in their debt.

Paul's use of the OT in Rom 9–11 parallels to some degree his use of the OT in Romans 4 as well as Galatians 3–4. Each passage is dense with OT quotations and allusions, and each deals with the Jew-Gentile issue in a salvation-historical framework. Paul heavily quotes the OT to refute gainsayers and reinforce his apostolic authority with the authority of OT Scripture.[73]

---

73. James W. Aageson, "Written Also for Our Sake: Paul's Use of Scripture in the Four Major Epistles, with a Study of 1 Corinthians 10," in *Hearing the Old Testament in the New Testament*, edited by Stanley E. Porter, 153–54.

3.2. The Use of the OT in NT Doxologies

Paul's use of the OT in Rom 11:34-35 is unique in that it leads directly to the doxology in 11:36. Of the many doxologies in the NT,[74] none is immediately preceded by OT quotations as in Rom 11:33-36. For example, Gal 1:4 praises Christ for his salvific work; Eph 3:20 praises God for his unlimited power; Phil 4:19 assures the generous Philippians that God will supply their every need; 1 Tim 1:12-16 highlights Christ's mercy in saving Paul; 2 Tim 4:15-18a underscores the Lord's physical and spiritual preservation of Paul; and Jude 24 accentuates God's preservation of believers. The OT quotations in Rom 11:34-35 flow directly into the concluding doxology, and Paul does this in a letter (Romans) and section (chs. 9-11) in which he quotes the OT most frequently.

On the other hand, while OT quotations may not *immediately* precede other doxologies, OT quotations and allusions do often precede them in context. Yarbrough recalls,

> Every one of Romans' five benedictions [Rom 1:25; 9:5; 11:36; 15:33; 16:27], ascriptions of praise and glory to God, hinge on Old Testament affirmations preceding the benedictions in the discourse... Absent the Scriptures and Paul's conviction that they convey some real semblance of what God has done and willed, there would be no ground for such doxological summations.[75]

There is one other qualification: the use of the OT in doxologies in Revelation.[76] Though Revelation never directly and completely quotes the OT, it is the most OT-saturated book in the NT,[77] and several of the doxologies spring from or are based on OT passages.[78]

---

74. E.g., Rom 1:25; 9:5; 16:27; Gal 1:5; Eph 3:21; Phil 4:20; 1 Tim 1:17; 2 Tim 4:18; 1 Pet 4:11; Jude 24-25.

75. Yarbrough, "Paul," 333; see 332-39 for how Paul connects Gods' glory with salvation history.

76. Doxologies in Revelation include 1:6; 4:8-11; 5:13; 7:12; 15:3-4, 7; 16:7; and 19:1-3. Several of these passages do not follow the three-fold form of Paul's doxologies as delineated by O'Brien ("Benediction," 69): (1) mentioning the person being praised; (2) praising that person; and (3) closing with a temporal expression, usually followed by ἀμήν. For example, the three parts of Rom 11:36 are (1) αὐτῷ, (2) ἡ δόξα, and (3) εἰς τοὺς αἰῶνας, ἀμήν. Cf. Aune, "Hymns," 314-17.

77. Cf. Beale, "Revelation," 318-36; idem, *Revelation*, 76-99; Osborne, *Revelation*, 25-27; Beale and McDonough, "Revelation," 1081-1161.

78. Cf. Rev 1:6 with Exod 19:6; Rev 4:8 with Isa 6:3; Rev 15:4 with Ps 86:9 and Isa 66:23; Rev 19:2a with Ps 19:9; Rev 19:2c with Deut 32:43 and 2 Kgs 9:7; and Rev 19:3 with Isa 34:10.

4. CONCLUSION

Of the many possible hermeneutical warrants explaining why NT authors use the OT the way they do, two apply to Paul's use of the OT in Rom 11:34–35: the larger OT contexts and typology (a core component of the canonical approach). When Paul quotes Isa 40:13 and Job 41:3a, he includes their larger OT contexts, which reveals a remarkable typological connection between the two OT passages and the end of Rom 11. The subjects in all three contexts (Job and Israelites) have been experiencing God's blessing, but God takes that away to some degree in a way that they think is unfair. After questioning God's righteousness while asserting their own, God gives them revelation that they find difficult and unsatisfying. But they must repent of their flawed view of God and themselves and trust God before they experience God's restored blessing to an even greater degree and in an unexpected way. God's salvation-historical plan demonstrates that he is wise, kind, and sovereign.

8

Paul's Theological Use of Isaiah 40:13 and Job 41:3a in Romans 11:34–35

> What comes into our minds when we think about God is the most important thing about us.
>
> –A. W. Tozer[1]

OUR SIXTH AND FINAL step answers the question, "To what theological use does the NT writer put the OT quotation or allusion? In one sense, this question is wrapped up in all the others, but it is worth asking separately as it highlights things that may otherwise be overlooked."[2] Silva rightly cautions, "We need to rid ourselves of the almost universal assumption that whenever a New Testament writer uses the Old Testament, he intends to prove a theological point. It may turn out, of course, that the assumption is correct, but this has to be demonstrated."[3] In the case of Isa 40:13 and Job 41:3a in Rom 11:34–35, there is no question that Paul is making some weighty theological points. Romans 11:34–35 and its immediate context are about God, especially what he is like in contrast to humans. The three rhetorical questions in Rom 11:34–35 communicate three of God's characteristics that correspond inversely to his attributes in Rom 11:33a, and they all correspond to his ways in salvation history:[4]

---

1. Tozer, *Knowledge*, 9.
2. Beale and Carson, "Introduction," xxv.
3. Silva, "NT Use," 157.
4. This chapter, which is not footnoted as heavily as the previous ones, builds on what precedes it. For further exegetical detail, see especially chs. 2–4.

1. God is incomprehensible (11:34a); his knowledge is deep (11:33a).
2. God is without counselors (11:34b); his wisdom is deep (11:33a).
3. God is without creditors (11:35); his riches are deep (11:33a).

The theological implications are simple and profound. They are rooted in God's supreme sovereignty (11:36a), and they culminate in doxology (11:36b).

1. GOD IS INCOMPREHENSIBLE: HIS KNOWLEDGE IS DEEP (ROM 11:34A)

God's ways in salvation history demonstrate that he is incomprehensible in the sense that no one can *fully* understand him.[5] The reason is that his knowledge is deep (Rom 11:33a). At least four theological implications follow:

1.1. Humans Cannot Understand Everything

God's knowledge is infinite, and human knowledge is finite. Humans cannot understand all of God's ways, so they should not be surprised if they cannot exhaustively understand a particular series of God-designed events in salvation history. Trying to track God's ways in salvation history is like trying to track an unseen person by following their footsteps on the beach right into the water where they disappear into the shallowest part of the ocean (cf. Ps 77:19). Those who have discovered God's ways in Rom 9–11 and therefore conclude that they fully understand God's ways would be as foolish as the Vikings discovering a slice of the shoreline of what is now America and therefore concluding that they fully understand North America. "Behold, these are but the outskirts ['outer fringe,' NIV] of his ways" (Job 26:14).[6]

> "These are the mere edges of His ways." The word edges (KJV, "parts") denotes a termination, a boundary line or coastline, an edge or corner. What we can discern of the infinite God from His works in nature and history are the mere coastlines of the continent of the mind and character of God. Imagine landing for the first time on the seventeenth-century American continent.

---

5. On God's incomprehensibility, see Bavinck, *God and Creation*, 27–52; Grudem, *Systematic Theology*, 149–51; Frame, *God*, 199–213; Culver, *Systematic Theology*, 90–91.

6. This repeats verbatim a portion of §3.2 in ch. 2 above.

> You have no idea that the sand onto which you step is the fringe of a continuous landmass over 3,000 miles wide and 9,500 miles long. Imagine formulating views of what this whole continent is like based on what you can see from the bay where you drop anchor. Suppose you forge your way five miles inland, or even fifty miles, to get a better idea of what this new country is like. As tangible and verifiable as what you see is, you are experiencing a minuscule fraction of an unimaginable stretch of vast and varied terrain yet to be explored—massive and multiple mountain ranges, trackless prairies, impenetrable forests, mammoth lakes and mighty rivers with deafening waterfalls, swamps and deserts, flora and fauna yet unknown. How much more there is to know about our magnificently infinite God than what we can see from where we are, only eternity can tell.[7]

1.2. God Is Not Obligated to Explain Anything

God does not owe anyone an explanation for how he orders his universe. And if a human presses him for an answer, God is completely just to reply not with an answer but with a rebuke.

> Dans Job, pour répondre à ceux qui critiquent sa conduite, Dieu se contente d'affirmer qu'il est le créateur et le maître de ce qu'il fait. Il ne doit rien à personne. Paul a pu reprendre ce texte pour montrer aux Juifs que Dieu n'a aucune dette à leur égard et que c'est de lui seul.[8]

> God's answer to Job's question is a counterquestion. Job asks "why." God asks "who." "Who are you" to question God's actions and attributes? "Who am I?"—that is, do you realize just Whom you have been challenging? The juxtaposition between "why" and "who" is echoed by Paul in Romans 9:20. "Shall the thing formed say to him that formed it, '*Why* have you made me like this?' Nay, O man, *who* are you to reply against God? Does not the potter have power [i.e., freedom] over the clay?" God's answer to Job is not an explanation nor a question seeking information. It is a rhetorical question. In reality, it is a declaration.[9]

Further, when humans demand an explanation from God regarding his ways, this presumes that they could understand his ways if he would

---

7. Talbert, *Beyond Suffering*, 146.
8. Viard, *Romains*, 254.
9. Talbert, *Beyond Suffering*, 202 (brackets in original).

simply explain them. But this is the very presumption for which God rebukes Job. Job could not understand the relatively simple natural phenomena he observed, let alone the complex ways of the infinite God with people. This is humbling.[10]

1.3. Christians Must Humbly Believe and Cherish What God Has Revealed

Consequently, Christians must humbly believe and cherish what God has revealed. Moo calls this "theological humility," Harris "humble orthodoxy," and Dever "humble dogmatism."[11] Maintaining this kind of theological humility is no easy task. It is like walking on an extremely narrow path with steep drop-offs on both sides. On the one side, theologians can be pugnacious, arrogantly close-minded, and overly confident about their positions. On the other side, they can be noncommittal, compromisingly ecumenical, and insufficiently confident about their positions, exhibiting an epistemological pseudo-humility.

Harris observes that people often associate orthodoxy with "jerks" who are "argumentative, annoying, arrogant" and divisive "because they've never seen it held humbly."[12] Harris, applying to theology what Timothy Keller says about politics, explains why this is the case and how to solve it:

> Keller's point is that if we make a good thing like right theology ultimate—if being right becomes more important to us than God—then our theology is not really about God anymore; it's about us. It becomes the source of our sense of worth and identity. And if theology becomes about us, then we'll despise and demonize those who oppose us.
>
> Knowledge about God that doesn't translate into exalting him in our words, thoughts, and actions will soon become self-exaltation. And then we'll attack anyone who threatens our tiny Kingdom of Self.
>
> If we stand before the awesome knowledge of God's character and our first thought isn't *I am small and unworthy to know the Creator of the universe*, then we should be concerned. Too many of us catch a glimpse of him and think, *Look at me, taking this all*

---

10. Cf. Boice, *Romans 9–11*, 1420–22; Carson, *How Long*, 153.
11. Moo, *Romans*, 391–92; Harris, *Dug*, 217–31, 241; Dever, "Humble Dogmatism."
12. Harris, *Dug*, 218, 223.

> in. Think of all the poor fools who have never seen this. God, you're certainly lucky to have me beholding you . . .
>
> The solution to arrogant orthodoxy is not less orthodoxy; it's more. If we truly know and embrace orthodoxy, it should humble us. When we know the truth about God—his power, his greatness, his holiness, his mercy—it doesn't leave us boasting; it leaves us amazed. It doesn't lead to a preoccupation with being right but to amazement that we have been rescued.[13]

Moo connects this humble orthodoxy to Rom 11:33–36:

> One of the most common sentiments I express these days is a greater humility about certain theological positions I hold. Like many young people, I felt confident of my positions in the first years of my career. I sometimes propagated views orally or in print that I had not thought through as thoroughly as I should have. While I have not changed many of these views, I am much more inclined now to notice evidence that might not fit my view. Therefore, I feel much more keenly the need to nuance what I teach by calling attention to this evidence and by admitting that my own view may not be correct. Increasing age should certainly not turn us into theological milquetoasts—uncertain about what we believe and swayed by the latest wind of doctrine. And I am as passionately committed to the essence of the Christian faith as I have ever been. But I would describe my current approach in theological study and teaching as "humble."
>
> What does all this have to do with Rom 11:33–36? Just this: Paul's reminder that God's thoughts are far beyond anything we could ever approximate and his plan more intricate and marvelous than we could even imagine certainly calls on each of us to exercise great humility in seeking to understand God and his Word. On this side of glory, all our theologizing is uncertain and tentative. Humility, willingness to listen, and respect for others are the appropriate attitudes for us finite creatures as we seek to plumb the depths of God's character and truth.
>
> To be sure, God has graciously given us in his Word a revelation of himself and his plan that everyone can understand. The essence of what that Word says is clear and undebatable. But the details are not always as clear as our theological traditions or denominational loyalties suggest. People holding views with more tenacity than Scripture justifies have done untold damage to the church and to the cause of Christ in the world. So even as we praise God for his amazing and gracious plan of redemption,

---

13. Ibid., 224–25; cf. 241n2.

we must also bow our knees in humility before him and keep a good perspective on our own limitations in understanding the specifics of that plan.[14]

1.4. God Deserves Praise for What He Does and Does Not Explain

God is infinite, and humans are finite. He sovereignly controls everything, and humans cannot control anything sovereignly. He can exhaustively explain everything, and humans cannot explain anything exhaustively. Consequently, humans have lots of questions—particularly about God's dealings with reference to themselves—and God knows the answers to every one of them. But he is not obligated to give humans an explanation, and he often does not. This is not only humbling; it is comforting and encouraging.[15] The right response for humans is not to become angry as their pride intensifies. The right response is to become submissive as their pride dissipates and to praise God that he is God and that they are not.

But sometimes God does reveal his ways with humans.[16] Even then humans cannot fully understand what he reveals, but what he does reveal fuels their praise for him. No one fully anticipated what God reveals in Rom 9–11 about his ways with Israelites and Gentiles. His ways in salvation history are surprising, confounding, and perfect, and they are further reasons that humans should praise him. "Whenever then we enter on a discourse respecting the eternal counsels of God," Calvin wisely counsels, "let a bridle be always set on our thoughts and tongue, so that after having spoken soberly and within the limits of God's word, our reasoning may at last end in admiration."[17]

2. GOD IS WITHOUT COUNSELORS: HIS WISDOM IS DEEP (ROM 11:34B)

God's ways in salvation history demonstrate that he is without counselors. He always chooses the best means to accomplish his holy will

---

14. Moo, *Romans*, 392.
15. Cf. Boice, *Romans 9–11*, 1421–23.
16. See §3.1.3 in ch. 2.
17. Calvin, *Romans*, 444.

because his wisdom is deep (Rom 11:33a).[18] At least two theological implications follow:

2.1. Humans Should Not Try to Give God Advice

Fallen humans may think that they know better than God and that God could benefit from their wisdom. But they should not attempt to give God advice for at least three reasons:

1. Humans cannot give God advice because they do not know better than he does. They are incapable of giving him guidance or recommendations that would help him in any way because his wisdom is infinite and theirs finite. They cannot match God's wisdom in any of his ways, so they should not be surprised that they cannot give God advice on how to run his universe and govern salvation history.

2. God does not need advice. This makes sense theoretically, but it can be difficult for humans to accept when God's ways do not make sense to them: "Struggle as we may with various facets of the problem of evil and suffering, there are times when particularly virulent evil or horribly inequitable suffering strikes us as staggeringly irrational, unfair."[19] But God does not need counseling. Everything always makes sense to him, and he always has everything completely under control. He does not get stuck and then turn to trusted advisors to suggest ways out of conundrums. He does not need advice.

3. Giving God advice is idolatry.[20] It presumes that God's wisdom is deficient, and it often accuses God of wrongdoing. That presumes that humans are sufficiently equipped to judge God—to discern that his plan is not quite right and that they know better—and thus are over him in some sense. Luther shrewdly observes that Isa 40:12 and following sets forth "the fountain and source of all idolatry" because the passage confutes

> heretics and the self righteous. It is as if he were saying: "Who are you who want to teach God?" It is the nature of every ungodly

---

18. On God's wisdom, see Bavinck, *God and Creation*, 203–7; Bray, *God*, 219–20; Grudem, *Systematic Theology*, 193–95; Feinberg, *No One Like Him*, 320–22; Frame, *God*, 505–9.

19. Carson, *How Long*, 135.

20. For a penetrating analysis of idolatry, see Keller, *Counterfeit Gods*.

man to mold God for himself and refuse to be molded by God . . . [The reason is that] our perversity refuses to be taught and formed but would rather teach and form God . . . Summary: All idolatry comes from our wisdom, whereby we appear upright to ourselves and have no regard for what God commands.[21]

2.2. God Deserves Praise for Not Needing Advice

A god who needs advice is not God. If God's wisdom were deficient in any way, then he would not be God because God by definition is all-wise, perfect in wisdom. In particular, he has perfectly planned the course of salvation history, and as humans watch it unfold, God deserves their praise for his grand masterplan.

3. GOD IS WITHOUT CREDITORS: HIS RICHES ARE DEEP (ROM 11:35)

God's ways in salvation history demonstrate that he is without creditors. His riches are deep (Rom 11:33a). God's riches in the context of Rom 11 refer to his abundant kindness to both Israelites and Gentiles in his revealed salvation-historical plan.[22] At least two theological implications follow:

3.1. Humans Should Not Try to Place God in Their Debt

Romans 11:35 is tied to 11:34b: if humans give God advice and he takes it, then God owes them. But God does not owe anything to anyone. His riches are infinite, and humans cannot add to them.

The book of Job illustrates that God does not owe humans anything, not even an explanation. Even though Job begs God for an explanation for his intense suffering, God never gives one. Job must live with mystery and trust a faithful, good, and gracious God, and so must everyone else.[23]

---

21. Luther, *Isaiah*, 16–17.

22. On God's mercy, grace, and patience, see Bavinck, *God and Creation*, 210–16; Grudem, *Systematic Theology*, 200–201; Feinberg, *No One Like Him*, 353–65; Frame, *God*, 424–37. Grudem defines mercy as "God's goodness toward those in misery and distress," grace as "God's goodness toward those who deserve only punishment," and patience as "God's goodness in withholding of punishment toward those who sin over a period of time."

23. Cf. Stuart, *Romans*, 387; Waltke, *OT Theology*, 939.

God does not have any creditors, but humans do. God does not owe anything to anyone because he is infinite and owns everything and everyone. Humans, on the other hand, owe everything they are and have to God (on a vertical level), and they may owe things to fellow humans (on a horizontal level). So they should not be surprised that they cannot place God in their debt. God designed exactly whom he will save and when and how he will do it, and nothing humans do can obligate him to save them or other individuals. His abundant kindness is deep, and he saves people freely by his grace.

Nevertheless, humans commonly try "in vain" to place God in their debt by somehow earning his favor by their good works, "as though there was mutual debt and credit."[24] Parsons calls Job 41:3 "an indictment of all ritualistic or moralistic attempts to force the hand of God. It is in germ form the concept of *sola gratia*."[25]

> The attempt to domesticate God by reducing his ways to human ways turns out to be the attempt to make him indebted to reward us for our works. If in the former citation [i.e., Rom 11:34] there was a warning not to imagine ourselves to be clever, here there is an implicit warning against imagining that our works gain us any privilege with God. The Creator retains the freedom of his mercy and cannot be bound to a mere distributive justice.[26]

Humans who try to place God in their debt in this way fit the following non-technical definition of a legalist: "A legalist is anyone who behaves as if they can earn God's forgiveness through personal performance."[27] Keller explains how "being very, very good" in a legalistic way is yet another form of idolatry:

> Religious people commonly live very moral lives, but their goal is to get leverage over God, to control him, to put him in a position where they think he owes them. Therefore, despite all their ethical fastidiousness and piety, they are actually rebelling against his authority . . .
> Elder brothers [like the elder brother in the parable of "the prodigal son" in Luke 15] obey God to get things. They don't

---

24. Calvin, *Romans*, 447–48.
25. Parsons, "Job 38:1—42:6," 203.
26. Seifrid, "Romans," 679.
27. Mahaney, *Living*, 112.

> obey God to get God himself—in order to resemble him, love him, know him, and delight him . . .
>
> Nearly everyone defines sin as breaking a list of rules. Jesus, though, shows us that a man who has violated virtually nothing on the list of moral misbehaviors can be every bit as spiritually lost as the most profligate, immoral person. Why? Because sin is not just breaking the rules, it is putting yourself in the place of God as Savior, Lord, and Judge . . .
>
> There are two ways to be your own Savior and Lord. One is by breaking all the moral laws and setting your own course, and one is by keeping all the moral laws and being very, very good.[28]

Carson, reflecting on Job 41:3 (Eng. 41:11), explains why imagining that God owes us something is yet another form of idolatry:

> Job 41:11 is a salutary reminder that we are not independent. Even if God were not the supremely good God he is, we would have no comeback. He owns us; he owns the universe; all the authority is his, all the branches of divine government are his, the ultimate judiciary is his. There is no "outside" place from which to judge him. To pretend otherwise is futile; worse, it is part of our race's rebellion against God—imagining he owes us something, imagining we are well placed to tell him off. Such wild fantasy is neither sensible nor good.[29]

3.2. God Deserves Praise for Not Owing Anything to Anyone

God is debtor to no one. If he were, he would be less glorious and less praiseworthy; worst of all, he would not be God because God by definition does not need anything. God's aseity means that he is self-existent, completely independent and non-contingent.[30] Nothing humans do can merit his abundant kindness. He saves whomever he wants at the time and in the manner he has designed in his salvation-historical plan. He deserves praise for freely and kindly saving Israelites and Gentiles by his grace and for his glory.

---

28. Keller, *Prodigal God*, 38, 42–44.
29. Carson, *Love of God*, March 12 entry.
30. On God's independence, see Bavinck, *God and Creation*, 148–53; Grudem, *Systematic Theology*, 160–63; Feinberg, *No One Like Him*, 239–43; Frame, *God*, 600–608.

4. CONCLUSION

The three rhetorical questions in Rom 11:34–35 communicate three of God's characteristics that correspond to his ways in salvation history, and each of them carries simple and profound theological implications.

1. God is incomprehensible (11:34a). This has at least four theological implications: (1) humans cannot understand everything; (2) God is not obligated to explain anything; (3) Christians must humbly believe and cherish what God has revealed; and (4) God deserves praise for what he does and does not explain.

2. God is without counselors (11:34b). This has at least two theological implications: (1) humans should not try to give God advice, and (2) God deserve praises for not needing advice.

3. God is without creditors (11:35). This has at least two theological implications: (1) humans should not try to place God in their debt, and (2) God deserves praise for not owing anything to anyone.

These three characteristics share at least two implications: (1) God's attributes are humbling,[31] and (2) God is gloriously praiseworthy. God's characteristics and their theological implications tie perfectly into the final climactic verse: Rom 11:36. All three of God's characteristics in Rom 11:34–35 are rooted in God's sovereignty (11:36a) and culminate in doxology (11:36b).

God is supremely sovereign (Rom 11:36a). He does whatever he wants.[32] He is the source of all things, the means of all things, and the goal of all things. He sovereignly designed salvation history and his special revelation of that history, namely, the Bible, especially how the NT uses the OT and how it all coheres. "The wrong inference from God's transcendence is that he is too great to care; the right one is that he is too great to fail."[33] A God like this is supremely trustworthy: it makes sense to trust a God who is infinitely knowledgeable, wise, kind, and sovereign.[34] And a God like this is supremely praiseworthy: he alone

---

31. Stuart (*Romans*, 386) testifies, "I scarcely know of anything in the whole Bible which strikes deeper at the root of human pride than vers. 33–36."

32. On God's sovereignty, see Bavinck, *God and Creation*, 228–49; Bray, *God*, 218–19; Grudem, *Systematic Theology*, 216–18, 315–54; Feinberg, *No One Like Him*, 294–98, 625–796; Frame, *God*, 20–182.

33. Kidner, "Isaiah," 656.

34. Cf. Smith, *Isaiah 40–66*, 123.

deserves glory eternally (Rom 11:36b).[35] "Not to us, O Lord, not to us, but to your name give glory, for the sake of your steadfast love and your faithfulness!" (Ps 115:1). *Non nobis, non nobis, Domine Sed nomini tuo da gloriam. Soli Deo gloria!*

> It is of great importance to note from Romans 1–11 that theology (our belief about God) and doxology (our worship of God) should never be separated. On the one hand, there can be no doxology without theology. It is not possible to worship an unknown god. All true worship is a response to the self-revelation of God in Christ and Scripture, and arises from our reflection on who he is and what he has done. It was the tremendous truths of Romans 1–11 which provoked Paul's outburst of praise. The worship of God is evoked, informed and inspired by the vision of God. Worship without theology is bound to degenerate into idolatry . . .
>
> On the other hand, there should be no theology without doxology. There is something fundamentally flawed about a purely academic interest in God. God is not an appropriate object for cool, critical, detached, scientific observation and evaluation. No, the true knowledge of God will always lead us to worship, as it did Paul. Our place is on our faces before him in adoration.[36]

James Montgomery Boice, former pastor of Tenth Presbyterian Church in Philadelphia, died in 2000 just six weeks after he was diagnosed with cancer. Less than a year before his death, he began writing new Reformation hymns, and he based his first on Rom 11:33–36. His doxological rhapsody expresses what wells up in Paul in Rom 9–11:

> Give praise to God who reigns above
> For perfect knowledge, wisdom, love;
> His judgments are divine, devout,
> His paths beyond all tracing out.

---

35. See Jonathan Edwards's famous essay on the glory of God in Piper, *God's Passion*, esp. 184, 191–92.

36. Stott, *Romans*, 311–12. Pitting doctrine against devotion is a false dichotomy because God intends them to go together. B. B. Warfield convincingly argues this in five articles reprinted in his *Selected Shorter Writings*, listed here chronologically: "Authority, Intellect, Heart," 2:668–71; "The Indispensableness of Systematic Theology to the Preacher," 2:280–8; "Spiritual Culture in the Theological Seminary," 2:468–96; "The Religious Life of Theological Students," 1:411–25; "The Purpose of the Seminary," 1:374–8. See also Cameron and Rosner, eds., *Trials*, esp. Rosner's reflections on Rom 11:33–36 (187–91).

No one can counsel God all-wise
Or truths unveil to his sharp eyes;
He marks our paths behind, before;
He is our steadfast Counselor.

Nothing exists that God might need
For all things good from him proceed.
We praise him as our Lord, and yet
We never place God in our debt.

Creation, life, salvation too,
And all things else both good and true,
Come from and through our God always,
And fill our hearts with grateful praise.

Come, lift your voice to heaven's high throne,
And glory give to God alone![37]

---

37. Ryken, Thomas, and Duncan, *Give Praise*, 237.

9

Conclusion

THIS BOOK EXAMINES THE use of Isa 40:13 and Job 41:3a in Rom 11:34–35. Its structure generally follows the six-step approach used in Beale and Carson's *Commentary on the New Testament Use of the Old Testament*, and what follows summarizes the book's conclusions for each step.

STEP 1. THE NT CONTEXT OF ROM 11:34-35 (CH. 2)

The theme of Romans is the gospel in its salvation-historical context, and chapters 9–11 are—from a literary standpoint—critical but not central to Paul's unfolding argument. Romans 9:6—11:32 vindicates God's righteousness in his past, present, and future dealings with Israel. The uncontainable praise for God in 11:33–36 naturally flows out of and euphorically concludes chapters 9–11. Responding primarily to the revealed nature of God's ways, Paul praises God for being deep (11:33), incomprehensible (11:34a), without counselors (11:34b), without creditors (11:35), and supreme (11:36).

STEP 2. THE OT CONTEXT OF ISAIAH 40:13 AND JOB 41:3A (CHS. 3-4)

Isaiah's theological message is that people should trust the Holy One of Israel because he is the incomparable King and Savior. Chapters 40–66 emphasize God's comfort and restoration of his people, and chapter 40 exalts God's incomparability to demonstrate that he can easily restore his people. Isaiah 40:13 exclaims that no one gives God advice, evoking God's unrivaled wisdom and incomparable greatness.

Job's theological message is that people should respond to innocent, unexplained suffering by trusting God because he is supremely wise, sovereign, just, and good. The significance of God's interrogation of Job in 38:1—42:6 is at least fourfold: God is too small in Job's eyes; Job is too large in his own eyes; God is not obligated to give Job anything, not even answers to his questions; and only God is all-wise. God's argument in Job 41:2–3 is twofold: (1) God argues from the lesser to the greater to teach Job a lesson on humility. If Job would be terrified to stand before Leviathan, he should be even more terrified to demand a trial with God and stand before him. (2) God argues from the greater to the lesser to teach Job a lesson on ownership. Because God created Job, God owns Job, and because God owns Job, God does not owe Job anything.

STEP 3. TEXTUAL ISSUES IN ISA 40:13, JOB 41:3A, AND ROM 11:34–35 (CH. 5)

The integrity of Isa 40:13, Job 41:3, and Rom 11:34–35 is unassailable. Although some question whether Paul directly cites Isa 40:13 and Job 41:3a in Rom 11:34–35, the external and internal evidence strongly favors direct, slightly adapted citations.

STEP 4. RELEVANT USES OF ISA 40:13 AND JOB 41:3A IN JEWISH LITERATURE (CH. 6)

The few uses of Job 41:3a in extracanonical Jewish literature are not significant for understanding the use of the OT in Rom 11:35, but the use of Leviathan in Jewish literature is at least partially consistent with the larger cosmic realities present in Job 40–41.

The apparent quotations of and allusions to Isa 40:13 in extracanonical Jewish literature share at least two themes. First, humans cannot fully understand God's thoughts and ways, especially in salvation history. Second, the only humans who can acquire a degree of God's wisdom are those to whom God reveals himself. These themes are also present in both Isa 40:13 and Rom 11:34.

There is both continuity and discontinuity between the uses of Isa 40:13 in Jewish literature and in Rom 11:34. The continuity is that Paul writes within a rich Jewish heritage that understands all these texts that praise God for his thoughts and ways. The discontinuity is what triggers

Paul's praise: Paul's salvation-historical reflection on God's sovereign ways with reference to the salvation of Jews and Gentiles.

STEP 5. PAUL'S HERMENEUTICAL WARRANT FOR USING ISA 40:13 AND JOB 41:3A IN ROM 11:34–35 (CH. 7)

Of the many possible hermeneutical warrants explaining why NT authors use the OT the way they do, two apply to Paul's use of the OT in Rom 11:34–35: the larger OT contexts and typology, a core component of the canonical approach. When Paul quotes Isa 40:13 and Job 41:3a, he includes their larger OT contexts, which reveals a remarkable typological connection between the two OT passages and the end of Rom 11. The subjects in all three contexts (Job and Israelites) have been experiencing God's blessing, but God takes that away to some degree in a way that they think is unfair. After questioning God's righteousness while asserting their own, God gives them revelation that they find difficult and unsatisfying. But they must repent of their flawed view of God and themselves and trust God before they experience God's restored blessing to an even greater degree and in an unexpected way. God's salvation-historical plan demonstrates that he is wise, kind, and sovereign.

STEP 6. PAUL'S THEOLOGICAL USE OF ISA 40:13 AND JOB 41:3A IN ROM 11:34–35 (CH. 8)

The three rhetorical questions in Rom 11:34–35 communicate three of God's characteristics that correspond to his ways in salvation history, and each of them carries simple and profound theological implications.

First, God is incomprehensible in the sense that no one can *fully* understand him (11:34a). At least four theological implications follow: (1) humans cannot understand everything; (2) God is not obligated to explain anything; (3) Christians must humbly believe and cherish what God has revealed; and (4) God deserves praise for what he does and does not explain.

Second, God is without counselors (11:34b). At least two theological implications follow: (1) humans should not try to give God advice, and (2) God deserves praise for not needing advice.

Third, God is without creditors (11:35). At least two theological implications follow: (1) humans should not try to place God in their debt, and (2) God deserves praise for not owing anything to anyone.

These three characteristics share at least two implications: (1) God's attributes are humbling, and (2) God is gloriously praiseworthy. These characteristics and their implications tie perfectly into Rom 11:36, the final climactic verse. All three of God's characteristics in Rom 11:34-35 are rooted in God's sovereignty (11:36a) and culminate in doxology (11:36b).

CONCLUSION

The conclusions to the above six steps correlate in a way that enriches our understanding of Rom 11:33–36, especially when measured by the way that commentators typically treat it. By quoting Isa 40:13 and Job 41:3a in Rom 11:34–35, Paul typologically connects Isa 40 and Job 38:1—42:6 with Rom 9–11 in order to exalt God's incomprehensibility, wisdom, mercy, grace, patience, independence, and sovereignty.

> Oh, the depth of the riches and wisdom and knowledge of God! How unsearchable are his judgments and how inscrutable his ways!
>
> > "For who has known the mind of the Lord,
> >   or who has been his counselor?"
> > "Or who has given a gift to him
> >   that he might be repaid?"
>
> For from him and through him and to him are all things. To him be glory forever. Amen. (Rom 11:33–36)

Bibliography

Aageson, James W. "Paul's Use of Scripture: A Comparative Study of Biblical Interpretation in Early Palestinian Judaism and the New Testament with Special Reference to Romans 9–11." PhD diss., Oxford University, 1983.

———. "Scripture and Structure in the Development of the Argument in Romans 9–11." *Catholic Biblical Quarterly* 48 (1986) 265–89.

———. "Typology, Correspondence, and the Application of Scripture in Romans 9–11." *Journal for the Study of the New Testament* 31 (1987) 51–72.

Abasciano, Brian J. "Corporate Election in Romans 9: A Reply to Thomas Schreiner." *Journal of the Evangelical Theological Society* 49 (2006) 351–71.

———. *Paul's Use of the Old Testament in Romans 9:1–9: An Intertextual and Theological Exegesis.* Library of New Testament Studies 301. New York: T. & T. Clark, 2005.

———. "Paul's Use of the Old Testament in Romans 9:1–9: An Intertextual and Theological Exegesis." PhD diss., University of Aberdeen, 2004.

Abegg Jr., Martin G., Peter Flint, and Eugene Ulrich, eds. *The Dead Sea Scrolls: The Oldest Known Bible Translated for the First Time into English.* San Francisco: HarperSanFrancisco, 1999.

Achtemeier, Elizabeth. "Typology." In *Interpreter's Dictionary of the Bible: An Illustrated Encyclopedia: Supplementary Volume*, edited by Keith Crim, 926–27. Nashville: Abingdon, 1976.

Albertz, Rainer. "The Sage and Pious Wisdom in the Book of Job: Three Friends' Perspective." In *The Sage in Israel and the Ancient Near East*, edited by John G. Gammie and Leo G. Perdue, translated by Leo G. Perdue, 243–61. Winona Lake, IN: Eisenbrauns, 1990.

———. *Weltschöpfung und Menschenschöpfung untersucht bei Deuterojesaja, Hiob und in den Psalmen.* Stuttgart: Calwer, 1974.

Alden, Robert L. *Job.* New American Commentary 11. Nashville: Broadman & Holman, 1993.

Aletti, Jean-Noël. "Romains 11: Le développement de l'argumentation et ses enjeux exégético-théologiques." In *The Letter to the Romans*, edited by Udo Schnelle, 197–223. Bibliotheca ephemeridum theologicarum lovaniensium 226. Leuven: Peeters, 2009.

Al-Fayyūmī, Saadia ben Joseph. *The Book of Theodicy: Translation and Commentary on the Book of Job.* Translated by L. E. Goodman. Yale Judaica Series 25. New Haven: Yale University Press, 1988.

Alonso-Schökel, Luis. "God's Answer to Job." In *Job and the Silence of God*, edited by Christian Duquoc et al., translated by G. W. S. Knowles, 45–51. Concilium 169. Edinburgh: T. & T. Clark, 1983.

Alsup, John E. "Typology." In *Anchor Bible Dictionary*, edited by D. N. Freedman, 6:682–85. 6 vols. New York: Doubleday, 1992.

Alter, Robert. "Truth and Poetry in the Book of Job." In *The Book of Job*, edited by Harold Bloom, 63–89. Modern Critical Interpretations. New York: Chelsea House, 1988.

Althaus, Paul. *Der Brief an die Römer*. 11th ed. Das Neue Testament Deutsch 6. Göttingen: Vandenhoeck & Ruprecht, 1970.

Ambrosiaster. *Commentaries on Romans and 1–2 Corinthians*. Edited and translated by Gerald L. Bray. Ancient Christian Texts. Downers Grove, IL: InterVarsity, 2009.

Andersen, Francis I. *Job: An Introduction and Commentary*. Tyndale Old Testament Commentaries. Downers Grove, IL: InterVarsity, 1976.

Archer, Gleason L. *The Book of Job: God's Answer to the Problem of Undeserved Suffering*. Grand Rapids: Baker, 1982.

———. *A Survey of Old Testament Introduction*. 3rd ed. Chicago: Moody, 1994.

Archer, Gleason L., and Gregory Chirichigno. *Old Testament Quotations in the New Testament: A Complete Survey*. Chicago: Moody, 1983.

Aune, David E. "Doxology." In *The Westminster Dictionary of New Testament and Early Christian Literature and Rhetoric*, 140–41. Louisville: Westminster John Knox, 2003.

———. "Excursus 4B: Hymns in Revelation." In *Revelation 1–5*, 314–17. Word Biblical Commentary 52. Dallas: Word, 1997.

———. "Paul's Exegesis of the Old Testament as Illustrated by His Quotations in Romans 9–11." MA thesis, Wheaton Graduate School of Theology, 1963.

Baker, David L. *Two Testaments, One Bible: The Theological Relationship between the Old and New Testaments*. 3rd ed. Downers Grove, IL: InterVarsity, 2010.

Baker, David W. "Isaiah." In *Zondervan Illustrated Bible Backgrounds Commentary: Old Testament*, edited by John H. Walton, 2–227. Grand Rapids: Zondervan, 2009.

Baker, Murray. "Paul and the Salvation of Israel: Paul's Ministry, the Motif of Jealousy, and Israel's Yes." *Catholic Biblical Quarterly* 67 (2005) 469–84.

Balentine, Samuel E. "Job." In *(Wisdom) Writings*, edited by Watson E. Mills and Richard H. Wilson, 1–40. Mercer Commentary on the Bible 3. Macon, GA: Mercer University Press, 2001.

———. *Job*. Smyth & Helwys Bible Commentary. Macon, GA: Smyth & Helwys, 2006.

Ball, C. J. *The Book of Job: A Revised Text and Version*. Oxford: Clarendon, 1922.

Baltzer, Klaus. *Deutero-Isaiah: A Commentary on Isaiah 40–55*. Edited by Peter Machinist. Translated by Margaret Kohl. Hermeneia. Minneapolis: Fortress, 2001.

———. "Jes 40:13–14—ein Schlüssel zur Einheit Deutero-Jesajas?" *Biblische Notizen* 37 (1987) 7–10.

Barnett, Paul. *Romans: The Revelation of God's Righteousness*. Focus on the Bible. Scotland: Christian Focus, 2003.

Barr, James. "The Book of Job and Its Modern Interpreters." *Bulletin of the John Rylands University Library of Manchester* 54 (1971) 28–46.

Barrett, C. K. *The Epistle to the Romans*. 2nd ed. Black's New Testament Commentaries 6. Peabody, MA: Hendrickson, 1991.

———. "The Interpretation of the Old Testament in the New." In *The Cambridge History of the Bible: The Interpretation of the Old Testament in the New: Volume 1, From the Beginnings to Jerome*, edited by P. R. Ackroyd and C. F. Evans, 377–411. Cambridge: Cambridge University Press, 1970.

Barrett, Michael P. V. "Job: The Problem with Problems." *Biblical Viewpoint* 21: 2 (1987) 17–26.

———. "The Theology of Isaiah." *Biblical Viewpoint* 12 (1978) 144–51.

Barth, Karl. *A Shorter Commentary on Romans.* 2nd ed. Richmond: John Knox, 1960.

———. "The Election of the Community." In *Church Dogmatics*, edited by Geoffrey W. Bromiley and Thomas F. Torrance, translated by G. W. Bromiley et al., 195–305. Edinburgh: T. & T. Clark, 2004.

———. *The Epistle to the Romans.* Translated by Edwyn C. Hoskyns. 6th ed. London: Oxford University Press, 1933.

Barth, Markus. "Theologie—ein Gebet (Röm 11,33–36)." *Theologische Zeitschrift* 41 (1985) 330–48.

Bass, Debra Moody. *God Comforts Israel: The Audience and the Message of Isaiah 40–55.* Lanham, MD: University Press of America, 2006.

Bavinck, Herman. *Reformed Dogmatics, vol. 2: God and Creation.* Edited by John Bolt. Translated by John Vriend. Grand Rapids: Baker, 2004.

Beale, G. K., ed. *The Right Doctrine from the Wrong Texts? Essays on the Use of the Old Testament in the New.* Grand Rapids: Baker, 1994.

Beale, G. K. *The Book of Revelation: A Commentary on the Greek Text.* New International Greek Testament Commentary. Grand Rapids: Eerdmans, 1999.

———. "Did Jesus and His Followers Preach the Right Doctrine from the Wrong Texts?" *Themelios* 14 (1989) 89–96.

———. *The Erosion of Inerrancy in Evangelicalism: Responding to New Challenges to Biblical Authority.* Wheaton: Crossway, 2008.

———. "Revelation." In *It Is Written: Scripture Citing Scripture: Essays in Honour of Barnabas Lindars, SSF*, edited by D. A. Carson and H. G. M. Williamson, 318–36. Cambridge: Cambridge University Press, 1988.

Beale, G. K., and D. A. Carson, eds. *Commentary on the New Testament Use of the Old Testament.* Grand Rapids: Baker, 2007.

Beale, G. K., and D. A. Carson. "Introduction." In *Commentary on the New Testament Use of the Old Testament*, edited by G. K. Beale and D. A. Carson, xxiii–xxviii. Grand Rapids: Baker, 2007.

Beale, G. K., and Sean M. McDonough. "Revelation." In *Commentary on the New Testament Use of the Old Testament*, edited by G. K. Beale and D. A. Carson, 1081–1161. Grand Rapids: Baker, 2007.

Beekman, John, and John Callow. *Translating the Word of God.* Dallas: Summer Institute of Linguistics, 1974.

Begrich, Joachim. *Studien zu Deuterojesaja.* Edited by Walther Zimmerli. 2nd ed. Theologische Bücherei 20. München: Kaiser, 1963. Beker, J. Christiaan. "The Faithfulness of God and the Priority of Israel in Paul's Letter to the Romans." In *The Romans Debate*, edited by Karl P. Donfried, 327–32. Peabody, MA: Hendrickson, 1991.

———. *Paul the Apostle: The Triumph of God in Life and Thought.* Philadelphia: Fortress, 1980.

———. "Romans 9–11 in the Context of the Early Church." *Princeton Seminary Bulletin* Supplement 1 (1990) 40–55.

Bell, Richard H. *Provoked to Jealousy: The Origin and Purpose of the Jealousy Motif in Romans 9–11.* Wissenschaftliche Untersuchungen zum Neuen Testament 63. Tübingen: Mohr Siebeck, 1994.

Bell, Robert D. "The Truth about Satan (and God) (Job 1:1—2:13; 42:7–17)." *Biblical Viewpoint* 21:2 (1987) 3–8.
Bengel, J. A. *Gnomon of the New Testament: A New Translation*. Translated by C. T. Lewis and M. R. Vincent. Philadelphia: Perkinpine & Higgins, 1864.
Berding, Kenneth. "An Analysis of Three Views on the New Testament Use of the Old Testament." In *Three Views on the New Testament Use of the Old Testament*, edited by Kenneth Berding and Jonathan Lunde, 233–43. Counterpoints. Grand Rapids: Zondervan, 2008.
Berges, Ulrich. *Jesaja 40–48*. Herders Theologischer Kommentar zum Alten Testament. Freiburg: Herder, 2008.
Berlin, Adele. "Parallelism." In *Anchor Bible Dictionary*, edited by D. N. Freedman, 5:155–62. 6 vols. New York: Doubleday, 1992. .
Berry, Donald K. *An Introduction to Wisdom and Poetry of the Old Testament*. Nashville: Broadman & Holman, 1995.
Best, Ernest. *The Letter of Paul to the Romans*. Cambridge Bible Commentary. Cambridge: Cambridge University Press, 1967.
Beuken, W. A. M. *Jesaja: Deel II A*. De Prediking van het Oude Testament. Nijkerk: Callenbach, 1979.
Black, Matthew. *The Book of Enoch, or I Enoch: A New English Edition with Commentary and Textual Notes*. Studia in Veteris Testamenti pseudepigraphica 7. Leiden: Brill, 1985.
———. *Romans*. 2nd ed. New Century Bible. Grand Rapids: Eerdmans, 1989.
Blenkinsopp, Joseph. *Isaiah 40–55: A New Translation with Introduction and Commentary*. Anchor Bible 19A. New York: Doubleday, 1974.
Bock, Darrell L. "Part 1: Evangelicals and the Use of the Old Testament in the New." *Bibliotheca Sacra* 142 (1985) 209–20.
———. "Part 2: Evangelicals and the Use of the Old Testament in the New." *Bibliotheca Sacra* 142 (1985) 306–16.
———. "Scripture Citing Scripture: Use of the Old Testament in the New." In *Interpreting the New Testament Text: Introduction to the Art and Science of Exegesis*, edited by Darrell L. Bock and Buist M. Fanning, 255–76. Wheaton: Crossway, 2006.
———. "Single Meaning, Multiple Contexts and Referents: The New Testament's Legitimate, Accurate, and Multifaceted Use of the Old." In *Three Views on the New Testament Use of the Old Testament*, edited by Kenneth Berding and Jonathan Lunde, 105–51 (responses 90–95, 226–31). Counterpoints. Grand Rapids: Zondervan, 2008.
Bockmuehl, Markus N. A. *Revelation and Mystery in Ancient Judaism and Pauline Christianity*. Wissenschaftliche Untersuchungen zum Neuen Testament 36. Tübingen: Mohr Siebeck, 1990.
Boice, James Montgomery. *God and History: Romans 9–11*. Vol. 3. *Romans*. Grand Rapids: Baker, 1993.
Bonnard, Pierre É. *Le Second Isaïe: Son disciple et leurs editeurs: Isaïe 40–66*. Etudes bibliques. Paris: Gabalda, 1972.
———. "Les Trésors de la miséricorde (Rm 11,33–36)." *Assemblées du Seigneur* 53 (1964) 13–19.
Boor, Werner de. *Der Brief des Paulus an die Römer*. Wuppertaler Studienbibel. Wuppertal: Brockhaus, 1973.

Bornkamm, Günther. "The Praise of God (Romans 11.33–36)." In *Early Christian Experience*, translated by Paul L. Hammer, 105–11. New York: Harper & Row, 1969.
Bourke, Myles M. *A Study of the Metaphor of the Olive Tree in Romans XI*. Washington, D.C.: Catholic University of America Press, 1947.
Brackett, James Kristian. "Paul's Use of the Old Testament in Romans 9–11." ThM thesis, The Master's Seminary, 1998.
Brand, Chad Owen, ed. *Perspectives on Election: Five Views*. Nashville: Broadman & Holman, 2006.
Brassey, Paul Del. "Metaphor and the Incomparable God in Isaiah 40–55." PhD diss., Harvard University, 1997.
Bray, Gerald. *The Doctrine of God*. Contours of Christian Theology. Downers Grove, IL: InterVarsity, 1993.
Bray, Gerald, ed. *Romans*. Ancient Christian Commentary on Scripture: New Testament 6. Downers Grove, IL: InterVarsity, 1998.
Brenner, Athalya. "God's Answer to Job." *Vetus Testamentum* 31 (1981) 129–37.
———. "Job the Pious? The Characterization of Job in the Narrative Framework of the Book." *Journal for the Study of the Old Testament* 43 (1989) 37–52.
Brettler, Marc Zvi. "Incompatible Metaphors for YHWH in Isaiah 40–66." *Journal for the Study of the Old Testament* 78 (1998) 97–120.
Briley, Terry R. *Isaiah: The Salvation of Jehovah*. 2 vols. College Press NIV Commentary. Joplin, MO: College Press, 2000.
Brown, Raymond E. *An Introduction to the New Testament*. New York: Doubleday, 1997.
———. "The *Sensus Plenior* in the Last Ten Years." *Catholic Biblical Quarterly* 25 (1963) 262–85.
———. *The* Sensus Plenior *of Sacred Scripture*. Baltimore: St. Mary's University, 1955.
Brown, William P. *Character in Crisis: A Fresh Approach to the Wisdom Literature of the Old Testament*. Grand Rapids: Eerdmans, 1996.
Bruce, F. F. *The Letter of Paul to the Romans: An Introduction and Commentary*. 2nd ed. Tyndale New Testament Commentaries. Grand Rapids: Eerdmans, 1985.
Brueggemann, Walter. *Isaiah 40–66*. Westminster Bible Companion. Louisville: Westminster John Knox, 1998.
———. *Theology of the Old Testament: Testimony, Dispute, Advocacy*. Minneapolis: Fortress, 1997.
Bruno, Christopher R. "The Deliverer from Zion: The Source(s) and Function of Paul's Citation in Romans 11:26–27." *Tyndale Bulletin* 59 (2008) 119–34.
Bullock, C. Hassell. *An Introduction to the Old Testament Poetic Books*. 2nd ed. Chicago: Moody, 1988.
Bultema, Harry. *Commentary on Isaiah*. Translated by Cornelius Lambregtse. Grand Rapids: Kregel, 1981.
Bultmann, Rudolf. *Theology of the New Testament*. Translated by Kendrick Grobel. Waco: Baylor University Press, 2007.
Burns, J. Lanier. "The Future of Ethnic Israel in Romans 11." In *Dispensationalism, Israel and the Church: The Search for Definition*, edited by Craig A. Blaising and Darrell L. Bock, 188–229. Grand Rapids: Zondervan, 1992.
Burrell, David B. *Deconstructing Theodicy: Why Job Has Nothing to Say to the Puzzle of Suffering*. Grand Rapids: Brazos, 2008.
Byrne, Brendan J. *Reckoning with Romans: A Contemporary Reading of Paul's Gospel*. Collegeville, MN: Liturgical, 1986.

———. *Romans*. Sacra Pagina 6. Collegeville, MN: Liturgical, 1996.
Calvin, John. *Commentaries on the Epistle of Paul the Apostle to the Romans*. Edited and translated by John Owen. Grand Rapids: Eerdmans, 1947.
———. *Commentary on the Prophet Isaiah*. Translated by William Pringle. 4 vols. Grand Rapids: Eerdmans, 1948.
———. *Sermons on Job*. Carlisle, PA: Banner of Truth, 1993.
Cambier, J. *L'évangile de Dieu selon l'épître aux Romains: Exégèse et théologie biblique: L'évangile de la justice et de la grace*. Vol. 1. Studia Neotestamentica. Brussels: Desclée de Brouwer, 1967.
Cameron, Andrew J. B., and Brian S. Rosner, eds. *The Trials of Theology: Becoming a "Proven Worker" in a Dangerous Business*. Fearn, Scotland: Christian Focus, 2010.
Caquot, André. "Le Léviathan de Job 40, 25–41, 26." *Revue biblique* 99 (1992) 40–69.
———. "Léviathan et Behémoth dans la troisième 'Parabole' d'Hénoch." *Semitica* 25 (1975) 111–22.
Carson, D. A. "1 Peter." In *Commentary on the New Testament Use of the Old Testament*, edited by G. K. Beale and D. A. Carson, 1015–1045. Grand Rapids: Baker, 2007.
———. "Athens Revisited." In *Telling the Truth: Evangelizing Postmoderns*, edited by D. A. Carson, 384–98. Grand Rapids: Zondervan, 2000.
———. *The Cross and Christian Ministry: Leadership Lessons from 1 Corinthians*. Grand Rapids: Baker, 2004.
———. "Current Issues in Biblical Theology: A New Testament Perspective." *Bulletin for Biblical Research* 5 (1995) 17–41.
———. *How Long, O Lord? Reflections on Suffering and Evil*. 2nd ed. Grand Rapids: Baker, 2006.
———. *For the Love of God: A Daily Companion for Discovering the Riches of God's Word*. Vol. 2. Wheaton: Crossway, 1999.
———. "Matthew." In *Matthew–Mark*, 23–670. Revised Expositor's Bible Commentary 9. Grand Rapids: Zondervan, 2010.
———. "Mystery and Fulfillment: Toward a More Comprehensive Paradigm of Paul's Understanding of the Old and New." In *The Paradoxes of Paul*. Vol. 2. *Justification and Variegated Nomism*, edited by D. A Carson et al., 393–436. Wissenschaftliche Untersuchungen zum Neuen Testament 181. Grand Rapids: Baker, 2004.
———. "New Testament Theology." In *Dictionary of the Later New Testament and Its Developments*, edited by Ralph P. Martin and Peter H. Davids, 796–814. Downers Grove, IL: InterVarsity, 1997.
———. "The Role of Exegesis in Systematic Theology." In *Doing Theology in Today's World: Essays in Honor of Kenneth S. Kantzer*, edited by John D. Woodbridge and Thomas Edward McComiskey, 39–76. Grand Rapids: Zondervan, 1991.
———."Systematic Theology and Biblical Theology." In *New Dictionary of Biblical Theology*, edited by T. Desmond Alexander and Brian S. Rosner, 89–104. Downers Grove, IL: InterVarsity, 2000.
———. "Unity and Diversity in the New Testament: The Possibility of Systematic Theology." In *Scripture and Truth*, edited by D. A. Carson and John D. Woodbridge, 65–95, 368–75. Grand Rapids: Zondervan, 1983.
Carson, D. A., and Douglas J. Moo. *An Introduction to the New Testament*. 2nd ed. Grand Rapids: Zondervan, 2005.

Carson, D. A., and H. G. M. Williamson, eds. *It Is Written: Scripture Citing Scripture: Essays in Honour of Barnabas Lindars, SSF*. Cambridge: Cambridge University Press, 1988.

Charles, J. Daryl. "Pagan Sources in the New Testament." In *Dictionary of New Testament Background*, edited by Craig A. Evans and Stanley E. Porter, 756–63. Downers Grove, IL: InterVarsity, 2000.

Cheney, Michael. *Dust, Wind and Agony: Character, Speech and Genre in Job*. Coniectanea biblica: Old Testament Series 36. Stockholm: Almqvist & Wiksell International, 1994.

Chesterton, G. K. "Introduction to the Book of Job." The American Chesterton Society. No pages. Online: http://www.chesterton.org/wordpress/2011/07/introduction-to-the-book-of-job/

Childs, Brevard S. *Isaiah*. Old Testament Library. Louisville: Westminster John Knox, 2001.

———. "Israel and the Church: Romans 9–11." In *The Church's Guide for Reading Paul: The Canonical Shaping of the Pauline Corpus*, 178–93. Grand Rapids: Eerdmans, 2008.

Chilton, Bruce D. *The Isaiah Targum: Introduction, Translation, Apparatus and Notes*. The Aramaic Bible 11. Collegeville, MN: Liturgical, 1990.

———. "Romans 9–11 as Scriptural Interpretation and Dialogue with Judaism." *Ex Auditu* 4 (1988) 27–37.

Chisholm, Robert B., Jr. "A Theology of Isaiah." In *A Biblical Theology of the Old Testament*, edited by Roy B. Zuck, 305–40. Chicago: Moody, 1991.

Ciampa, Roy E., and Brian S. Rosner. "1 Corinthians." In *Commentary on the New Testament Use of the Old Testament*, edited by G. K. Beale and D. A. Carson, 695–752. Grand Rapids: Baker, 2007.

Clarke, Ernest G. *The Wisdom of Solomon*. Cambridge Bible Commentary. Cambridge: Cambridge University Press, 1973.

Clements, Ronald E. "'A Remnant Chosen by Grace' (Romans 11:5): The Old Testament Background and Origin of the Remnant Concept." In *Pauline Studies: Essays Presented to Professor F. F. Bruce on His 70th Birthday*, edited by Donald A. Hagner and Murray J. Harris, 106–21. Grand Rapids: Eerdmans, 1980.

Clifford, Richard J. *Fair Spoken and Persuading: An Interpretation of Second Isaiah*. 2nd ed. Theological Inquiries. New York: Paulist, 1984.

———. "Isaiah, Book of (Second Isaiah)." In *Anchor Bible Dictionary*, edited by D. N. Freedman, 3:488–501. 6 vols. New York: Doubleday, 1992.

———. "The Function of Idol Passages in Second Isaiah." *Catholic Biblical Quarterly* 42 (1980) 450–64.

———. *The Wisdom Literature*. Interpreting Biblical Texts. Nashville: Abingdon, 1998.

Clines, David J. A. "Job." In *New Bible Commentary: Twenty-first Century Edition*, edited by D. A. Carson, et al., 459–84. Downers Grove, IL: InterVarsity, 1994.

———. *Job 1–20*. Word Biblical Commentary 17. Dallas: Word, 1989.

———. *Job 21–37*. Word Biblical Commentary 18A. Dallas: Word, 2006.

———. *Job 38–42*. Word Biblical Commentary 18B. Dallas: Word, forthcoming.

———. "Job's God." In *Job's God*, edited by Ellen van Wolde, 39–51. London: SCM, 2004.

———. "Why Is There a Book of Job, and What Does It Do to You If You Read It?" In *The Book of Job*, edited by W. A. M. Beuken, 1–20. Bibliotheca ephemeridum theologicarum lovaniensium 114. Leuven: Leuven University Press, 1994.

Cohen, Matityahu. "More on the Subject 'Behemoth and Leviathan' in God's Second Lecture to Job [written in modern Hebrew]." In *History of the Jewish People: Proceedings of the Twelfth World Congress of Jewish Studies, Jerusalem, July 29–August 5, 1997: Division A*, edited by Ron Margolin and Haim Weiss, 65–78. Jerusalem: World Union of Jewish Studies, 1999.

Compton, Jared M. "Shared Intentions? Reflections on Inspiration and Interpretation in Light of Scripture's Dual Authorship." *Themelios* 33:3 (2008) 23–33.

Conrad, Edgar W. *Reading Isaiah*. Overtures to Biblical Theology. Minneapolis: Fortress, 1991.

Cook, Michael J. "Paul's Argument in Romans 9–11." *Review and Expositor* 103 (2006) 91–111.

Cornelius, Izak. "Job." Vol. 5. *Zondervan Illustrated Bible Backgrounds Commentary: Old Testament*, edited by John H. Walton, 246–315. Grand Rapids: Zondervan, 2009.

Cotton, Bill. *Will You Torment a Windblown Leaf? A Commentary on Job*. Focus on the Bible. Scotland: Christian Focus, 2001.

Cottrell, Jack. *Romans*. 2 vols. College Press NIV Commentary. Joplin, MO: College, 1998.

Couroyer, Bernard. "Behemoth = Hippopotamus ou Buffle?" *Revue biblique* 94 (1987) 214–21.

———. "Isaïe xl, 12." *Revue biblique* 73 (1966) 186–96.

———. "Le 'Glaive' de Béhémoth: Job, XL, 19–20." *Revue biblique* 84 (1977) 59–79.

———. "Qui est Béhémoth? Job, XL, 15–24." *Revue biblique* 82 (1975) 418–43.

Cranfield, C. E. B. *A Critical and Exegetical Commentary on the Epistle to the Romans*. 2 vols. International Critical Commentary. London: T. & T. Clark, 1975.

Crenshaw, James L. "Beginnings, Endings, and Life's Necessities in Biblical Wisdom." In *Wisdom Literature in Mesopotamia and Israel*, edited by Richard J. Clifford, 93–105. Society of Biblical Literature Symposium Series 36. Atlanta: Society of Biblical Literature, 2007.

———. *Old Testament Wisdom: An Introduction*. 2nd ed. Louisville: Westminster John Knox, 1998.

———. "The Wisdom Literature." In *The Hebrew Bible and Its Modern Interpreters*, edited by Douglas A. Knight and Gene M. Tucker, 369–407. Chico: Scholars, 1985.

———. "When Form and Content Clash: The Theology of Job 38:1—40:5." In *Creation in the Biblical Traditions*, edited by Richard J. Clifford and John J. Collins, 70–84. Catholic Biblical Quarterly Monograph Series 24. Washington, D.C.: Catholic Biblical Association of America, 1992.

Crossan, John Dominic, ed. *The Book of Job and Paul Ricoeur's Hermeneutics*. Semeia 19. Chico: Society of Biblical Literature, 1981.

Cullmann, Oscar. *Christ and Time: The Primitive Christian Conception of Time and History*. Translated by Floyd V. Filson. 2nd ed. Philadelphia: Westminster, 1964.

———. *Salvation in History*. Translated by Sidney G. Sowers. New York: Harper & Row, 1967.

Culver, Robert Duncan. *Systematic Theology: Biblical and Historical*. Fearn, Scotland: Mentor, 2005.

Curtis, John Briggs. "On Job's Response to Yahweh." *Journal of Biblical Literature* 98 (1979) 497–511.

Dahood, Mitchell. "The Breakup of Two Composite Phrases in Is 40:13." *Biblica* 54 (1973) 537–38.

Dailey, Thomas F. "And Yet He Repents—On Job 42,6." *Zeitschrift für die alttestamentliche Wissenschaft* 105 (1993) 205–9.

———. "The Aesthetics of Repentance: Re-Reading the Phenomenon of Job." *Biblical Theology Bulletin* 23:2 (1993) 64–70.

———. *The Repentant Job: A Ricoeurian Icon for Biblical Theology*. Lanham, MD: University Press of America, 1994.

———. "The Wisdom of Divine Disputation? On Job 40.2–5." *Journal for the Study of the Old Testament* 63 (1994) 105–19.

———. "The Wisdom of Job: Moral Maturity or Religious Reckoning." *Union Seminary Quarterly Review* 51:1–2 (1997) 45–55.

———. "Theophanic Bluster: Job and the Wind of Change." *Studies in Religion* 22 (1993) 187–95.

Das, A. Andrew. *Solving the Romans Debate*. Minneapolis: Fortress, 2007.

Davidson, A. B. *The Book of Job*. 2nd ed. The Cambridge Bible for Schools and Colleges. Cambridge: University Press, 1951.

Davidson, Richard M. *Typology in Scripture: A Study of Hermeneutical Τύπος Structures*. Andrews University Seminary Doctoral Dissertation Series 2. Berrien Springs, MI: Andrews University Press, 1981.

Day, John. "God and Leviathan in Isaiah 27:1." *Bibliotheca Sacra* 155 (1998) 423–36.

———. *God's Conflict with the Dragon and the Sea: Echoes of a Canaanite Myth in the Old Testament*. University of Cambridge Oriental Publications 35. Cambridge: Cambridge University Press, 1985.

———. "Leviathan." In *Anchor Bible Dictionary*, edited by D. N. Freedman, 4:295–96. 6 vols. New York: Doubleday, 1992.

De Lorenzi, Lorenzo, ed. *Die Israelfrage nach Römer 9–11*. Rome: Abtei von St Paul, 1977.

Deichgräber, Reinhard. *Gotteshymnus und Christushymnus in der frühen Christenheit: Untersuchungen zur Form, Sprache und Stil der frühchristlichen Hymnen*. Studien zur Umwelt des Neuen Testaments 5. Göttingen: Vandenhoeck & Ruprecht, 1967.

Delitzsch, Franz. *Isaiah*. Translated by James Martin. Commentary on the Old Testament 7. Grand Rapids: Eerdmans, 1988.

———. *Job*. Translated by Francis Bolton. Commentary on the Old Testament 4. 1866–91. Reprint, Grand Rapids: Eerdmans, 1988.

Dell, Katharine J. *The Book of Job as Sceptical Literature*. Beihefte zur Zeitschrift für die alttestamentliche Wissenschaft 197. Berlin: De Gruyter, 1991.

Dempster, Stephen G. *Dominion and Dynasty: A Biblical Theology of the Hebrew Bible*. New Studies in Biblical Theology 15. Downers Grove, IL: InterVarsity, 2003.

Denney, James. "St. Paul's Epistle to the Romans." Vol. 2. *The Expositor's Greek Testament*, edited by W. Robertson Nicoll, 555–725. Grand Rapids: Eerdmans, 1956.

Denny, David R. "The Significance of Isaiah in the Writings of Paul." ThD diss., New Orleans Theological Seminary, 1985.

deSilva, David A. *Introducing the Apocrypha: Message, Context, and Significance*. Grand Rapids: Baker, 2002.

Dever, Mark. "Humble Dogmatism." *Together for the Gospel*. February 8, 2006. No Pages. Online: http://www.t4g.org/2006/02/humble-dogmatism.

Dhorme, Édouard. *A Commentary on the Book of Job*. Translated by Harold Knight. Nashville: Thomas Nelson, 1984.

Di Lella, Alexander A. "An Existential Interpretation of Job." *Biblical Theology Bulletin* 15:2 (1985) 49–55.
Dodd, C. H. *According to the Scriptures: The Sub-Structure of New Testament Theology.* London: Nisbet, 1952.
———. *The Epistle of Paul to the Romans.* Moffatt New Testament Commentary. London: Collins, 1959.
———. *The Old Testament in the New.* Biblical Series 3. Philadelphia: Fortress, 1963.
Donaldson, Terence L. "'Riches for the Gentiles' (Rom 11:12): Israel's Rejection and Paul's Gentile Mission." *Journal of Biblical Literature* 112 (1993) 81–98.
Donfried, Karl P. "A Short Note on Romans 16." In *The Romans Debate*, edited by Karl P. Donfried, 44–52. Peabody, MA: Hendrickson, 1991.
———. "Solving the Romans Debate." Review of *Solving the Romans Debate* by A. Andrew Das. *Theological Studies* 69 (2008) 189–90.
Donfried, Karl P., ed. *The Romans Debate.* 2nd ed. Peabody, MA: Hendrickson, 1991.
Dorsey, David A. *The Literary Structure of the Old Testament: A Commentary on Genesis– Malachi.* Grand Rapids: Baker, 1999.
Drane, John W. "The Religious Background." In *New Testament Interpretation: Essays on Principles and Methods*, edited by I. Howard Marshall, 116–24. Milton Keynes, UK: Paternoster, 1979.
Driver, Samuel Rolles, and George Buchanan Gray. *A Critical and Exegetical Commentary on the Book of Job.* International Critical Commentary. Edinburgh: T. & T. Clark, 1921.
Duhm, Bernhard. *Das Buch Jesaia.* 5th ed. Göttingen: Vandenhoeck u. Rupprecht, 1968.
Dumbrell, William J. *Romans: A New Covenant Commentary.* Eugene, OR: Wipf and Stock, 2005.
———. "The Purpose of Isaiah." *Tyndale Bulletin* 36 (1985) 111–28.
———. "The Purpose of the Book of Job." In *The Way of Wisdom: Essays in Honor of Bruce K. Waltke*, edited by J. I. Packer and Sven Soderlund, 91–105. Grand Rapids: Zondervan, 2000.
Dunham, Kyle C. "Eliphaz as Counselor in Job within the Context of Ancient Near Eastern Wisdom Theodicy." ThD diss., The Master's Seminary, 2010.
Dunn, James D. G. *Romans 1–8.* Word Biblical Commentary 38A. Dallas: Word, 1988.
———. *Romans 9–16.* Word Biblical Commentary 38B. Dallas: Word, 1988.
Dupont, Jacques. *Gnosis: La connaissance religieuse dans les épîtres de Saint Paul.* 2nd ed. Louvain: Nauwelaerts, 1960.
Durham, James. *Lectures on Job.* Edited by Christopher Coldwell. 2nd ed. Dallas: Naphtali, 2003.
Durham, John I. "Isaiah 40–55: A New Creation, a New Exodus, a New Messiah." In *The Yahweh/Baal Confrontation and Other Studies in Biblical Literature and Archaeology: When Religions Collide: Essays in Honour of Emmett Willard Hamrick*, edited by Julia M. O'Brien and Fred L. Horton Jr., 47–56. Studies in Bible and Early Christianity 35. Lewiston: Mellen Biblical Press, 1995.
Eaton, J. H. *Job.* Old Testament Guides. Sheffield, England: JSOT, 1985.
Edwards, James R. *Romans.* New International Biblical Commentary 6. Peabody, MA: Hendrickson, 1992.
Edwards, Jonathan. *Writings on the Trinity, Grace, and Faith.* Edited by Sang Hyun Lee. The Works of Jonathan Edwards 21. New Haven: Yale University Press, 2002.

Eisemann, Moshe. *Job: A New Translation with a Commentary Anthologized from Talmudic, Midrashic, and Rabbinic Sources*. The ArtScroll Tanach Series. Brooklyn: Mesorah, 1994.

Elliger, Karl. *Deuterojesaja: Jesaja 40,1—45,7*. Biblischer Kommentar: Altes Testament 11. Neukirchen-Vluyn: Neukirchener Verlag, 1978.

Elliott, Mark W., ed. *Isaiah 40–66*. Ancient Christian Commentary on Scripture: Old Testament 11. Downers Grove, IL: InterVarsity, 2007.

———. "Typology." Vol. 5. *The New Interpreter's Dictionary of the Bible*, edited by Katharine Doob Sakenfeld, 692. Nashville: Abingdon, 2009.

Ellis, E. Earle. "How the New Testament Uses the Old." In *New Testament Interpretation: Essays on Principles and Methods*, edited by I. Howard Marshall, 198–214. Milton Keynes, UK: Paternoster, 1979.

———. *Paul's Use of the Old Testament*. Grand Rapids: Eerdmans, 1957.

———. *Prophecy and Hermeneutic in Early Christianity: New Testament Essays*. Wissenschaftliche Untersuchungen zum Neuen Testament 18. Grand Rapids: Eerdmans, 1978.

Emerton, J. A. "Wisdom." In *Tradition and Interpretation: Essays by Members of the Society for Old Testament Study*, edited by G. W. Anderson, 214–37. Oxford: Clarendon, 1979.

Engseth, Jerome M. "The Role of Behemoth and Leviathan in the Book of Job." In *Church Divinity 1987*, edited by John H. Morgan, 119–37. Graduate Theological Foundation. Bristol, IN: Wyndham Hall, 1987.

Enns, Peter. "Fuller Meaning, Single Goal: A Christotelic Approach to the New Testament Use of the Old in Its First-Century Interpretive Environment." In *Three Views on the New Testament Use of the Old Testament*, edited by Kenneth Berding and Jonathan Lunde, 167–217 (responses 96–101, 159–64). Counterpoints. Grand Rapids: Zondervan, 2008.

———. *Inspiration and Incarnation: Evangelicals and the Problem of the Old Testament*. Grand Rapids: Baker, 2005.

Esler, Philip F. "Ancient Oleiculture and Ethnic Differentiation: The Meaning of the Olive-Tree Image in Romans 11." *Journal for the Study of the New Testament* 26 (2003) 103–24.

———. *Conflict and Identity in Romans: The Social Setting of Paul's Letter*. Minneapolis: Fortress, 2003.

Estes, Daniel J. *Handbook on the Wisdom Books and Psalms: Job, Psalms, Proverbs, Ecclesiastes, Song of Songs*. Grand Rapids: Baker, 2005.

Evans, Craig A., ed. *From Prophecy to Testament: The Function of the Old Testament in the New*. Peabody, MA: Hendrickson, 2004.

Evans, Craig A. *Ancient Texts for New Testament Studies: A Guide to the Background Literature*. 2nd ed. Peabody, MA: Hendrickson, 2005.

———. "Paul and the Hermeneutics of 'True Prophecy': A Study of Romans 9–11." *Biblica* 65 (1984) 560–70.

———. "Paul and the Prophets: Prophetic Criticism in the Epistle to the Romans (with Special Reference to Romans 9–11)." In *Romans and the People of God: Essays in Honor of Gordon D. Fee on the Occasion of His 65th Birthday*, edited by Sven Soderlund and N. T. Wright, 115–28. Grand Rapids: Eerdmans, 1999.

———. "The Old Testament in the New." In *The Face of New Testament Studies: A Survey of Recent Research*, edited by Scot McKnight and Grant R. Osborne, 130–45. Grand Rapids: Baker, 2004.

Evans, Craig A., and Stanley E. Porter, eds. *Dictionary of New Testament Background.* Downers Grove, IL: InterVarsity, 2000.

Fairbairn, Patrick. *The Typology of Scripture: Viewed in Connection with the Whole Series of the Divine Dispensations.* 2 vols. Grand Rapids: Baker, 1975.

Fantin, Joseph D. "Background Studies: Grounding the Text in Reality." In *Interpreting the New Testament Text: Introduction to the Art and Science of Exegesis,* edited by Darrell L. Bock and Buist M. Fanning, 167–96. Wheaton: Crossway, 2006.

Fee, Gordon D. *The First Epistle to the Corinthians.* New International Commentary on the New Testament. Grand Rapids: Eerdmans, 1987.

Feinberg, Charles L. "The Book of Job." *Bibliotheca Sacra* 91 (1934) 78–86.

Feinberg, John S. *No One Like Him: The Doctrine of God.* Foundations of Evangelical Theology. Wheaton: Crossway, 2001.

Feinberg, John S., ed. *Continuity and Discontinuity: Perspectives on the Relationship Between the Old and New Testaments: Essays in Honor of S. Lewis Johnson Jr.* Westchester, IL: Crossway, 1988.

Ferguson, Everett. *Backgrounds of Early Christianity.* 3rd ed. Grand Rapids: Eerdmans, 2003.

Fitzmyer, Joseph A. *Essays on the Semitic Background of the New Testament.* London: Scholars, 1974.

———. *First Corinthians: A New Translation with Introduction and Commentary.* Anchor Yale Bible 34. New Haven: Yale University Press, 2008.

———. *Romans: A New Translation with Introduction and Commentary.* Anchor Bible 33. New York: Doubleday, 1993.

Fohrer, Georg. *Das Buch Hiob.* Kommentar zum Alten Testament 16. Gütersloh: Gütersloher Verlagshaus Gerd Mohn, 1989.

———. *Das Buch Jesaja.* 3 vols. Zürcher Bibelkommentare. Zürich: Zwingli, 1960.

———. "Gottes Antwort aus dem Sturmwind, Hi. 38–41." *Theologische Zeitschrift* 18 (1962) 1–24.

Folker, Siegert. *Argumentation bei Paulus gezeigt an Röm 9–11.* Wissenschaftliche Untersuchungen zum Neuen Testament 34. Tübingen: Mohr Siebeck, 1985.

Foulkes, Francis. *The Acts of God: A Study of the Basis of Typology in the Old Testament.* Tyndale Old Testament Lecture. London: Tyndale, 1958.

Frame, John M. *The Doctrine of God.* Phillipsburg, NJ: Presbyterian & Reformed, 2002.

France, R. T. "Relationship between the Testaments." In *Dictionary for Theological Interpretation of the Bible,* edited by Kevin J. Vanhoozer, 666–72. Grand Rapids: Baker, 2005.

Friesen, Ivan D. *Isaiah.* Believers Church Bible Commentary. Scottdale, PA: Herald, 2009.

Fung, William Chi-Chau. "Israel's Salvation: The Meaning of 'All Israel' in Romans 11:26." PhD diss., The Southern Baptist Theological Seminary, 2004.

Fyall, Robert S. *Now My Eyes Have Seen You: Images of Creation and Evil in the Book of Job.* New Studies in Biblical Theology 12. Downers Grove, IL: InterVarsity, 2002.

Gadenz, Pablo T. *Called from the Jews and from the Gentiles: Pauline Ecclesiology in Romans 9–11.* Wissenschaftliche Untersuchungen zum Neuen Testament 267. Tübingen: Mohr Siebeck, 2009.

Gammie, John G. "Behemoth and Leviathan: On the Didactic and Theological Significance of Job 40:15—41:26." In *Israelite Wisdom: Theological and Literary*

Essays in Honor of Samuel Terrien, edited by John G. Gammie et al., 217–31. Missoula, MT: Scholars, 1978.

Garrett, Richard N. "A Syntactical Analysis of Romans 9–11." PhD diss., Baylor University, 1982.

Gibson, John C. L. "A New Look at Job 41.1–4 (English 41.9–12)." In *Text as Pretext: Essays in Honour of Robert Davidson*, edited by Robert P. Carroll, 129–39. Journal for the Study of the Old Testament Supplement Series 138. Sheffield, England: JSOT, 1992.

———. *Job*. Daily Study Bible Series. Philadelphia: Westminster, 1985.

———. "On Evil in the Book of Job." In *Ascribe to the Lord: Biblical and Other Essays in Memory of Peter C. Craigie*, edited by Lyle Eslinger and Glen Taylor, 399–419. Journal for the Study of the Old Testament Supplement Series 67. Sheffield: JSOT, 1988.

Gignilliat, Mark S. *Paul and Isaiah's Servants: Paul's Theological Reading of Isaiah 40–66 in 2 Corinthians 5:14—6:10*. Library of New Testament Studies 330. London: T. & T. Clark, 2007.

Gileadi, Avraham. *The Literary Message of Isaiah*. New York: Hebraeus Press, 1994.

Ginsberg, Harold Louis, et al. "Job, Book of." In *Encyclopaedia Judaica*, edited by Michael Berenbaum and Fred Skolnik, 341–59. Detroit: Macmillan Reference, 2007.

Ginzberg, Louis. *The Legends of the Jews*. Translated by Henrietta Szold. 7 vols. Philadelphia: Jewish Publication Society of America, 1909-38.

Gitay, Jehoshua. *Prophecy and Persuasion: A Study of Isaiah 40–48*. Forum theologiae linguisticae 14. Bonn: Linguistica Biblica, 1981.

Gladson, Jerry A. "Job." In *A Complete Literary Guide to the Bible*, edited by Leland Ryken and Tremper Longman III, 230–40. Grand Rapids: Zondervan, 1993.

Glatzer, Nahum N. "The Book of Job and Its Interpreters." In *Biblical Motifs: Origins and Transformations*, edited by Alexander Altmann, 197–220. Studies and Texts 3. Cambridge: Harvard University Press, 1966.

Glatzer, Nahum N., ed. *The Dimensions of Job: A Study and Selected Readings*. New York: Schocken, 1969.

Gloer, W. Hulitt. "Homologies and Hymns in the New Testament: Form, Content, and Criteria for Identification." *Perspectives in Religious Studies* 11 (1984) 115–32.

Godet, Frédéric Louis. *Commentary on St. Paul's Epistle to the Romans*. Translated by A. Cusin. 2 vols. Edinburgh: T. & T. Clark, 1883.

Goldingay, John. *Isaiah*. New International Biblical Commentary on the Old Testament 13. Peabody, MA: Hendrickson, 2001.

———. "The Breath of Yahweh Scorching, Confounding, Anointing: The Message of Isaiah 40–42." *Journal of Pentecostal Theology* 11 (1997) 3–34.

———. *The Message of Isaiah 40–55: A Literary-Theological Commentary*. New York: T. & T. Clark, 2005.

———. *Old Testament Theology: Israel's Faith*. Downers Grove, IL: InterVarsity, 2006.

———. "The Theology of Isaiah." In *Interpreting Isaiah: Issues and Approaches*, edited by David G. Firth and H. G. M. Williamson, 168–90. Downers Grove, IL: InterVarsity, 2009.

Goldingay, John, and David Payne. *A Critical and Exegetical Commentary on Isaiah 40–55*. Vol. 1. International Critical Commentary. 2 vols. New York: T. & T. Clark, 2006.

Good, Edwin M. *In Turns of Tempest: A Reading of Job with a Translation*. Stanford: Stanford University Press, 1990.

———. "The Problem of Evil in the Book of Job." In *The Voice from the Whirlwind: Interpreting the Book of Job*, edited by Leo G. Perdue and W. Clark Gilpin, 50–69, 236–38. Nashville: Abingdon, 1992.

Goodrick, A. T. S., ed. *The Book of Wisdom: With Introduction and Notes*. London: Rivington, 1913.

Goppelt, Leonhard. *Typos: The Typological Interpretation of the Old Testament in the New*. Translated by Donald H. Madvig. Grand Rapids: Eerdmans, 1982.

———. "τύπος, ἀντίτυπος, τυπικός, ὑποτύπωσις." In *Theological Dictionary of the New Testament*, edited by G. Kittel and G. Friedrich, translated by G. W. Bromiley, 8:246–59. 10 vols. Grand Rapids: Eerdmans, 1964-1975.

Gordis, Robert. *The Book of God and Man: A Study of Job*. Chicago: University of Chicago Press, 1965.

———. *The Book of Job: Commentary, New Translation, and Special Studies*. New York: Jewish Theological Seminary of America, 1978.

Gordon, Cyrus W. "Leviathan: Symbol of Evil." In *Biblical Motifs: Origins and Transformations*, edited by Alexander Altmann, 1–9. Studies and Texts 3. Cambridge: Harvard University Press, 1966.

Gradl, Felix. "Ijobs Begegnung mit Gott: Anmerkungen zu Ijob 40,6–8.9–14." In *Ein Gott, eine Offenbarung: Beiträge zur biblischen Exegese, Theologie und Spiritualität: Festschrift für Notker Füglister OSB zum 60. Geburtstag*, edited by Friedrich Vinzenz Reiterer, 65–82. Würzburg: Echter, 1991.

Greathouse, William M. *Romans 9–16*. New Beacon Bible Commentary. Kansas City: Beacon Hill, 2008.

Grieb, A. Katherine. *The Story of Romans: A Narrative Defense of God's Righteousness*. Louisville: Westminster John Knox, 2002.

Grimm, Werner. *Deuterojesaja: Deutung–Wirkung–Gegenwart: Ein Kommentar zu Jesaja 40–55*. Calwer Bibelkommentare. Stuttgart: Calwer Verlag, 1990.

Grisanti, Michael A. "The Progress of God's Program for Jews and Gentiles in Romans Eleven." ThM thesis, Central Baptist Theological Seminary, 1986.

Grogan, Geoffrey W. "Isaiah." In *Proverbs–Isaiah*, 433–863. Expositor's Bible Commentary 6. Grand Rapids: Zondervan, 2008.

Grudem, Wayne. *Systematic Theology: An Introduction to Biblical Doctrine*. Grand Rapids: Zondervan, 1994.

Guillaume, Alfred. *Studies in the Book of Job with a New Translation*. Edited by John Macdonald. Annual of Leeds University Oriental Society Supplement 2. Leiden: Brill, 1968.

Gundry, Judith M. "'Or who gave first to him, so that he shall receive recompense?' (Rom 11,35): Divine Benefaction and Human Boasting in Paul and Philo." In *The Letter to the Romans*, edited by Udo Schnelle, 25–53. Bibliotheca ephemeridum theologicarum lovaniensium 226. Leuven: Peeters, 2009.

Guthrie, Donald. *New Testament Introduction*. 4th ed. Downers Grove, IL: InterVarsity, 1990.

Gutiérrez, Gustavo. *On Job: God-Talk and the Suffering of the Innocent*. Translated by Matthew J. O'Connell. Maryknoll: Orbis, 1987.

Güttgemanns, Erhardt. "Heilsgeschichte bei Paulus oder Dynamik des Evangeliums? Zur strukturellen Relevanz von Röm 9–11 für die Theologie des Römerbriefs (1970)." In *Studia linguistica Neotestamentica: Gesammelte Aufsätze zur linguistischen Grundlage einer Neutestamentlichen Theologie*, 34–58. Munich: Kaiser Verlag München, 1971.

Haacker, Klaus. *Der Brief des Paulus an die Römer*. Theologischer Handkommentar zum Neuen Testament 6. Leipzig: Evangelisches Verlagsanstalt, 1999.

———. *The Theology of Paul's Letter to the Romans*. New Testament Theology. Cambridge: Cambridge University Press, 2003.

Habel, Norman C. "In Defense of God the Sage." In *The Voice from the Whirlwind: Interpreting the Book of Job*, edited by Leo G. Perdue and W. Clark Gilpin, 21–38, 232–33. Nashville: Abingdon, 1992.

———. "Of Things beyond Me: Wisdom in the Book of Job." *Currents in Theology and Mission* 10 (1983) 142–54.

———. *The Book of Job*. Cambridge Bible Commentary. London: Cambridge University Press, 1975.

———. *The Book of Job: A Commentary*. Old Testament Library. Philadelphia: Westminster, 1985.

———. "The Role of Elihu in the Design of the Book of Job." In *In the Shelter of Elyon: Essays on Ancient Palestinian Life and Literature in Honour of G.W. Ahlström*, edited by W. Boyd Barrick and John R. Spencer, 81–98. Journal for the Study of the Old Testament Supplement Series 31. Sheffield: JSOT, 1984.

———. "The Verdict on/of God at the End of Job." In *Job's God*, edited by Ellen van Wolde, 27–38. London: SCM, 2004.

Habtu, Tewoldemedhin. "Job." In *Africa Bible Commentary: A One-Volume Commentary Written by 70 African Scholars*, edited by Tokunboh Adeyemo, 571–604. Grand Rapids: Zondervan, 2006.

Hafemann, Scott J. "The Salvation of Israel in Romans 11:25–32: A Response to Krister Stendahl." *Ex Auditu* 4 (1988) 38–58.

Hagner, Donald A. "The Old Testament in the New Testament." In *Interpreting the Word of God: Festschrift in Honor of Steven Barabas*, edited by Samuel J. Schultz and Morris A. Inch, 78–104. Chicago: Moody, 1976.

———. "Wisdom of Solomon." Vol. 5. *The Zondervan Encyclopedia of the Bible*, edited by Merrill C. Tenney and Moisés Silva, 1096–1102. Grand Rapids: Zondervan, 2009.

Haldane, Robert. *Exposition of the Epistle to the Romans*. London: Banner of Truth, 1958.

Hall, Winfield Scott, Jr. "Paul as a Christian Prophet in His Interpretation of the Old Testament in Romans 9–11." ThD diss., Lutheran School of Theology at Chicago, 1982.

Hamilton Jr., James M., *God's Glory in Salvation through Judgment: A Biblical Theology*. Wheaton: Crossway, 2010.

Hamlin, E. John. *Comfort My People: A Guide to Isaiah 40–66*. Atlanta: John Knox, 1980.

Hanson, Anthony Tyrrell. *Studies in Paul's Technique and Theology*. Grand Rapids: Eerdmans, 1974.

———. *The Living Utterances of God: The New Testament Exegesis of the Old*. London: Darton, Longman and Todd, 1983.

———. *The New Testament Interpretation of Scripture*. London: SPCK, 1980.

Hanson, Paul D. *Isaiah 40–66*. Interpretation. Louisville: Westminster John Knox, 1995.

Harder, Günther. *Paulus und das Gebet*. Gütersloh: Bertelsmann, 1936.

Harding, Mark. "The Salvation of Israel and the Logic of Romans 11:11–36." *Australian Biblical Review* 46 (1998) 55–69.

Harlow, Daniel C. "Jewish Context of the NT." In *Dictionary for Theological Interpretation of the Bible*, edited by Kevin J. Vanhoozer, 373–80. Grand Rapids: Baker, 2005.

Harman, Allan. *Isaiah: A Covenant to Be Kept for the Sake of the Church*. Focus on the Bible. Scotland, UK: Christian Focus, 2005.

Harris, Dana M. "The Eternal Inheritance in Hebrews: The Appropriation of the Old Testament Inheritance Motif by the Author of Hebrews." PhD diss., Trinity Evangelical Divinity School, 2009.

Harris, Joshua. *Dug Down Deep: Unearthing What I Believe and Why It Matters*. Colorado Springs: Multnomah, 2010.

Harris, R. Laird. "The Book of Job and Its Doctrine of God." *Grace Journal* 13 (1972) 3–33.

Harrison, Everett F., and Donald A. Hagner. "Romans." In *Romans–Galatians*, 19–237. Expositor's Bible Commentary 11. Grand Rapids: Zondervan, 2008.

Harrison, R. K. *Introduction to the Old Testament*. Grand Rapids: Eerdmans, 1969.

Harrisville, Roy A. *Romans*. Augsburg Commentary on the New Testament. Minneapolis: Augsburg, 1980.

Hartley, John E. *Job*. New International Commentary on the Old Testament. Grand Rapids: Eerdmans, 1988.

———. "Theology of Job." Vol. 4. *The New International Dictionary of Old Testament Theology and Exegesis*, edited by Willem A. VanGemeren, 780–96. Grand Rapids: Zondervan, 1997.

Harvey, John D. *Listening to the Text: Oral Patterning in Paul's Letters*. Erfurter theologische Studien. Grand Rapids: Baker, 1998.

Hatina, Thomas R. "Jewish Religious Backgrounds of the New Testament: Pharisees and Sadducees as Case Studies." In *Approaches to New Testament Study*, edited by Stanley E. Porter and David Tombs, 46–76. Journal for the Study of the New Testament Supplement Series 120. Sheffield, England: Sheffield Academic Press, 1995.

Hays, Richard B. *Echoes of Scripture in the Letters of Paul*. New Haven: Yale University Press, 1989.

———. *First Corinthians*. Interpretation. Louisville: John Knox, 1997.

Hays, Richard B., and Joel B. Green. "The Use of the Old Testament by New Testament Writers." In *Hearing the New Testament: Strategies for Interpretation*, edited by Joel B. Green, 222–38. Grand Rapids: Eerdmans, 1995.

Helyer, Larry R. *Exploring Jewish Literature of the Second Temple Period: A Guide for New Testament Students*. Downers Grove, IL: InterVarsity, 2002.

Hendriksen, William. *Exposition of Paul's Epistle to the Romans*. New Testament Commentary. Grand Rapids: Baker, 1981.

Hengstenberg, E. W. "Interpreting the Book of Job." In *Classical Evangelical Essays in Old Testament Interpretation*, edited by Walter C. Kaiser Jr, 91–112. Grand Rapids: Baker, 1972.

Herbert, A. S. *The Book of the Prophet Isaiah*. 2 vols. Cambridge: Cambridge University Press, 1973–75.

Herntrich, Volkmar. *Das Buch Jesaja: Kap. 40-66*. Berlin: Evangelische Verlagsanstalt, 1968.

Herzer, Jens. "Jakobus, Paulus und Hiob: Die Intertextualität der Weisheit." *Das Buch Hiob und seine Interpretationen: Beiträge zum Hiob-Symposium auf dem Monte Verità vom 14.–19. August 2005*. Edited by Thomas Krüger et al. Abhandlungen zur Theologie des Alten und Neuen Testaments 88. Zürich: Theologischer Verlag Zürich, 2007.

Hirsch Jr., E. D. *Validity in Interpretation.* New Haven: Yale University Press, 1967.
Hodge, Charles. *A Commentary on the Epistle to the Romans.* 19th ed. New York: Carter & Bros., 1880.
Hoehner, Harold W. "Israel in Romans 9–11." In *Israel, the Land and the People: An Evangelical Affirmation of God's Promises,* edited by H. Wayne House, 145–67. Grand Rapids: Kregel, 1998.
Hofius, Otfried. "'All Israel Will Be Saved': Divine Salvation and Israel's Deliverance in Romans 9–11." *Princeton Seminary Bulletin* Supplement 1 (1990) 19–39.
———. "Das Evangelium und Israel: Erwägungen zu Römer 9–11." *Zeitschrift für Theologie und Kirche* 83 (1986) 297–324.
Hooks, Stephen M. *Job.* College Press NIV Commentary. Joplin, MO: College Press, 2007.
House, Paul R. *Old Testament Theology.* Downers Grove, IL: InterVarsity, 1998.
Hübner, Hans. *Gottes Ich und Israel: Zum Schriftgebrauch des Paulus in Römer 9–11.* Forschungen zur Religion und Literatur des Alten und Neuen Testaments 136. Göttingen: Vandenhoeck & Ruprecht, 1984.
———. *Die Weisheit Salomons: Liber sapientiae Salomonis.* Das Alte Testament Deutsch: Apokryphen 4. Göttingen: Vandenhoeck & Ruprecht, 1999.
Huby, Joseph. *Saint Paul: Épître Aux Romains.* Edited by Stanislas Lyonnet. 2nd ed. Verbum Salutis 10. Paris: Beauchesne, 1957.
Hugenberger, G. P. "Introductory Notes on Typology." In *The Right Doctrine from the Wrong Texts? Essays on the Use of the Old Testament in the New,* edited by G. K. Beale, 331–41. Grand Rapids: Baker, 1994.
Hunt, Allen R. *The Inspired Body: Paul, the Corinthians, and Divine Inspiration.* Macon, GA: Mercer University Press, 1996.
Instone-Brewer, David. *Techniques and Assumptions in Jewish Exegesis before 70 CE.* Texte und Studien zum Antiken Judentum 30. Tübingen: Mohr Siebeck, 1992.
Jacobs, Irving. "Elements of Near-Eastern Mythology in Rabbinic Aggadah." *Journal of Jewish Studies* 28 (1977) 1–11.
Jaeggli, John Randolph. "An Historical-Theological Analysis of the Holy One of Israel in Isaiah 40–66." PhD diss., Bob Jones University, 1987.
Janzen, J. Gerald. *Job.* Interpretation. Atlanta: Westminster John Knox, 1985.
Jeremias, Joachim. "Chiasmus in den Paulusbriefen." *Zeitschrift für die neutestamentliche Wissenschaft und die Kunde der älteren Kirche* 49 (1958) 145–56.
———. "Einige vorwiegend sprachliche Beobachtungen zu Röm 11:25–36." In *Die Israelfrage nach Römer 9–11,* edited by Lorenzo De Lorenzi, 193–216. Rome: Abtei von St Paul, 1977.
Jewett, Robert. *Romans: A Commentary on the Book of Romans.* Hermeneia. Minneapolis: Fortress, 2007.
Johnson, Alan F. *Romans.* 2nd ed. Everyman's Bible Commentary. Chicago: Moody, 2000.
Johnson, E. Elizabeth. "Romans 9–11: The Faithfulness and Impartiality of God." In *Romans,* edited by David M. Hay and E. Elizabeth Johnson, 211–39. Pauline Theology. Minneapolis: Fortress, 1995.
———. *The Function of Apocalyptic and Wisdom Traditions in Romans 9–11.* Society of Biblical Literature Dissertation Series 109. Atlanta: Society of Biblical Literature, 1989.

Johnson, S. Lewis. "A Response to Patrick Fairbairn and Biblical Hermeneutics as Related to the Quotations of the Old Testament in the New." In *Hermeneutics, Inerrancy, and the Bible: Papers from ICBI Summit II*, edited by Earl D. Radmacher and Robert D. Preus, 791–99. Grand Rapids: Zondervan, 1984.

———. "Evidence from Romans 9–11." In *A Case for Premillennialism: A New Consensus*, edited by Donald K. Campbell and Jeffrey Townsend, 199–223. Chicago: Moody, 1992.

———. *The Old Testament in the New: An Argument for Biblical Inspiration*. Grand Rapids: Zondervan, 1980.

Johnston, Philip S. "Faith in Isaiah." In *Interpreting Isaiah: Issues and Approaches*, edited by David G. Firth and H. G. M. Williamson, 104–21. Downers Grove, IL: InterVarsity, 2009.

Kaiser, Walter C., Jr. "The Current Crisis in Exegesis and the Apostolic Use of Deuteronomy 25:4 in 1 Corinthians 9:8–10." *Journal of the Evangelical Theological Society* 21 (1978) 3–18.

———. "Magnifying the Incomparability of Our God: Isaiah 40:9–31." In *The Majesty of God in the Old Testament: A Guide for Preaching and Teaching*, 23–36. Grand Rapids: Baker, 2007.

———. "The Single Intent of Scripture." In *Evangelical Roots: A Tribute to Wilbur Smith*, edited by Kenneth S. Kantzer, 123–41. Nashville: Nelson, 1978.

———. "Single Meaning, Unified Referents: Accurate and Authoritative Citations of the Old Testament by the New Testament." In *Three Views on the New Testament Use of the Old Testament*, edited by Kenneth Berding and Jonathan Lunde, 45–89 (responses: 152–58, 218–25). Counterpoints. Grand Rapids: Zondervan, 2008.

———. *The Uses of the Old Testament in the New*. Chicago: Moody, 1985.

Käsemann, Ernst. *Commentary on Romans*. Edited and translated by Geoffrey W. Bromiley. Grand Rapids: Eerdmans, 1980.

Keck, Leander E. *Romans*. Abingdon New Testament Commentaries. Nashville: Abingdon, 2005.

Keel, Othmar. *Jahwes Entgegnung an Ijob: Eine Deutung Von Ijob 38–41 vor dem Hintergrund der Zeitgenössischen Bildkunst*. Forschungen zur Religion und Literatur des Alten und Neuen Testaments 121. Göttingen: Vandenhoeck & Ruprecht, 1978.

Keener, Craig S. *Romans*. New Covenant Commentary Series. Eugene, OR: Wipf and Stock, 2009.

———. *The IVP Bible Background Commentary: New Testament*. Downers Grove, IL: InterVarsity, 1993.

Keller, Timothy. *Counterfeit Gods: The Empty Promises of Money, Sex, and Power, and the Only Hope that Matters*. New York: Dutton, 2009.

———. *The Prodigal God: Recovering the Heart of the Christian Faith*. New York: Dutton, 2008.

Kidner, Derek. "Isaiah." In *New Bible Commentary: Twenty-First Century Edition*, edited by D. A. Carson et al., 629–70. Downers Grove, IL: InterVarsity, 1994.

———. *The Wisdom of Proverbs, Job, and Ecclesiastes: An Introduction to Wisdom Literature*. Downers Grove, IL: InterVarsity, 1985.

Kim, Johann D. *God, Israel, and the Gentiles: Rhetoric and Situation in Romans 9–11*. Society of Biblical Literature Dissertation Series 176. Atlanta: Society of Biblical Literature, 2000.

Kim, Seyoon. "The 'Mystery' of Rom 11:25-6 Once More." *New Testament Studies* 43 (1997) 412-29.
Klein, Hans. "Der Beweis der Einzigkeit Jahwes bei Deuterojesaja." *Vetus Testamentum* 35 (1985) 267-73.
Klein, Ralph W. *Israel in Exile: A Theological Interpretation*. Overtures to Biblical Theology. Philadelphia: Fortress, 1979.
Klein, William W. *The New Chosen People: A Corporate View of Election*. Grand Rapids: Zondervan, 1990.
Klijn, A. F. J. "2 (Syriac Apocalypse of) Baruch." Vol. 1. *The Old Testament Pseudepigrapha*, edited by James H. Charlesworth, 615-52. Garden City, NY: Doubleday, 1983.
Knight, George A. F. *Servant Theology: A Commentary on the Book of Isaiah 40-55*. 2nd ed. International Theological Commentary. Edinburgh: Handsel, 1984.
Koch, Dietrich-Alex. *Die Schrift als Zeuge des Evangeliums: Untersuchungen zur Verwendung und zum Verständnis der Schrift bei Paulus*. Beiträge zur historischen Theologie 69. Tübingen: Mohr Siebeck, 1986.
Köhler, Ludwig. *Deuterojesaja (Jesaja 40-55) stilkritisch untersucht*. Beiheft zur Zeitschrift für die alttestamentliche Wissenschaft 37. Giessen: Töpelmann, 1923.
Kolb, Robert, and Timothy J. Wengert, eds. *The Book of Concord: The Confessions of the Evangelical Lutheran Church*. Translated by Charles Arand, et al. Minneapolis: Fortress, 2000.
Konkel, August H. "Job." In *Job, Ecclesiastes, Song of Songs*, 1-249. Cornerstone Biblical Commentary 6. Carol Stream, IL: Tyndale House, 2006.
Kooij, Arie van der. *Die alten Textzeugen Jesajabuches: Ein Beitrag zur Textgeschichte des alten Testaments*. Orbis Biblicus et Orientalis 35. Freiburg, Schweiz: Universitätsverlag, 1981.
Koole, Jan Leunis. *Isaiah III: Isaiah 40-48*. Translated by Anthony P. Runia. Vol. 1. Historical Commentary on the Old Testament. Kampen, The Netherlands: Kok Pharos, 1997.
Köstenberger, Andreas J. "Testament Relationships." In *Dictionary of Biblical Criticism and Interpretation*, edited by Stanley E. Porter, 350-52. London: Routledge, 2007.
Köstenberger, Andreas J., L. Scott Kellum, and Charles L. Quarles. *The Cradle, the Cross, and the Crown: An Introduction to the New Testament*. Nashville: Broadman & Holman, 2009.
Köstenberger, Andreas J., and Peter T. O'Brien. *Salvation to the Ends of the Earth: A Biblical Theology of Mission*. New Studies in Biblical Theology 11. Downers Grove, IL: InterVarsity, 2001.
Kramer, Philip A. "Mystery without Mystery in Galatians: An Examination of the Relationship between Revelatory Language in Galatians 1:11-17 and Scriptural References in Galatians 3:6-18; 4:21-31." PhD diss., Trinity Evangelical Divinity School, 2004.
Kroeze, Jan Hendrik. *Het Boek Job*. Commentaar op het Oude Testament. Kampen: Kok, 1961.
Krüger, Thomas. "Did Job Repent?" In *Das Buch Hiob und seine Interpretationen: Beiträge zum Hiob-Symposium auf dem Monte Verità vom 14.-19. August 2005*, edited by Thomas Krüger et al., 217-29. Abhandlungen zur Theologie des Alten und Neuen Testaments 88. Zürich: Theologischer Verlag Zürich, 2007.

Kubina, Veronika. *Die Gottesreden im Buche Hiob: Ein Beitrag zur Diskussion um die Einheit von Hiob 38:1—42:6.* Freiburger theologische Studien 115. Freiburg: Herder, 1979.

Kuhn, Karl Georg. "Ἰσραήλ, Ἰουδαῖος, Ἑβραῖος in Jewish Literature after the OT." In *Theological Dictionary of the New Testament*, edited by G. Kittel and G. Friedrich, translated by G. W. Bromiley, 6:359–69. 10 vols. Grand Rapids: Eerdmans, 1964-1975.

Kuss, Otto. *Der Römerbrief.* 2nd ed. 3 vols. Regensburg: Pustet, 1963.

Labuschagne, C. J. *The Incomparability of Yahweh in the Old Testament.* Pretoria Oriental Series 5. Leiden: Brill, 1966.

Lagrange, Marie-Joseph. *Saint Paul: Épître aux Romains.* Etudes bibliques. Paris: Gabalda, 1950.

Lasine, Stuart. "Bird's-eye and Worm's-eye Views of Justice in the Book of Job." *Journal for the Study of the Old Testament* 42 (1988) 29–53.

Laurin, Robert. "The Theological Structure of Job." *Zeitschrift für die alttestamentliche Wissenschaft* 84 (1972) 86–89.

Leclerc, Thomas L. "Mišpāt (Justice) in the Book of Isaiah." ThD diss., Harvard University, 1998.

Leenhardt, Franz J. *The Epistle to the Romans: A Commentary.* Translated by Harold Knight. Cleveland: World, 1961.

Lenski, R. C. H. *The Interpretation of St. Paul's Epistle to the Romans.* Minneapolis: Augsburg, 1961.

Lewis, C. S. *The Problem of Pain.* 1940. Reprint, New York: HarperCollins, 1996.

Leupold, H. C. *Exposition of Isaiah.* 2 vols. Grand Rapids: Baker, 1968.

Lévêque, Jean. *Job et Son Dieu: Essai d'exégèse et de théologie Biblique.* 2 vols. Études bibliques. Paris: Gabalda, 1970.

———. "L'interprétation des discours de Yhwh (Job 38,1—42,6)." In *The Book of Job*, edited by W. A. M. Beuken, 203–22. Bibliotheca ephemeridum theologicarum lovaniensium 114. Leuven: Leuven University Press, 1994.

———. "Tradition and Betrayal in the Speeches of the Friends." In *Job and the Silence of God*, edited by Christian Duquoc, Casiano Floristán, and Marcus Lefébure, 39–44. Concilium 169. Edinburgh: T. & T. Clark, 1983.

Liddon, H. P. *Explanatory Analysis of St. Paul's Epistle to the Romans.* Grand Rapids: Zondervan, 1961.

Lietzmann, Hans. *Einführung in die Textgeschichte der Paulusbriefe: An die Römer.* 4th ed. Handbuch zum Neuen Testament. Tübingen: Mohr, 1933.

Lim, Bo H. "The 'Way of the Lord' in the Book of Isaiah." PhD diss., Trinity Evangelical Divinity School, 2006.

Lim, Timothy H. *Holy Scripture in the Qumran Commentaries and Pauline Letters.* New York: Oxford University Press, 1997.

Lindars, Barnabas. *New Testament Apologetic: The Doctrinal Significance of Old Testament Quotations.* Philadelphia: Westminster, 1961.

Lloyd-Jones, David Martyn. *Romans: An Exposition of Chapter 10: Saving Faith.* Edinburgh: Banner of Truth, 1997.

———. *Romans: An Exposition of Chapter 11: To God's Glory.* Carlisle, PA: Banner of Truth, 1998.

———. *Romans: An Exposition of Chapter 9: God's Sovereign Purpose.* Edinburgh: Banner of Truth, 1991.

Lo, Alison. *Job 28 as Rhetoric: An Analysis of Job 28 in the Context of Job 22-31*. Supplements to Vetus Testamentum 97. Leiden: Brill, 2003.

Lodge, John G. *Romans 9-11: A Reader-Response Analysis*. University of South Florida: International Studies in Formative Christianity and Judaism 6. Atlanta: Scholars, 1996.

Longenecker, Bruce W. "Different Answers to Different Issues: Israel, the Gentiles and Salvation History in Romans 9-11." *Journal for the Study of the New Testament* 36 (1989) 95-123.

Longenecker, Richard N. *Biblical Exegesis in the Apostolic Period*. 2nd ed. Grand Rapids: Eerdmans, 1999.

Longman III, Tremper. "Literary Approaches and Interpretation." Vol. 1. *The New International Dictionary of Old Testament Theology and Exegesis*, edited by Willem A. VanGemeren, 103-24. Grand Rapids: Zondervan, 1997.

Longman III, Tremper, and Raymond B. Dillard. *An Introduction to the Old Testament*. 2nd ed. Grand Rapids: Zondervan, 2006.

Lübking, Hans-Martin. *Paulus und Israel im Römerbrief: Eine Untersuchung zu Römer 9-11*. Europäische Hochschulschriften 23. New York: Lang, 1986.

Lund, Nils Wilhelm. *Chiasmus in the New Testament: A Study in the Form and Function of Chiastic Structures*. Peabody, MA: Hendrickson, 1992.

Lunde, Jonathan. "An Introduction to Central Questions in the New Testament Use of the Old Testament." In *Three Views on the New Testament Use of the Old Testament*, edited by Kenneth Berding and Jonathan Lunde, 7-41. Counterpoints. Grand Rapids: Zondervan, 2008.

Lupieri, Edmondo. *Il cielo è il mio trono: Isaia 40:12 e 66:1 nella tradizione testimoniaria*. Temi e Testi 28. Rome: Edizioni di storia e letteratura, 1980.

Luther, Martin. *Lectures on Isaiah: Chapters 40-66*. Edited by Hilton C. Oswald. Translated by Herbert J. A. Bouman. Luther's Works 17. St. Louis: Concordia, 1972.

———. *Lectures on the Minor Prophets III: Zechariah*. Edited by Hilton C. Oswald. Luther's Works 20. St. Louis: Concordia, 1973.

———. *Lectures on Romans: Glosses and Scholia*. Edited by Hilton C. Oswald. Luther's Works 25. St. Louis: Concordia, 1972.

———. *Sermons I*. Edited by John W. Doberstein. Luther's Works 51. Philadelphia: Fortress, 1959.

Maag, Viktor. *Hiob: Wandlung und Verarbeitung des Problems in Novelle, Dialogdichtung und Spätfassungen*. Forschungen zur Religion und Literatur des Alten und Neuen Testaments 128. Göttingen: Vandenhoeck & Ruprecht, 1982.

Maarten, J. Paul. "לִוְיָתָן." Vol. 2. *The New International Dictionary of Old Testament Theology and Exegesis*, edited by Willem A. VanGemeren, 778-80. Grand Rapids: Zondervan, 1997.

Machinist, Peter, and Jehuda Feliks. "Leviathan." In *Encyclopaedia Judaica*, edited by Michael Berenbaum and Fred Skolnik, 696-97. Detroit: Macmillan Reference, 2007.

Mackay, John L. *A Study Commentary on Isaiah: Volume 2: Chapters 40-66*. Carlisle, PA: Evangelical Press, 2009.

MacKenzie, Roderick A. F. "The Purpose of the Yahweh Speeches in the Book of Job." *Biblica* 40 (1959) 435-45.

Mahaney, C. J. *Living the Cross-Centered Life: Keeping the Gospel the Main Thing*. Sisters, OR: Multnomah, 2006.

Malchow, Bruce V. "Nature from God's Perspective: Job 38–39." *Dialog* 21 (1982) 130–33.

Mangan, Céline. "The Interpretation of Job in the Targums." In *The Book of Job*, edited by W. A. M. Beuken, 267–80. Bibliotheca ephemeridum theologicarum lovaniensium 114. Leuven: Leuven University Press, 1994.

Marshall, I. Howard. "An Assessment of Recent Developments." In *It Is Written: Scripture Citing Scripture: Essays in Honour of Barnabas Lindars, SSF*, edited by D. A. Carson and H. G. M. Williamson, 1–21. Cambridge: Cambridge University Press, 1988.

Martens, Elmer A. "בְּהֵמוֹת." In *Theological Workbook of the Old Testament*, edited by R. L. Harris and G. L. Archer, 93. 2 vols. Chicago: Moody, 1980.

Martin, Ralph P. "Aspects of Worship in the New Testament Church." *Vox Evangelica* 2 (1963) 6–32.

———. "Hymns, hymn fragments, songs, spiritual songs." In *Dictionary of Paul and His Letters*, edited by Gerald F. Hawthorne and Ralph P. Martin, 419–22. Downers Grove, IL: InterVarsity, 1993.

———. *Worship in the Early Church*. Grand Rapids: Eerdmans, 1974.

Martínez, García, and Eibert J. C. Tigchelaar, eds. *The Dead Sea Scrolls: Study Edition (Translations)*. 2 vols. Leiden: Brill, 1997.

Mayhew, Eugene J. "God's Use of General Revelation in His Response to Job: A Critique of 2000 Years of Interpretation in Judaism and Christianity." *Journal of Christian Apologetics* 2 (1998) 94–131.

McCartney, Dan G. "New Testament Use of the Old Testament." In *Inerrancy and Hermeneutic: A Tradition, a Challenge, a Debate*, edited by Harvie Conn, 101–16. Grand Rapids: Baker, 1988.

McClain, Alva J. *Romans: The Gospel of God's Grace*. Edited by Herman A. Hoyt. Winona Lake, IN: BMH, 1973.

McKenna, David L. *Job*. Communicator's Commentary Series 12. Waco: Word, 1986.

McKenzie, John L. *Second Isaiah*. Anchor Bible 20. Garden City: Doubleday, 1968.

Melugin, Roy F. *The Formation of Isaiah 40–55*. Beihefte zur Zeitschrift fuer die altestamentliche Wissenschaft 141. Berlin: de Grutyer, 1976.

Merkle, Ben L. "Romans 11 and the Future of Ethnic Israel." *Journal of the Evangelical Theological Society* 43 (2000) 709–21.

Merrill, Eugene H. *Everlasting Dominion: A Theology of the Old Testament*. Nashville: Broadman & Holman, 2006.

———. "Isaiah 40–55 as Anti-Babylonian Polemic." *Grace Theological Journal* 8 (1987) 3–18.

———. "The Language and Literary Characteristics of Isaiah 40–55 as Anti-Babylonian Polemic." PhD diss., Columbia University, 1984.

———. "The Literary Character of Isaiah 40–55: Part 1: Survey of a Century of Studies." *Bibliotheca Sacra* 144 (1987) 24–43.

———. "The Literary Character of Isaiah 40–55: Part 2: Literary Genres in Isaiah 40–55." *Bibliotheca Sacra* 144 (1987) 144–55.

———. "The Unfading Word: Isaiah and the Incomparability of Israel's God." In *The Church at the Dawn of the 21st Century: Essays in Honor of W. A. Criswell*, edited by Paige Patterson, John Pretlove, and Luis Pantoja Jr., 131–55. Dallas: Criswell, 1989.

Mettinger, Tryggve N. D. "The Enigma of Job: The Deconstruction of God in Intertextual Perspective." *Journal of Northwest Semitic Languages* 23:2 (1997) 1–19.

———. "The God of Job: Avenger, Tyrant, or Victor?" In *The Voice from the Whirlwind: Interpreting the Book of Job*, edited by Leo G. Perdue and W. Clark Gilpin, 39–49, 232–33. Nashville: Abingdon, 1992.

Meyer, Heinrich August Wilhelm. *Critical and Exegetical Handbook to the Epistle to the Romans*. Edited by William P. Dickson. Translated by John C. Moore and Edwin Johnson. 2 vols. Critical and Exegetical Commentary on the New Testament 9–10. Edinburgh: T. & T. Clark, 1881.

Michel, Otto. *Der Brief an die Römer*. 14th ed. Kritisch-exegetischer Kommentar über das Neue Testament 4. Göttingen: Vandenhoeck & Ruprecht, 1978.

Mickel, Tobias. *Seelsorgerliche Aspekte im Hiobbuch: Ein Beitrag zur biblischen Dimension der Poimenik*. Theologische Arbeiten 48. Berlin: Evangelische Verlagsanstalt, 1990.

Miller, James E. "The Structure and Meaning of the Animal Discourse in the Theophany of Job (38,39–39,30)." *Zeitschrift für die alttestamentliche Wissenschaft* 103 (1991) 418–21.

Milling, D. H. "The Origin and Character of the New Testament Doxology." PhD diss., University of Cambridge, 1972.

Miscall, Peter D. *Isaiah*. Readings: A New Biblical Commentary. Sheffield, England: JSOT, 1993.

Moo, Douglas J. *Encountering the Book of Romans: A Theological Survey*. Encountering Biblical Studies. Grand Rapids: Baker, 2002.

———. "Israel and the Law in Romans 5–11: Interaction with the New Perspective." In *The Paradoxes of Paul*. Vol. 2. *Justification and Variegated Nomism*, edited by D. A. Carson, Peter T. O'Brien, and Mark A. Seifrid, 185–216. Wissenschaftliche Untersuchungen zum Neuen Testament 181. Grand Rapids: Baker, 2004.

———. "The Law of Christ as the Fulfillment of the Law of Moses: A Modified Lutheran View." Vol. 8. *Five Views on Law and Gospel*, edited by Stanley N. Gundry, 3–90, 165–73, 218–25, 309–15, 319–76. Counterpoints. Grand Rapids: Zondervan, 1999.

———. *The Letter of James*. Pillar New Testament Commentary. Grand Rapids: Eerdmans, 2000.

———. "Paul's Universalizing Hermeneutic in Romans." *The Southern Baptist Journal of Theology* 11:3 (2007) 62–90.

———. *Romans*. NIV Application Commentary. Grand Rapids: Zondervan, 2000.

———. *The Epistle to the Romans*. New International Commentary on the New Testament. Grand Rapids: Eerdmans, 1996.

———. *The Old Testament in the Gospel Passion Narratives*. Sheffield: Almond, 1983.

———. "The Problem of Sensus Plenior." In *Hermeneutics, Authority, and Canon*, edited by D. A. Carson and John D. Woodbridge, 175–211, 397–405. Grand Rapids: Zondervan, 1986.

———. "The Theology of Romans 9–11: A Response to E. Elizabeth Johnson." In *Romans*, edited by David M. Hay and E. Elizabeth Johnson, 240–58. Pauline Theology. Minneapolis: Fortress, 1995.

Moo, Douglas J., and Andrew David Naselli. "The Problem of the New Testament's Use of the Old Testament." *"But My Words Will Never Pass Away": The Enduring Authority of the Christian Scriptures*, edited by D. A. Carson. Grand Rapids: Eerdmans, forthcoming.

Moore, Carey A. *Judith: A New Translation with Introduction and Commentary*. Anchor Yale Bible. New Haven: Yale University Press, 2008.

Morgan, Donn F. *Wisdom in the Old Testament Traditions*. Atlanta: John Knox, 1981.

Morris, Henry M. *The Remarkable Record of Job: The Ancient Wisdom, Scientific Accuracy, and Life-Changing Message of an Amazing Book*. Grand Rapids: Baker, 1988.

Morris, Leon. *The Epistle to the Romans*. Pillar New Testament Commentary. Grand Rapids: Eerdmans, 1988.

———. "The Theme of Romans." In *Apostolic History and the Gospel: Biblical and Historical Essays Presented to F. F. Bruce on His 60th Birthday*, edited by W. Ward Gasque and Ralph P. Martin, 249–63. Grand Rapids: Eerdmans, 1970.

Morriston, Wesley. "God's Answer to Job." *Religious Studies* 32 (1996) 339–56.

Mortenson, Sonja. "The Text and Interpretation of Isaiah 40 in the Dead Sea Scrolls." MA thesis, Trinity Western University (Canada), 2003.

Motyer, J. Alec. *Isaiah: An Introduction and Commentary*. Tyndale Old Testament Commentaries 18. Downers Grove, IL: InterVarsity, 1999.

———. *The Prophecy of Isaiah: An Introduction and Commentary*. Downers Grove, IL: InterVarsity, 1993.

Moyise, Steve. "Quotations." In *As It Is Written: Studying Paul's Use of Scripture*, edited by Stanley E. Porter and Christopher D. Stanley, 15–28. Society of Biblical Literature Symposium Series 50. Atlanta: Society of Biblical Literature, 2008.

Muilenberg, James. "The Book of Isaiah: Chapters 40–66." Vol. 5. *The Interpreter's Bible*, 381–772. Nashville: Abingdon, 1956.

Mullen, E. Theodore, Jr. "Divine Assembly." In *Anchor Bible Dictionary*, edited by D. N. Freedman, 2:214–17. 6 vols. New York: Doubleday, 1992.

———. *The Divine Council in Canaanite and Early Hebrew Literature*. Harvard Semitic Monographs 24. Chico: Scholars, 1980.

Müller, Christian. *Gottes Gerechtigkeit und Gottes Volk: Eine Untersuchung zu Römer 9–11*. Forschungen zur Religion und Literatur des Alten und Neuen Testaments 86. Göttingen: Vandenhoeck & Ruprecht, 1964.

Müller, Hans-Peter. "Die Hiobrahmenerzählung und ihre altorientalischen Parallelen als paradigmen einer weisheitlichen Wirklichkeitswahrnahme." In *The Book of Job*, edited by W. A. M. Beuken, 21–39. Bibliotheca ephemeridum theologicarum lovaniensium 114. Leuven: Leuven University Press, 1994.

Munck, Johannes. *Christ and Israel: An Interpretation of Romans 9–11*. Philadelphia: Fortress, 1967.

Murphy, Roland E. *The Tree of Life: An Exploration of Biblical Wisdom Literature*. 3rd ed. Grand Rapids: Eerdmans, 2002.

Murray, John. *The Epistle to the Romans: The English Text with Introduction, Exposition and Notes*. 2 vols. New International Commentary on the New Testament. Reprint, 1997. Grand Rapids: Eerdmans, 1959–65.

Myers, Jacob M. *I and II Esdras: Introduction, Translation and Commentary*. Anchor Yale Bible. New Haven: Yale University Press, 2008.

Naidoff, Bruce D. "The Rhetoric of Encouragement in Isaiah 40:12–31: A Form-Critical Study." *Zeitschrift für die alttestamentliche Wissenschaft* 93 (1981) 62–76.

Nanos, Mark D. *The Mystery of Romans: The Jewish Context of Paul's Letter*. Minneapolis: Fortress, 1996.

Naselli, Andrew David. "Paul's Use of Isaiah 40:13 and Job 41:3a (Eng. 41:11a) in Romans 11:34–35." PhD diss., Trinity Evangelical Divinity School, 2010.

Newell, B. Lynne. "Job: Repentant or Rebellious?" *Westminster Theological Journal* 46 (1984) 298–316.

Newman, Barclay M., and Eugene A. Nida. *A Handbook on Paul's Letter to the Romans*. New York: United Bible Societies, 1973.

Newsom, Carol A. *The Book of Job: A Contest of Moral Imaginations*. Oxford: Oxford University Press, 2003.

———. "The Book of Job: Introduction, Commentary, and Reflections." Vol. 4. *The New Interpreter's Bible*, 317-637. Nashville: Abingdon, 1996.

Nicholson, E. W. "The Limits of Theodicy as a Theme of the Book of Job." In *Wisdom in Ancient Israel: Essays in Honour of J. A. Emerton*, edited by John Day, Robert P. Gordon, and H. G. M. Williamson, 71-82. Cambridge: Cambridge University Press, 1995.

Nickelsburg, George W. E. *1 Enoch: A Commentary on the Book of 1 Enoch, Chapters 1-36; 81-108*. Edited by Klaus Baltzer. Hermeneia. Minneapolis: Fortress, 2001.

———. *Jewish Literature between the Bible and the Mishnah: A Literary and Historical Introduction*. 2nd ed. Minneapolis: Fortress, 2005.

Nicole, Roger. "New Testament Use of the Old Testament." In *Revelation and the Bible: Contemporary Evangelical Thought*, edited by Carl F. H. Henry, 137-51. Grand Rapids: Baker, 1958.

———. "Patrick Fairbairn and Biblical Hermeneutics as Related to the Quotations of the Old Testament in the New." In *Hermeneutics, Inerrancy, and the Bible: Papers from ICBI Summit II*, edited by Earl D. Radmacher and Robert D. Preus, 767-76. Grand Rapids: Zondervan, 1984.

———. "The Old Testament in the New Testament." In *Expositor's Bible Commentary* 1, edited by Frank E. Gaebelein, 617-28. Grand Rapids: Eerdmans, 1979.

Norden, Eduard. *Agnostos Theos: Untersuchungen zur Formengeschichte religiöser Rede*. Leipzig: Teubner, 1923.

North, Christopher R. *Isaiah 40-55: Introduction and Commentary*. 2nd ed. Torch Bible Commentaries. London: SCM, 1964.

Nygren, Anders. *Commentary on Romans*. Translated by Carl C. Rasmussen. London: SCM, 1952.

O'Brien, Peter T. "Benediction, Blessing, Doxology, Thanksgiving." In *Dictionary of Paul and His Letters*, edited by Gerald F. Hawthorne and Ralph P. Martin, 68-71. Downers Grove, IL: InterVarsity, 1993.

O'Connor, Kathleen M. "Wild, Raging Creativity: The Scene in the Whirlwind (Job 38-41)." In *A God so Near: Essays on Old Testament Theology in Honor of Patrick D. Miller*, edited by Brent A. Strawn and Nancy R. Bowen, 171-79. Winona Lake, IN: Eisenbrauns, 2003.

O'Neill, J. C. *Paul's Letter to the Romans*. Pelican New Testament Commentaries. Baltimore: Penguin, 1975.

Oehler, Gustav Friedrich. *Theology of the Old Testament*. Translated by George E. Day. 2nd ed. New York: Funk & Wagnaiss, 1883.

Oesterley, W. O. E. *Studies in Isaiah XL-LXVI: With an Introductory Chapter on the Composite Character of Isaiah I-XXXIX*. London: Scott, 1916.

Origen. *Commentary on the Epistle to the Romans, Books 6-10*. Translated by Thomas P. Scheck. The Fathers of the Church: A New Translation 104. Washington, D.C.: The Catholic University of America Press, 2002.

Oropeza, B. J. "Paul and Theodicy: Intertextual Thoughts on God's Justice and Faithfulness to Israel in Romans 9-11." *New Testament Studies* 53 (2007) 57-80.

Osborne, Grant R. *Romans*. IVP New Testament Commentary. Downers Grove, IL: InterVarsity, 2004.

———. *The Hermeneutical Spiral: A Comprehensive Introduction to Biblical Interpretation.* 2nd ed. Downers Grove, IL: InterVarsity, 2006.
———. *Revelation.* Baker Exegetical Commentary on the New Testament. Grand Rapids: Baker, 2002.
———. "Type, Typology." In *Evangelical Dictionary of Theology*, 2nd ed., edited by Walter A. Elwell, 1222–1223. Grand Rapids: Baker, 2001.
———. "Type; Typology." Vol. 4. *The International Standard Bible Encyclopedia*, edited by Geoffrey W. Bromiley, 930–32. Grand Rapids: Eerdmans, 1979.
Oss, Douglas A. "A Note on Paul's Use of Isaiah." *Bulletin for Biblical Research* 2 (1992) 105–12.
———. "Paul's Use of Isaiah and Its Place in His Theology: With Special Reference to Romans 9–11." PhD diss., Westminster Theological Seminary, 1992.
Oswalt, John N. "Isaiah." In *New Dictionary of Biblical Theology*, edited by T. Desmond Alexander and Brian S. Rosner, 217–23. Downers Grove, IL: InterVarsity, 2000.
———. *Isaiah.* NIV Application Commentary. Grand Rapids: Zondervan, 2003.
———. "The Book of Isaiah: A Short Course on Biblical Theology." *Calvin Theological Journal* 39 (2004) 54–71.
———. *The Book of Isaiah: Chapters 1–39.* New International Commentary on the Old Testament. Grand Rapids: Eerdmans, 1986.
———. *The Book of Isaiah: Chapters 40–66.* New International Commentary on the Old Testament. Grand Rapids: Eerdmans, 1988.
———. "The Kerygmatic Structure of the Book of Isaiah." In *"Go to the Land I Will Show You": Studies in Honor of Dwight W. Young*, edited by Joseph E. Coleson and Victor H. Matthews, 143–57. Winona Lake, IN: Eisenbrauns, 1996.
———. "Key Themes in the Book of Isaiah: Their Relevance for Christian Theology." Vol. 3. *Newell Lectureships*, edited by Timothy Dwyer, 13–90, 202–11. Anderson, IN: Warner, 1996.
———. "The Myth of the Dragon and Old Testament Faith." *Evangelical Quarterly* 49 (1977) 163–72.
———. "Theology of Isaiah." Vol. 4. *The New International Dictionary of Old Testament Theology and Exegesis*, edited by Willem A. VanGemeren, 725–32. Grand Rapids: Zondervan, 1997.
Painter, Ricky C. "A Hermeneutical and Exegetical Assessment and Application of Folklore Theory to Job 1–31 and 42:7–17 as an Account of Testing." PhD diss., Trinity Evangelical Divinity School, 2005.
Pao, David W. *Acts and the Isaianic New Exodus.* Wissenschaftliche Untersuchungen zum Neuen Testament 130. Tübingen: Mohr Siebeck, 2000.
Parry, Donald W., and Elisha Qimron, eds. *The Great Isaiah Scroll (1QIsaa): A New Edition.* Studies on the Texts of the Desert of Judah 32. Leiden: Brill, 1999.
Parsons, Gregory W. "A Biblical Theology of Job 38:1—42:6." ThD diss., Dallas Theological Seminary, 1980.
———. "Job, Theology of." In *Evangelical Dictionary of Biblical Theology*, edited by Walter A. Elwell, 415–19. Grand Rapids: Baker, 1996.
———. "Literary Features of the Book of Job." *Bibliotheca Sacra* 138 (1981) 213–29.
———. "The Structure and Purpose of the Book of Job." *Bibliotheca Sacra* 138 (1981) 139–51.
Patrick, James E. "The Fourfold Structure of Job: Variations on a Theme." *Vetus Testamentum* 55 (2005) 185–206.

Patton, Corrine L. "The Beauty of the Beast: Leviathan and Behemoth in Light of Catholic Theology." In *The Whirlwind: Essays on Job, Hermeneutics and Theology in Memory of Jane Morse*, edited by Stephen L. Cook, Corrine L. Patton, and James W. Watts, 142–67. Journal for the Study of the Old Testament Supplement Series 336. London: Sheffield Academic, 2001.

Payne, J. Barton. "Eighth Century Israelitish Background of Isaiah 40–66." *Westminster Theological Journal* 29 (1967) 179–90.

———. "Eighth Century Israelitish Background of Isaiah 40–66: Part II." *Westminster Theological Journal* 30 (1967) 50–58.

———. "Eighth Century Israelitish Background of Isaiah 40–66: Part III." *Westminster Theological Journal* 30 (1968) 185–203.

———. "לוה." In *Theological Workbook of the Old Testament*, edited by R. L. Harris and G. L. Archer, 471–72. 2 vols. Chicago: Moody, 1980.

Pegler, Stephen T. "The Nature of Paul's Universal Salvation Language in Romans." PhD diss., Trinity Evangelical Divinity School, 2002.

Penchansky, David. *The Betrayal of God: Ideological Conflict in Job*. Literary Currents in Biblical Interpretation. Louisville: Westminster John Knox, 1990.

Pépin, Jean. "Le 'Conseiller' de Dieu." In *Lectures anciennes de la Bible*, edited by P. Maraval, 53–73. Cahiers de Biblia Patristica 1. Strasbourg: Centre d'Analyse et de Documentation Patristiques, 1987.

Perdue, Leo G. *Wisdom and Creation: The Theology of Wisdom Literature*. Nashville: Abingdon, 1994.

———. *Wisdom in Revolt: Metaphorical Theology in the Book of Job*. Journal for the Study of the Old Testament Supplement Series 112. Sheffield: JSOT, 1991.

———. "Wisdom in the Book of Job." In *In Search of Wisdom: Essays in Memory of John G. Gammie*, edited by Leo G. Perdue, William Johnston Wiseman, and Bernard Brandon Scott, 73–98. Louisville: Westminster John Knox, 1993.

———. *Wisdom Literature: A Theological History*. Louisville: Westminster John Knox Press, 2007.

Pesch, Rudolf. *Römerbrief*. Die neue Echter Bibel. Würzburg: Echter, 1983.

Pfeiffer, Charles F. "Lotan and Leviathan." *Evangelical Quarterly* 32 (1960) 208–11.

Pidcock-Lester, Karen. "'Earth Has No Sorrow That Earth Cannot Heal': Job 38–41." In *God Who Creates: Essays in Honor of W. Sibley Towner*, edited by William P. Brown and S. Dean McBride Jr., 125–32. Grand Rapids: Eerdmans, 2000.

Pieper, August. *Isaiah II: An Exposition of Isaiah 40–66*. Translated by Erwin E. Kowalke. Milwaukee: Northwestern, 1979.

Pietersma, Albert, and Benjamin G. Wright, eds. "Iob." In *A New Translation of the Septuagint and the Other Greek Translations Traditionally Included under That Title*, translated by Claude E. Cox, 667–97. Oxford: Oxford University Press, 2007.

Pinto, Carlos Osvaldo Cardoso. "The Contribution of the Isaiah Quotations to Paul's Argument in Romans 9–11." PhD diss., Dallas Theological Seminary, 2003.

Piper, John. "The Deep Riches and Wisdom and Knowledge of God." Sermon on Rom 11:33–36, Bethlehem Baptist Church, Minneapolis, MN, March 21, 2004. No pages. Online: http://www.desiringgod.org/ResourceLibrary/Sermons/ByDate/2004/167_The_Deep_Riches_and_Wisdom_and_Knowledge_of_God/. Accessed June 25, 2009.

———. *God's Passion for His Glory: Living the Vision of Jonathan Edwards: With the Complete Text of The End for Which God Created the World*. Wheaton: Crossway, 1998.

———. *The Justification of God: An Exegetical and Theological Study of Romans 9:1–23*. 2nd ed. Grand Rapids: Baker, 1993.

Pleins, J. David. "'Why Do You Hide Your Face?': Divine Silence and Speech in the Book of Job." *Interpretation* 48 (1994) 229–38.

Polzin, Robert, and David Robertson, eds. *Studies in the Book of Job*. Semeia 7. Missoula, MT: Society of Biblical Literature, 1977.

Pope, Marvin H. *Job: Introduction, Translation, and Notes*. 3rd ed. Anchor Bible 15. Garden City, NY: Doubleday, 1973.

Porter, Stanley E., ed. *Hearing the Old Testament in the New Testament*. McMaster New Testament Studies 8. Grand Rapids: Eerdmans, 2006.

Porter, Stanley E. "The Message of the Book of Job: Job 42:7b as Key to Interpretation?" *Evangelical Quarterly* 63 (1991) 291–304.

———. "The Use of the Old Testament in the New Testament: A Brief Comment on Method and Terminology." In *Early Christian Interpretation of the Scriptures of Israel: Investigations and Proposals*, edited by Craig A. Evans and James Sanders, 79–96. Journal for the Study of the New Testament Supplement Series 148; Studies in Scripture in Early Judaism and Christianity 5. Sheffield: Sheffield Academic Press, 1997.

Porter, Stanley E., and Christopher D. Stanley, eds. *As It Is Written: Studying Paul's Use of Scripture*. Society of Biblical Literature Symposium Series 50. Atlanta: Society of Biblical Literature, 2008.

Porter, Wendy J. "Creeds and Hymns." In *Dictionary of New Testament Background*, edited by Craig A. Evans and Stanley E. Porter, 231–38. Downers Grove, IL: InterVarsity, 2000.

Poythress, Vern Sheridan. "Divine Meaning of Scripture." *Westminster Theological Journal* 48 (1986) 241–79.

Preuß, Horst Dietrich. "Jahwes Antwort an Hiob und die sogenannte Hiobliteratur des alten Vorderen Orients." In *Beiträge zur alttestamentlichen Theologie: Festschrift für Walther Zimmerli zum 70. Geburtstag*, edited by Herbert Donner, Robert Hanhart, and Rudolf Smend, 323–43. Göttingen: Vandenhoeck & Ruprecht, 1977.

Pury, Roland de. *Hiob, der Mensch im Aufruhr*. Biblische Studien 15. Neukirchen: Neukirchener Verlag, 1957.

Rad, Gerhard von. *Wisdom in Israel*. Nashville: Abingdon, 1972.

Räisänen, Heikki. "Paul, God, and Israel: Romans 9–11 in Recent Research." In *The Social World of Formative Christianity and Judaism: Essays in Tribute to Howard Clark Kee*, edited by Jacob Neusner, Peter Borgen, and Ernest S. Fredrichs, 178–206. Philadelphia: Fortress, 1988.

Reasoner, Mark. *Romans in Full Circle: A History of Interpretation*. Louisville: Westminster John Knox, 2005.

Refoulé, François. "*. . . Et Ainsi Tout Israël Sera Sauvé*": *Romains 11, 25–32*. Lectio Divina 117. Paris: Cerf, 1984.

Reichert, Angelika. *Der Römerbrief als Gratwanderung: Eine Untersuchung zur Abfassungsproblematik*. Forschungen zur Religion und Literatur des Alten und Neuen Testaments 194. Göttingen: Vandenhoeck & Ruprecht, 2001.

Reyburn, William D. *A Handbook on the Book of Job*. UBS Handbook Series. New York: United Bible Societies, 1992.
Ridderbos, Herman N. *Aan De Romeinen. Commentaar op het Nieuwe Testament*. Kampen: Kok, 1959.
———. *Paul: An Outline of His Theology*. Translated by John Richard de Witt. Grand Rapids: Eerdmans, 1975.
Ridderbos, Jan. *Isaiah*. Translated by John Vriend. Bible Students Commentary. Grand Rapids: Zondervan, 1985.
Roberts, Alexander, James Donaldson, and A. Cleveland Coxe, eds. *The Ante-Nicene Fathers: Translations of the Writings of the Fathers Down to A.D. 325*. 8 vols. Grand Rapids: Eerdmans, 1997.
Roberts, J. J. M. "Isaiah in Old Testament Theology." *Interpretation* 36 (1982) 130–43.
Robertson, David. "The Book of Job: A Literary Study." *Soundings* 56 (1973) 446–69.
Robinson, John A. T. *Wrestling with Romans*. Philadelphia: Westminster, 1979.
Rodd, C. S. *The Book of Job*. Narrative Commentaries. Philadelphia: Trinity Press International, 1990.
Rosner, Brian S. "Salvation, History of." In *Dictionary for Theological Interpretation of the Bible*, edited by Kevin J. Vanhoozer, 714–17. Grand Rapids: Baker, 2005.
Rowley, H. H. *Job*. 2nd ed. New Century Bible. Grand Rapids: Eerdmans, 1980.
———. "The Book of Job and Its Meaning." In *From Moses to Qumran: Studies in the Old Testament*, 141–83. London: Lutterworth, 1963.
Rowold, Henry L. "The Theology of Creation in the Yahweh Speeches as a Solution to the Problem Posed by the Book of Job." ThD diss., Concordia Seminary in Exile, 1977.
———. "מי הוא? לי הוא!: Leviathan and Job in Job 41:2–3." *Journal of Biblical Literature* 105 (1986) 104–9.
Rude, Terry. "God's Answer to a Complaining Sufferer (Job 38:1—42:6)." *Biblical Viewpoint* 21:2 (1987) 37–41.
Ruppert, Lothar. "Die Disputationsworte bei Deuterojesaja in neuem religionsgeschichtlichem Licht." In *Prophetie und geschichtliche Wirklichkeit im alten Israel: Festschrift für Siegfried Herrmann zum 65. Geburtstag*, edited by Rüdiger Liwak and Siegfried Wagner, 317–25. Stuttgart, Germany: Kohlhammer, 1991.
Ryan, Judith M. "The Faithfulness of God: Paul's Prophetic Response to Israel: An Exegesis of Romans 11:1–36." PhD diss., Fordham University, 1995.
Ryken, Philip Graham, Derek Thomas, and J. Ligon Duncan, eds. *Give Praise to God: A Vision for Reforming Worship: Celebrating the Legacy of James Montgomery Boice*. Phillipsburg, NJ: Presbyterian & Reformed, 2003.
Ryken, Leland, J. C. Wilhoit, and Tremper Longman III, eds. "Rhetorical Patterns." In *Dictionary of Biblical Imagery*, 720–27. Downers Grove, IL: InterVarsity, 1998.
Sanday, William, and Arthur C. Headlam. *A Critical and Exegetical Commentary on the Epistle to the Romans*. 5th ed. International Critical Commentary. Edinburgh: T. & T. Clark, 1907.
Sanders, E. P. *Paul and Palestinian Judaism*. Philadelphia: Fortress, 1977.
———. *Paul, the Law, and the Jewish People*. Minneapolis: Fortress, 1983.
Sandmel, Samuel. "Parallelomania." *Journal of Biblical Literature* 81 (1962) 1–13.
Scheindlin, Raymond P., ed. *The Book of Job*. Translated by Raymond P. Scheindlin. New York: Norton, 1998.

Schelkle, Karl Hermann. *Paulus, Lehrer der Väter: Die altkirchliche Auslegung von Römer 1–11*. Düsseldorf: Patmos, 1956.

Schifferdecker, Kathryn. *Out of the Whirlwind: Creation Theology in the Book of Job*. Harvard Theological Studies 61. Cambridge: Harvard University Press, 2008.

Schlatter, Adolf von. *Gottes Gerechtigkeit: Ein Kommentar zum Römerbrief*. 4th ed. Stuttgart: Calwer, 1965.

Schlier, Heinrich. *Der Römerbrief: Kommentar von Heinrich Schlier*. Herders theologischer Kommentar zum Neuen Testament 6. Basel: Herder, 1979.

Schmidt, Hans Wilhelm. *Der Brief des Paulus an die Römer*. Theologischer Handkommentar zum Neuen Testament 6. Berlin: Evangelische, 1963.

Schmithals, Walter. *Der Römerbrief als historisches Problem*. Studien zum Neuen Testament 9. Gütersloher: Mohn, 1975.

———. *Der Römerbrief: Ein Kommentar*. Gütersloher: Mohn, 1988.

Schmitt, John J. *Isaiah and His Interpreters*. New York: Paulist, 1986.

Schmitt, Rainer. *Gottesgerechtigkeit—Heilsgeschichte—Israel in der Theologie des Paulus*. Europäische Hochschulschriften 23. New York: Peter Lang, 1984.

Schnabel, Eckhard J. *Law and Wisdom from Ben Sira to Paul: A Tradition Historical Enquiry into the Relation of Law, Wisdom, and Ethics*. Wissenschaftliche Untersuchungen zum Neuen Testament 16. Tübingen: Mohr Siebeck, 1985.

Schnelle, Udo, ed. *The Letter to the Romans*. Bibliotheca ephemeridum theologicarum lovaniensium 226. Leuven: Peeters, 2009.

Scholnick, Sylvia Huberman. "Poetry in the Courtroom: Job 38–41." In *Directions in Hebrew Poetry*, edited by Elaine Follis, 185–204. Journal for the Study of the Old Testament Supplement Series 40. Sheffield: JSOT, 1987.

Schoors, Antoon. *I Am God Your Saviour: A Form-Critical Study of the Main Genres in Is. XL–LV*. Vetus Testamentum Supplements 24. Leiden: Brill, 1973.

Schreiner, Susan Elizabeth. *Where Shall Wisdom Be Found? Calvin's Exegesis of Job from Medieval and Modern Perspectives*. Chicago: University of Chicago Press, 1994.

Schreiner, Thomas R. "Corporate and Individual Election in Romans 9: A Response to Brian Abasciano." *Journal of the Evangelical Theological Society* 49 (2006) 373–86.

———. "Does Romans 9 Teach Individual Election unto Salvation?" In *Still Sovereign: Contemporary Perspectives on Election, Foreknowledge, and Grace*, edited by Thomas R. Schreiner and Bruce A. Ware, 89–106. Grand Rapids: Baker, 2000.

———. "Reading Romans Theologically: A Review Article." *Journal of the Evangelical Theological Society* 41 (1998) 641–50.

———. *Romans*. Baker Exegetical Commentary on the New Testament 6. Grand Rapids: Baker, 1998.

Schultz, Richard L. "Isaiah, Book of." In *Dictionary for Theological Interpretation of the Bible*, edited by Kevin J. Vanhoozer, 336–44. Grand Rapids: Baker, 2005.

Schweitzer, Albert. *The Mysticism of Paul the Apostle*. Translated by W. Montgomery. New York: Holt, 1931.

Scobie, Charles H. H. *The Ways of Our God: An Approach to Biblical Theology*. Grand Rapids: Eerdmans, 2002.

Scott, J. Julius, Jr. *Jewish Backgrounds of the New Testament*. Grand Rapids: Baker, 2000.

Scott, James M. "'And Then All Israel Will Be Saved' (Rom 11:26)." In *Restoration: Old Testament, Jewish, and Christian Perspectives*, edited by James M. Scott, 489–527. Supplements to the Journal for the Study of Judaism 72. Leiden: Brill, 2001.

Scroggs, Robin. "Paul: ΣΟΦΟΣ and ΠΝΕΥΜΑΤΙΚΟΣ." *New Testament Studies* 14 (1967) 33–55.
Seifrid, Mark A. *Christ, Our Righteousness: Paul's Theology of Justification*. New Studies in Biblical Theology 9. Downers Grove, IL: InterVarsity, 2000.
———. "Paul's Use of Righteousness Language Against Its Hellenistic Background." In *The Paradoxes of Paul*. Vol. 2. *Justification and Variegated Nomism*, edited by D. A Carson, Peter T. O'Brien, and Mark A. Seifrid, 39–74. Wissenschaftliche Untersuchungen zum Neuen Testament 181. Grand Rapids: Baker, 2004.
———. "Righteousness Language in the Hebrew Scriptures and Early Judaism." In *The Complexities of Second Temple Judaism*. Vol. 1. *Justification and Variegated Nomism*, edited by D. A Carson, Peter T. O'Brien, and Mark A. Seifrid, 415–42. Wissenschaftliche Untersuchungen zum Neuen Testament 140. Grand Rapids: Baker, 2001.
———. "Romans." In *Commentary on the New Testament Use of the Old Testament*, edited by G. K. Beale and D. A. Carson, 607–94. Grand Rapids: Baker, 2007.
———. "The Gospel as the Revelation of Mystery: The Witness of the Scriptures to Christ in Romans." *The Southern Baptist Journal of Theology* 11:3 (2007) 92–103.
Seitz, Christopher R. "How Is the Prophet Isaiah Present in the Latter Half of the Book? The Logic of Chapters 40–66 within the Book of Isaiah." *Journal of Biblical Literature* 115 (1996) 219–40.
———. *Isaiah 1–39*. Interpretation. Louisville: Westminster John Knox, 1993.
Seitz, Christopher R., ed. *Reading and Preaching the Book of Isaiah*. Philadelphia: Fortress, 1988.
Seitz, Christopher R. "The Book of Isaiah 40–66: Introduction, Commentary, and Reflections." Vol. 6. *The New Interpreter's Bible*, 307–552. Nashville: Abingdon, 2001.
———. "The Divine Council: Temporal Transition and New Prophecy in the Book of Isaiah." *Journal of Biblical Literature* 109 (1990) 229–47.
Shaw, Bernard. *The Adventures of the Black Girl in Her Search for God*. London: Constable, 1932.
Shedd, W. G. T. *A Critical and Doctrinal Commentary upon the Epistle of St. Paul to the Romans*. New York: Scribner's, 1879.
Sheldon, Linda Jean. "The Book of Job as Hebrew Theodicy: An Ancient Near Eastern Intertextual Conflict Between Law and Cosmology." PhD diss., University of California, Berkeley, 2002.
Shum, Shiu-Lun. *Paul's Use of Isaiah in Romans: A Comparative Study of Paul's Letter to the Romans and the Sibylline and Qumran Sectarian Texts*. Wissenschaftliche Untersuchungen zum Neuen Testament 156. Tübingen: Mohr Siebeck, 2002.
Sickenberger, Joseph. *Die Briefe des Heiligen Paulus an die Korinther und Römer*. 4th ed. Die Heilige Schrift des Neuen Testamentes 6. Bonn: Hanstein, 1932.
Silva, Moisés. "Old Testament in Paul." In *Dictionary of Paul and His Letters*, edited by Gerald F. Hawthorne, Ralph P. Martin, and Daniel G. Reid, 630–42. Downers Grove, IL: InterVarsity, 1993.
———. "The New Testament Use of the Old Testament: Text Form and Authority." In *Scripture and Truth*, edited by D. A. Carson and John D. Woodbridge, 147–65, 381–86. Grand Rapids: Zondervan, 1983.
Simonetti, Manlio, and Marco Conti, eds. *Job*. Ancient Christian Commentary on Scripture: Old Testament 6. Downers Grove, IL: InterVarsity, 2006.

Simundson, Daniel J. *The Message of Job: A Theological Commentary*. Augsburg Old Testament Studies. Minneapolis: Augsburg, 1986.

Skehan, Patrick William. "Job's Final Plea (Job 29–31) and the Lord's Reply (Job 38–41)." *Biblica* 45 (1964) 51–62.

Skinner, John. *The Book of the Prophet Isaiah*. 2nd ed. Cambridge Bible for Schools and Colleges. Cambridge: Cambridge University Press, 1917.

Smart, James D. *History and Theology in Second Isaiah: A Commentary on Isaiah 35, 40–66*. Philadelphia: Westminster, 1965.

Smick, Elmer B. "Another Look at the Mythological Elements in the Book of Job." *Westminster Theological Journal* 40 (1978) 213–28.

———. "Architectonics, Structural Poems, and Rhetorical Devices in the Book of Job." In *A Tribute to Gleason Archer*, edited by Walter C. Kaiser Jr. and Ronald F. Youngblood, 87–104. Chicago: Moody, 1986.

———. "Job." In *1 Kings–Job*, 843–1060. Expositor's Bible Commentary 4. Grand Rapids: Eerdmans, 1988.

———. "Mythology and the Book of Job." *Journal of the Evangelical Theological Society* 13 (1970) 101–8.

———. "Semeiological Interpretation of the Book of Job." *Westminster Theological Journal* 48 (1986) 135–49.

Smith, D. Moody. "The Pauline Literature." In *It Is Written: Scripture Citing Scripture: Essays in Honour of Barnabas Lindars, SSF*, edited by D. A. Carson and H. G. M. Williamson, 265–91. Cambridge: Cambridge University Press, 1988.

———. "The Use of the Old Testament in the New." In *The Use of the Old Testament in the New and Other Essays: Studies in Honor of William Franklin Stinespring*, edited by James M. Efird, 3–65. Durham: Duke University Press, 1972.

Smith, Gary V. "Is There a Place for Job's Wisdom in Old Testament Theology?" *Trinity Journal* 13 (1992) 3–20.

———. *Isaiah 1–39*. New American Commentary 15A. Nashville: Broadman & Holman, 2007.

———. *Isaiah 40–66*. New American Commentary 15B. Nashville: Broadman & Holman, 2009.

Smith, Sidney. *Isaiah Chapters XL–LV: Literary Criticism and History*. The Schweich Lectures 1940. London: Oxford University Press, 1944.

Snaith, Norman H. *The Book of Job: Its Origin and Purpose*. Studies in Biblical Theology: Second Series 11. London: SCM, 1968.

Soskice, Janet Martin. *Metaphor and Religious Language*. New York: Oxford University Press, 1985.

Spencer, F. Scott. "Metaphor, Mystery and the Salvation of Israel in Romans 9–11: Paul's Appeal to Humility and Doxology." *Review and Expositor* 103 (2006) 113–33.

Sproul, R. C. *The Gospel of God: Expositions of Paul's Letter to the Romans*. Scotland: Christian Focus, 1999.

Stein, Robert H. *A Basic Guide to Interpreting the Bible: Playing by the Rules*. 2nd ed. Grand Rapids: Baker, 2011.

Steinmann, Andrew E. "The Structure and Message of the Book of Job." *Vetus Testamentum* 46 (1996) 85–100.

Stendahl, Krister. *Paul among Jews and Gentiles: And Other Essays*. Philadelphia: Fortress, 1976.

———. "The Apostle Paul and the Introspective Conscience of the West." *Harvard Theological Review* 56 (1963) 199–215.
Stenning, J. F., ed. *The Targum of Isaiah*. Oxford: Clarendon, 1949.
Stifler, James M. *The Epistle to the Romans: A Commentary Logical and Historical*. 2nd ed. New York: Revell, 1897.
Stone, Michael Edward. *Fourth Ezra: A Commentary on the Book of Fourth Ezra*. Edited by Frank Moore Cross. Hermeneia. Minneapolis: Fortress, 1990.
Stott, John R. W. *The Message of Romans: God's Good News for the World*. Bible Speaks Today. Downers Grove, IL: InterVarsity, 1994.
Stowers, Stanley K. *A Rereading of Romans: Justice, Jews, and Gentiles*. New Haven: Yale University Press, 1994.
Stuart, Moses. *A Commentary on the Epistle to the Romans*. Edited by R. D. C. Robbins. 4th ed. Andover, MA: Draper, 1862.
Stuhlmacher, Peter. *Paul's Letter to the Romans: A Commentary*. Translated by Scott J. Hafemann. Louisville: Westminster John Knox, 1994.
———. "The Theme of Romans." In *The Romans Debate*, edited by Karl P. Donfried, 333–45. Peabody, MA: Hendrickson, 1991.
Sweeney, Marvin A. *Isaiah 1–39 with an Introduction to Prophetic Literature*. Forms of the Old Testament Literature 16. Grand Rapids: Eerdmans, 1996.
Talbert, Charles H. *Romans*. Smyth & Helwys Bible Commentary. Macon, GA: Smyth & Helwys, 2002.
Talbert, Layton. *Beyond Suffering: Discovering the Message of Job*. Greenville, SC: Bob Jones University Press, 2007.
Terrien, Samuel. "The Book of Job." Vol. 3. *The Interpreter's Bible*, 875–1989. Nashville: Abingdon, 1956.
———. "The Yahweh Speeches and Job's Response." *Review and Expositor* 68 (1971) 497–509.
Theobald, Michael. *Römerbrief*. 2 vols. Stuttgarter Kleiner Kommentar: Neues Testament 6. Stuttgart: Verlag Katholisches Bibelwerk, 1992.
———. *Studien zum Römerbrief*. Wissenschaftliche Untersuchungen zum Neuen Testament 136. Tübingen: Mohr Siebeck, 2001.
———. "Unterschiedliche Gottesbilder in Röm 9–11? Die Israel-Kapitel als Anfrage an die Einheit des theologischen Diskurses bei Paulus." In *The Letter to the Romans*, edited by Udo Schnelle, 135–77. Bibliotheca ephemeridum theologicarum lovaniensium 226. Leuven: Peeters, 2009.
Thielman, Frank. "Unexpected Mercy: Echoes of a Biblical Motif in Romans 9–11." *Scottish Journal of Theology* 47 (1994) 169–81.
Thiselton, Anthony C. *The First Epistle to the Corinthians: A Commentary on the Greek Text*. New International Greek Testament Commentary. Grand Rapids: Eerdmans, 2000.
Tholuck, Friedrich August Gottreu. *Exposition of St. Paul's Epistle to the Romans: With Extracts from the Exegetical Works of the Fathers and Reformers*. Translated by Robert Menzies. 2nd ed. Philadelphia: Sorin and Ball, 1844.
Thomas, Derek. *Proclaiming the Incomprehensible God: Calvin's Teaching on Job*. Fearn: Mentor, 2004.
Thomas, Robert L. "The New Testament Use of the Old Testament." *The Master's Seminary Journal* 13 (2002) 79–98.

―――. "The Principle of Single Meaning." *The Master's Seminary Journal* 12 (2001) 33-47.

Thompson, Michael E. W. *Isaiah: Chapters 40-66*. Epworth Commentary. London: Epworth, 2001.

Thyen, Hartwig. "Das Mysterium Israel (Roem 11,25-32)." In *Das Gesetz im frühen Judentum und im Neuen Testament: Festschrift für Christoph Burchard zum 75. Geburtstag*, edited by Dieter Sänger and Matthias Konradt, 304-18. Novum Testamentum et Orbis Antiquus / Studien zur Umwelt des Neuen Testaments 57. Göttingen: Vandenhoeck & Ruprecht, 2006.

Tobin, Thomas H. *Paul's Rhetoric in Its Context: The Argument of Romans*. Peabody, MA: Hendrickson, 2004.

Tozer, A. W. *The Knowledge of the Holy: The Attributes of God, Their Meaning in the Christian Life*. New York: Harper & Row, 1961.

Trebilco, Paul R. "Jewish Backgrounds." In *Handbook to Exegesis of the New Testament*, edited by Stanley E. Porter, 359-88. New Testament Tools and Studies 25. New York: Brill, 1997.

Treier, Daniel J. "Typology." In *Dictionary for Theological Interpretation of the Bible*, edited by Kevin J. Vanhoozer, 823-27. Grand Rapids: Baker, 2005.

Treves, Marco. "The Book of Job." *Zeitschrift für die alttestamentliche Wissenschaft* 107 (1995) 261-72.

Trudinger, Paul. "'To Whom Then Will You Liken God?' A Note on the Interpretation of Isaiah XL 18-20." *Vetus Testamentum* 17 (1967) 220-25.

Tsevat, Matitiahu. "The Meaning of the Book of Job." *Hebrew Union College Annual* 37 (1966) 73-106.

Udd, Stanley V. "An Evaluation of the Mythological Hermeneutic in Light of the Old Testament Usage of the Leviathan Motif." ThD diss., Grace Theological Seminary, 1980.

Uehlinger, Christoph. "Leviathan." In *Dictionary of Deities and Demons in the Bible*, edited by Karel van der Toorn, Bob Becking, and Pieter W. van der Horst, 511-15. 2nd ed. Leiden: Brill, 1999.

Van Buren, Paul M. "The Church and Israel: Romans 9-11." *Princeton Seminary Bulletin* 11 (1990) 5-18.

VanGemeren, Willem A. *Interpreting the Prophetic Word: An Introduction to the Prophetic Literature of the Old Testament*. Grand Rapids: Zondervan, 1990.

―――. *The Progress of Redemption: The Story of Salvation from Creation to the New Jerusalem*. Grand Rapids: Baker, 1988.

Vanlaningham, Michael G. "Romans 11:25-27 and the Future of Israel in Paul's Thought." *The Master's Seminary Journal* 3 (1992) 141-74.

Vermeylen, Jacques. *Job, ses amis et son Dieu: La légende de Job et ses relectures postexiliques*. Studia biblica 2. Leiden: Brill, 1986.

―――. "Le méchant dans les discours des amis de Job." In *The Book of Job*, edited by W. A. M. Beuken, 101-27. Bibliotheca ephemeridum theologicarum lovaniensium 114. Leuven: Leuven University Press, 1994.

Viard, André. *Saint Paul Épitre aux Romains*. Sources bibliques. Paris: Gabalda, 1975.

Viberg, Åke. "Job." In *New Dictionary of Biblical Theology*, edited by T. Desmond Alexander and Brian S. Rosner, 200-203. Downers Grove, IL: InterVarsity, 2000.

Vincent, Jean M. *Studien zur literarischen Eigenart und zur geistigen Heimat von Jesaja, Kap. 40–55*. Beiträge zur biblischen Exegese und Theologie 5. Frankfurt am Main: Lang, 1977.

Wagner, Daniel L. "The Dynamic 'Structure' of Isaiah 40–66: An Analysis of Organization Based on Transitions in the Servant and Other Orienting Motifs." PhD diss., Bob Jones University, 2004.

Wagner, J. Ross. *Heralds of the Good News: Isaiah and Paul "In Concert" in the Letter to the Romans*. Supplements to Novum Testamentum 101. Leiden: Brill, 2002.

———. "Isaiah in Romans and Galatians." In *Isaiah in the New Testament*, edited by Steve Moyise and Maarten J. J. Menken, 117–32. New Testament and the Scriptures of Israel. New York: T. & T. Clark, 2005.

———. "Moses and Isaiah in Concert: Paul's Reading of Isaiah and Deuteronomy in the Letter to the Romans." *"As Those Who Are Taught": The Interpretation of Isaiah from the LXX to the SBL*. Edited by Claire Mathews McGinnis and Patricia K. Tull. Atlanta: Society of Biblical Literature, 2006.

Walker, Larry L. "Isaiah." In *Isaiah, Jeremiah, and Lamentations*, 1–291. Cornerstone Biblical Commentary 8. Wheaton: Tyndale House, 2005.

Walter, Nikolaus. "Zur Interpretation von Römer 9–11." *Zeitschrift für Theologie und Kirche* 81. Römer 9–11 (1984) 172–95.

Waltke, Bruce K. "A Canonical Approach to the Psalms." In *Tradition and Testament: Essays in Honor of Charles Lee Feinberg*, edited by John S. Feinberg and Paul D. Feinberg, 3–18. Chicago: Moody Bible Institute, 1981.

———. *An Old Testament Theology: An Exegetical, Canonical, and Thematic Approach*. Grand Rapids: Zondervan, 2007.

———. *The Book of Proverbs: Chapters 1–15*. New International Commentary on the Old Testament. Grand Rapids: Eerdmans, 2004.

Waltke, Bruce K., and David Diewert. "Wisdom Literature." In *The Face of Old Testament Studies: A Survey of Contemporary Approaches*, edited by David W. Baker and Bill T. Arnold, 295–328. Grand Rapids: Baker, 2004.

Walton, John H., Victor H. Matthews, and Mark W. Chavalas. *The IVP Bible Background Commentary: Old Testament*. Downers Grove, IL: InterVarsity, 2000.

Warfield, Benjamin B. *Selected Shorter Writings*. Edited by John E. Meeter. 2 vols. Phillipsburg, NJ: Presbyterian & Reformed, 1973.

Waters, Kenneth L. "The Salvation of Israel in Paul's Thought and Experience: A Post-Radical Literary Investigation of Romans 9–11 and Its Context." PhD diss., Fuller Theological Seminary, 1999.

Waters, Larry J. "Elihu's Categories of Suffering from Job 32–37." *Bibliotheca Sacra* 166 (2009) 405–20.

———. "Elihu's Theology and His View of Suffering." *Bibliotheca Sacra* 156 (1999) 143–59.

———. "Reflections on Suffering from the Book of Job." *Bibliotheca Sacra* 154 (1997) 436–51.

———. "The Authenticity of the Elihu Speeches in Job 32–37." *Bibliotheca Sacra* 156 (1999) 28–41.

Watson, Francis. "Election: Reimagining the Scriptural Witness (Romans 9–11)." In *Paul, Judaism, and the Gentiles: Beyond the New Perspective*, 301–43. Grand Rapids: Eerdmans, 2007.

Watts, John D. W. *Isaiah 34–66*. Word Biblical Commentary 25. Dallas: Word, 1987.

Waymeyer, Matthew W. "The Identity of 'All Israel' in Romans 11:26." ThM thesis, The Master's Seminary, 2003.
Wedderburn, A. J. M. *The Reasons for Romans*. Studies of the New Testament and Its World. Edinburgh: T. & T. Clark, 1988.
Wegner, Paul D. "Isaiah, Theology of." In *Evangelical Dictionary of Biblical Theology*, edited by Walter A. Elwell, 375-79. Grand Rapids: Baker, 1996.
Westcott, Frederick Brooke. *St. Paul and Justification, Being an Exposition of the Teaching in the Epistles to Rome and Galatia*. London: Macmillan, 1913.
Westerholm, Stephen. "Paul and the Law in Romans 9-11." In *Paul and the Mosaic Law*, edited by James D. G. Dunn, 215-37. Grand Rapids: Eerdmans, 2001.
———. *Understanding Paul: The Early Christian Worldview of the Letter to the Romans*. 2nd ed. Grand Rapids: Baker, 2004.
Westermann, Claus. *Der Aufbau des Buches Hiob*. 2nd ed. Calwer theologische Monographien 6. Stuttgart: Calwer Verlag, 1977.
———. *Isaiah 40-66: A Commentary*. Translated by David M. G. Stalker. Old Testament Library. Philadelphia: Westminster, 1969.
———. *Sprache und Struktur der Prophetie Deuterojesajas*. Stuttgart: Calwer, 1981.
———. "The Two Faces of Job." In *Job and the Silence of God*, edited by Christian Duquoc, Casiano Floristán, and Marcus Lefébure, 15-22. Translated by Graham Harrison. Concilium 169. Edinburgh: T. & T. Clark, 1983.
Whedbee, J. William. *Isaiah and Wisdom*. Nashville: Abingdon, 1971.
Whitney, K. William. *Two Strange Beasts: Leviathan and Behemoth in Second Temple and Early Rabbinic Judaism*. Harvard Semitic Monographs 63. Winona Lake, IN: Eisenbrauns, 2006.
Whybray, R. N. *Isaiah 40-66*. New Century Bible. London: Oliphants, 1975.
———. *Job*. Readings: A New Biblical Commentary. Sheffield: Sheffield Academic Press, 1998.
———. *The Heavenly Counsellor in Isaiah xl 13-14: A Study of the Sources of the Theology of Deutero-Isaiah*. Society for Old Testament Study 1. Cambridge: Cambridge University Press, 1971.
———. *The Intellectual Tradition in the Old Testament*. Beihefte zur Zeitschrift für die alttestamentliche Wissenschaft 135. New York: de Gruyter, 1974.
———. *The Second Isaiah*. Old Testament Guides 1. Sheffield: JSOT Press, 1983.
———. "The Social World of the Wisdom Writers." In *The World of Ancient Israel: Sociological, Anthropological, and Political Perspectives; Essays by Members of the Society for Old Testament Study*, edited by R. E. Clements, 227-50. Cambridge: Cambridge University Press, 1989.
Wilckens, Ulrich. *Der Brief an die Römer*. 3 vols. 3rd ed. Evangelisch-Katholischer Kommentar zum Neuen Testament 6. Zürich: Benziger, 1980.
———. "σοφία, σοφός, σοφίζω." In *Theological Dictionary of the New Testament*, edited by G. Kittel and G. Friedrich, translated by G. W. Bromiley, 7:465-528. 10 vols. Grand Rapids: Eerdmans, 1964-1975.
Wilcox, John T. *The Bitterness of Job: A Philosophical Reading*. Ann Arbor: University of Michigan Press, 1989.
Wilde, A. de. *Das Buch Hiob*. Oudtestamentische studiën 22. Leiden: Brill, 1981.
Wilk, Florian. *Die Bedeutung des Jesajabuches für Paulus*. Forschungen zur Religion und Literatur des Alten und Neuen Testaments 179. Göttingen: Vandenhoeck & Ruprecht, 1998.

Wilken, Robert Louis, ed. *Isaiah: Interpreted by Early Christian and Medieval Commentators*. Translated by Robert Louis Wilken. The Church's Bible. Grand Rapids: Eerdmans, 2007.

Williams, H. H. Drake. *The Wisdom of the Wise: The Presence and Function of Scripture within 1 Cor. 1:18-3:23*. Arbeiten zur Geschichte des antiken Judentums und des Urchristentums 49. Leiden: Brill, 2001.

Williams, James G. "Deciphering the Unspoken: The Theophany of Job." *Hebrew Union College Annual* 49 (1978) 59-72.

―――. "Job and the God of Victims." In *The Voice from the Whirlwind: Interpreting the Book of Job*, edited by Leo G. Perdue and W. Clark Gilpin, 208-31, 252-53. Nashville: Abingdon, 1992.

Williamson, H. G. M. "Isaiah 40:20: A Case of Not Seeing the Wood for the Trees." *Biblica* 67 (1986) 1-19.

―――. "Recent Issues in the Study of Isaiah." In *Interpreting Isaiah: Issues and Approaches*, edited by David G. Firth and H. G. M. Williamson, 21-39. Downers Grove, IL: InterVarsity, 2009.

Wilson, Gerald H. *Job*. New International Biblical Commentary. Peabody, MA: Hendrickson, 2007.

Wilson, J. V. Kinnier. "Return to the Problems of Behemoth and Leviathan." *Vetus Testamentum* 25 (1975) 1-14.

Wilson, Lindsay. "Job 38-39 and Biblical Theology." *Reformed Theological Review* 62:3 (2003) 121-38.

―――. "Job, Book of." In *Dictionary for Theological Interpretation of the Bible*, edited by Kevin J. Vanhoozer, 384-89. Grand Rapids: Baker, 2005.

―――. "Protest and Faith in the Book of Job: An Holistic Reading." ThM thesis, Australian College of Theology, 1991.

―――. "Realistic Hope or Imaginative Exploration: The Identity of Job's Arbiter." *Pacifica* 9 (1996) 243-52.

―――. "The Book of Job and the Fear of God." *Tyndale Bulletin* 46 (1995) 59-79.

―――. "The Role of the Elihu Speeches in the Book of Job." *Reformed Theological Review* 55 (1996) 81-94.

―――. "Wisdom in Isaiah." In *Interpreting Isaiah: Issues and Approaches*, edited by David G. Firth and H. G. M. Williamson, 145-67. Downers Grove, IL: InterVarsity, 2009.

Winston, David. *The Wisdom of Solomon: A New Translation with Introduction and Commentary*. Anchor Yale Bible. New Haven: Yale University Press, 2008.

Wise, Michael O., Martin G. Abegg Jr., and Edward M. Cook, eds. *The Dead Sea Scrolls: A New Translation*. 2nd ed. San Francisco: HarperSanFrancisco, 2005.

Witherington III, Ben, with Darlene Hyatt. *Paul's Letter to the Romans: A Socio-Rhetorical Commentary*. Grand Rapids: Eerdmans, 2004.

Wolde, Ellen van. "Job 42,1-6: The Reversal of Job." In *The Book of Job*, edited by W. A. M. Beuken, 223-50. Bibliotheca ephemeridum theologicarum lovaniensium 114. Leuven: Leuven University Press, 1994.

Wolf, Herbert M. *Interpreting Isaiah: The Suffering and Glory of the Messiah*. Grand Rapids: Zondervan, 1985.

Wolfers, David. *Deep Things Out of Darkness: The Book of Job: Essays and a New English Translation*. Kampen, Netherlands: Pharos, 1995.

Wood, Thomas R. "The Regathering of the People of God: An Investigation into the New Testament's Appropriation of the Old Testament Prophecies Concerning the Regathering of Israel." PhD diss., Trinity Evangelical Divinity School, 2006.
Wrede, Wilhelm. *Paul*. Translated by Edward Lummis. London: Green, 1907.
Wright, N. T. "Christ, the Law and the People of God: The Problem of Romans 9–11." In *The Climax of the Covenant: Christ and the Law in Pauline Theology*, 231–57. Minneapolis: Fortress, 1992.

———. "Romans and the Theology of Paul." In *Romans*, edited by David M. Hay and E. Elizabeth Johnson, 30–67. Pauline Theology. Minneapolis: Fortress, 1995.

———. "The Letter to the Romans: Introduction, Commentary, and Reflections." Vol. 10. *The New Interpreter's Bible*, 393–770. Nashville: Abingdon, 2002.

Yarbrough, Robert W. "Paul and Salvation History." In *The Paradoxes of Paul*. Vol. 2. *Justification and Variegated Nomism*, edited by D. A Carson, Peter T. O'Brien, and Mark A. Seifrid, 297–342. Wissenschaftliche Untersuchungen zum Neuen Testament 181. Grand Rapids: Baker, 2004.

———.*The Salvation Historical Fallacy? Reassessing the History of New Testament Theology*. History of Biblical Interpretation Series 2. Leiden: Deo, 2004.

———. "The Theology of Romans in Future Tense." *The Southern Baptist Journal of Theology* 11:3 (2007) 46–60.

Yeager, Janet, and Thomas F. Dailey. "Job's World: A Chaotic Conundrum!" *Encounter* 56 (1995) 175–87.

Yoshikawa, Scott T. "The Prototypical Use of the Noahic Flood in the New Testament." PhD diss., Trinity Evangelical Divinity School, 2004.

Young, Edward J. *The Book of Isaiah: The English Text, with Introduction, Exposition, and Notes*. 3 vols. Grand Rapids: Eerdmans, 1965.

Youngblood, Ronald. *The Book of Isaiah: An Introductory Commentary*. 2nd ed. Grand Rapids: Baker, 1993.

Zahn, Theodor. *Der Briefe des Paulus an die Römer*. Kommentar zum Neuen Testament 6. Leipzig: Deichert, 1910.

Zaspel, Fred G. "Jews, Gentiles, and the Goal of Redemptive History: An Exegetical and Theological Analysis of Romans 9–11." Hatfield, PA: The Interdisciplinary Biblical Research Institute, 1995. No pages. Online: http://www.biblicalstudies.com/bstudy/eschatology/romans11.htm.

Zeller, Dieter. *Der Brief an die Römer*. Regensburger Neues Testament. Regensburg: Pustet, 1985.

———. *Juden und Heiden in der Mission des Paulus: Studien zum Römerbrief*. Forschung zur Bibel. Stuttgart: Verlag Katholisches Bibelwerk, 1973.

Zerafa, Peter Paul. *The Wisdom of God in the Book of Job*. Studia Universitatis S. Thomae in Urbe 8. Roma: Herder, 1978.

Ziesler, John A. *Paul's Letter to the Romans*. Trinity Press International New Testament Commentaries. Philadelphia: Trinity Press International, 1989.

Zoccali, Christopher. "'And So All Israel Will Be Saved': Competing Interpretations of Romans 11.26 in Pauline Scholarship." *Journal for the Study of the New Testament* 30 (2008) 289–318.

Zuck, Roy B. *Job*. Everyman's Bible Commentary. Chicago: Moody, 1978.

———. "Job." Vol. 1. *The Bible Knowledge Commentary*, edited by John F. Walvoord and Roy B. Zuck, 715–77. Wheaton: Victor, 1983–85.

Zuck, Roy B., ed. *Sitting with Job: Selected Studies on the Book of Job.* Grand Rapids: Baker, 1992.

Zuckerman, Bruce. *Job the Silent: A Study in Historical Counterpoint.* New York: Oxford University Press, 1991.

Zutphen, Vincent H. van. "Studies on the Hymn in Romans 11,33–36 with Special Emphasis on the History of the Prepositional Formula." PhD diss., University of Würzburg, 1972.

www.ingramcontent.com/pod-product-compliance
Lightning Source LLC
Chambersburg PA
CBHW070326230426
43663CB00011B/2230